MW01492053

About Island Press

Since 1984, the nonprofit organization Island Press has been stimulating, shaping, and communicating ideas that are essential for solving environmental problems worldwide. With more than 1,000 titles in print and some 30 new releases each year, we are the nation's leading publisher on environmental issues. We identify innovative thinkers and emerging trends in the environmental field. We work with world-renowned experts and authors to develop cross-disciplinary solutions to environmental challenges.

Island Press designs and executes educational campaigns, in conjunction with our authors, to communicate their critical messages in print, in person, and online using the latest technologies, innovative programs, and the media. Our goal is to reach targeted audiences—scientists, policy makers, environmental advocates, urban planners, the media, and concerned citizens—with information that can be used to create the framework for long-term ecological health and human well-being.

Island Press gratefully acknowledges major support from The Bobolink Foundation, The Curtis and Edith Munson Foundation, The Forrest C. and Frances H. Lattner Foundation, The Freedom Together Foundation, The Kresge Foundation, The Summit Charitable Foundation, Inc., and many other generous organizations and individuals.

The opinions expressed in this book are those of the author(s) and do not necessarily reflect the views of our supporters.

Agri-Energy

Agri-Energy

GROWING POWER, GROWING FOOD

Rebekah M. Pierce

ISLANDPRESS | Washington | Covelo

Library of Congress Control Number: 2025937874

All Island Press books are printed on environmentally responsible materials.

Manufactured in the United States of America
10 9 8 7 6 5 4 3 2 1

Keywords: agricultural economics, biochar, business of farming, carbon farming, cattle ranching, conservation farming, family farming, farm subsidies and grants, grazing livestock, land conservation, land use, New York farming, regenerative farming, renewable energy, rural communities, sheep grazing, solar farm, solar grazing, sustainable agriculture, wind farm

This book is dedicated to my family: to the challenges that have made us stronger, the laughs that have brought us closer, and the dreams that have made us one.

Without you, there would be no "family" in our family farm. Without you, I'd be lost.

Contents

Introduction

An old joke goes, "The best way to make a million dollars farming is to start with two million."

As is the case with most good jokes, there's a pretty big (and pretty painful) nugget of truth behind this adage. I never realized that until I became a farmer myself.

We didn't start a farm to get rich. My husband, Josh, and I started farming because we realized, at age twenty-two (before we were even married), that we enjoyed raising our own chickens. We were entranced by this agrarian lifestyle and in love with the idea of producing all our own food and some for our friends, family, and neighbors. Our small flock of laying hens quickly grew, multiplying into 50 laying hens, 450 meat chickens, dozens of pigs, some turkeys, a dozen beef cows, and 200 ewes. We dumped thousands of dollars into pursuing our dream, both of us working second, third, and fourth jobs to support our very expensive passion. By the time our son was born in 2020, we realized that not only did we have a profound love for farming, but we desperately needed to find a way to make money doing it.

Making money while farming is an oxymoron. It's something we didn't truly realize in full color until early 2021, when we met with our accountant to go over our returns for the previous year. "Well," he said with a sigh, leaning back in his chair, "it's common for a farm to show a significant loss in the first year."

"Significant loss" was putting it gently. Our expenses were more than double what we actually brought in. The farm owed us a *lot* of money. By 2021, I was working from home as a freelance writer and enjoying it (and the higher paycheck it brought) more than teaching, but Josh was getting more frustrated by the day. He wanted to leave teaching, too, and to do that, he needed to find a way to make the farm pay for itself. The expenses piled up. It seemed like no matter how hard we worked, we just had more debt, more stress, and a significantly smaller savings account.

It wasn't the lifestyle we imagined when we decided to get into farming, but unfortunately, it's a reality that's shared by just about every farmer we know. According to the US Department of Agriculture, the median total income from farming in 2023 was −$900.[1] Yes, that's a negative number, and no, it's not a typo. Based on that dismal income projection alone, it's no wonder farmers are leaving the profession in droves; between 2011 and 2018 alone, the United States lost more than one hundred thousand farms.[2]

Josh and I understood why so many of our fellow farmers were getting out, but that wasn't a choice we wanted to make. After all, we were just getting started. And we already had dreams of passing down the farm to our son, who, even before he could walk, was expressing a profound love for the natural world.

We had begun to research our options for making the farm more lucrative as early as 2019, when we had our first inkling that small-scale livestock farming in and of itself wasn't profitable. We knew we needed another way to make money with the farm.

At that point, there were plenty of talks on the table about marijuana being legalized in New York state for recreational and medicinal

Lew, age three. Credit: J&R Pierce Family Farm

purposes, so we had our fair share of (mostly) joking conversations about how we might have to pivot from raising grass-fed lamb to growing weed (a different type of grass entirely) for our customers. But then a farmer friend offered us a new solution. It was one that would not only allow us to keep farming and make a decent profit, but it would also help us give our animals the space they needed to be healthy and happy.

It wasn't magic.

It wasn't a trust fund.

It certainly wasn't a grant or a loan from the US Department of Agriculture.

Instead, it was something as simple as the sun: solar panels.

Enter: Agri-Energy

In this book, I use the term *agri-energy* to refer to any combination of renewable energy and agriculture, in whatever form that might take. Other terms—*agri-PV, agrisolar, dual-use solar,* and *agrivoltaics*—are also used, but they tend to apply exclusively to solar energy and agriculture. I wanted to use a broader term that could be applied to any combination of renewables and agriculture (including wind). Agri-energy fits the bill.

Josh and I first heard about the idea of agri-energy in the summer of 2019. Then, I was still working as a teacher, but had been hired by Acres USA to write a magazine article about this new idea called "solar grazing." Solar grazing is just one form of agri-energy that I'll tell you about in this book, and though it's the form discussed most often, it's certainly not the only form agri-energy can take. I also use the term *agri-energy* to refer to grazing livestock under wind turbines, growing crops under solar panels, and about a million other manifestations of the beautiful marriage between renewables and agriculture.

The research I did for that first initial article on solar grazing (titled "A Bright Future for Solar Sheep") put me into contact with some fascinating folks who are now big names in the world of agri-energy. After those interviews, it seemed to me that solar grazing was just the tip of the iceberg and something people weren't talking about nearly enough. Josh and I had once explored the idea of putting solar panels on our own property to help offset some of our energy expenses, but we didn't want to put them on our roof and didn't have great exposure anywhere else on the property. We had tabled the idea until one day when the concept of being able to graze our sheep under solar panels arose as a possibility.

It was our "aha" moment, light bulb and all. What if we could take advantage of solar somewhere else, perhaps in a not-so-traditional way? It was intriguing, but again we set the idea aside as there weren't any solar farms being built in our area. The timing wasn't right. It wasn't until a couple of years later, during a conversation with two of our farmer friends, George and Marcel Giroux, that the idea came up again. Right in the middle of one of those long, ambling summer conversations that goes on for hours until somebody finally slams the truck door closed and says with a sigh, "Well, I'll let you get back to it, then"—even though the "it" you need to get back to is seldom clear to either party of the conversation—George and Marcel told us that a new solar farm was being built on their property.

"We want you two to graze it," they told us repeatedly about the site. And, in 2022, they helped us make the initial connection to land our first solar grazing contract with a developer.

We were over the moon, telling everybody who would listen about this revolutionary new opportunity for our farm to make money, real money that could help support our growing flock. For the first time we would now be able to expand our farm in the way we wanted to, all while maintaining our diversity and beginning to make a (small) profit. This revelation was miraculous to us, and we weren't the only farmers who were finding cause to celebrate. Incorporating renewable energy into working agriculture is an opportunity for farmers across the United States and around the world to mitigate costs and diversify in ways they never dreamed possible. Short of taking on a second or third job, or even selling off the entire farm, renewable energy contracts are a way to help farmers make ends meet or even branch out into new ventures.

How lucratively those ends meet depends largely on circumstance, but for most, the payout is beyond what a farmer could get doing just about anything else with his property. In general, the more property a farmer has, the more wind turbines and solar panels can be installed.

Wind farms can bring in anywhere from $8,000 to $80,000 per year for the farmer, with the average payout being more than $30,000 per year.[3] Commercial solar developers typically look for parcels of at least ten acres for anything other than a very small community solar site, but on large sites, those more than one hundred acres, lease rates start at $300 to $2,000 an acre (and often exist as twenty- to thirty-year leases). In 2024, 58 percent of farmers reported lease offers of more than $1,000 per acre on average.[4] That's reliable, long-term income that farmers can count on—income that's immune to the changing tides of policy changes and fluctuating commodity prices. Renewables are a smart choice, especially for landowners who have lots to lose if they don't find another way to make the most of their land.

The real beauty of these deals, however, is that in most cases, *the farmer doesn't have to stop farming.*

What Does Agri-Energy Look Like?

In this book, I'll talk about a few different models of agri-energy, all of which can provide mutual benefit to the farmer and to the energy company, but each of which functions in a slightly different way. To get a clearer picture of how agri-energy might fit into the larger fabric of your own community, it's important to understand the differences.

Model 1: Farmers Leasing Their Land to Developers

Model 1, currently the most popular model, is the way "things have always been done." At least, that's been the case ever since renewables came on the scene in the United States in full force.

In this model, a farmer, often one who is nearing the end of their farming career, chooses to lease or sell land to a solar or wind developer. The farmer receives an annual check for the lease payments (or a final bill of sale) and moves on. Case closed.

Model 1.5: Farming the Developer's Land

As an extension of the first model, let's call it model 1.5, some renewable energy developers are choosing to have a third party come in and farm the land that is now covered with acres of solar panels or wind turbines. A sheep farmer might graze their sheep beneath the panels, or a vegetable farmer could grow spinach. These third-party farmers may or may not receive compensation. In the case of livestock grazing, the third-party almost always *is* compensated because they are performing a necessary service for the company: keeping the vegetation mowed down. In the case of vegetable farming, it's not always as clear-cut. Often, these farmers do not receive any kind of payment because it is presumed that the ability to farm the land for free (when they would otherwise have to pay to lease land) is payment enough.

Josh and I currently partake in this model, as do many other farmers around the country (and around the world) that I'll speak about in this book. We are farming on land that is being leased by other farmers to solar companies, and we receive payment from the solar companies for our "vegetation management" services (keeping the grass mowed so that the solar panels function optimally).

The benefit to us, then, is twofold: We are gaining access to land (and inexpensive feed) for our livestock, and we are being paid for our management services. This model is working well in New York, where we live, as well as in other states, including California, North Carolina, Texas, Vermont, and Virginia, and countries, including Canada and Denmark among countless others.

Model 2: Farmers Installing Their Own Renewables

Model 2 is the farmer who invests in and owns their own renewables. Later in this book, I'll introduce you to the Menards, a family that supplies a significant portion of their on-farm electricity needs with solar panels they paid to install themselves, although they do not farm under the panels. This arrangement has not only allowed them to dramatically reduce their annual energy expenditures, but also provides them with the added benefit of net metering, something I'll discuss more in depth later on.

Model 3: Farmers Installing Their Own Renewables and Farming on Them

The Menards are not farming under their own solar panels, but there *are* farmers who do and follow model 3. Dr. Anna Clare Monlezun, a rancher and researcher in Colorado, is one of these farmers. They don't receive any compensation from renewable energy companies for grazing or growing under solar panels; they own the panels themselves. However, they're making the most of their land while also dramatically reducing energy expenses (and creating a more sustainable, self-reliant energy system on the farm).

A Solution Beyond Farmers

While the impact of agri-energy on my own farm has been profound, we need to zoom out to get the full picture. We all know that land is limited, a finite resource, and the conversation around renewable energy versus traditional sources of energy (that is, fossil fuels) has often focused exclusively on that fact. "We don't have enough land to feed our growing population," the (very valid) argument goes, "so why should we tie it all up in wind and solar?"

It's an argument that I don't, at face value, disagree with. A one-megawatt solar farm produces about enough energy to power 170 homes, but takes up roughly five to ten acres of land. On that same five to ten acres, you could feasibly grow around fifteen hundred bushels of corn or several hundred tons of tomatoes. You could graze five to ten cows. That's quite a lot of food, especially if that food is produced in the model of agriculture that is currently in vogue, the goliath factory farm system. But (and this is a big but) the conversation surrounding land use and renewables has always centered on doing either—producing renewable energy or growing food—in isolation. That model is no longer the only option. It is no longer an either-or dilemma. Agri-energy makes it possible to do both, helping us get more bang for our metaphorical buck.

In fact, renewable energy farms cost less to operate and ultimately cost less to build than coal-powered plants. The cost of clean energy sources is falling every year, with solar falling by 13 percent and wind by about 9 percent.[5]

We need to eliminate our single-mindedness when it comes to renewables and think about solutions as they work in tandem, rather than in isolation. For example, can multiple renewables work hand in hand (that is, solar and wind on the same site to maximize land use)? Can we revamp existing renewable farms at a lower cost than building new ones? One of the most significant challenges to expanding renewables, after all, is finding enough land to develop these projects.

It's not just any land, though. It has to be the right kind of land.

The best sites for wind are the tops of hills that are smooth and rounded, open plains and water, and even mountain gaps that funnel wind (here, the wind is more intense and generates more power). For solar, there's a little more flexibility. Panels can be installed on roofs, but for utility-scale installations or even large community solar sites, much more space is needed. A lot of open space is needed around the panels, so installations near tall buildings aren't an option. Wide, open spaces are again the best choice.

If you're a farmer, you likely already have recognized the challenge in securing that kind of land, and that's where the major ag-renewable sticking point lies. Wide, open spaces are ideal for wind and solar, but they're also ideal for agriculture. That's why farmland is so widely sought after by renewable energy developers and why the renewable-agriculture argument is one of the most problematic as renewables scale up.

People have been fighting over land rights for about as long as human history has been recorded. Here in Clinton County, New York, the soil is known for being rocky and heavy with clay. Much of the acreage is wooded, and most of the arable farmland was swept up by farming families decades ago (and now has largely been sold to larger farm corporations). The unused, family-owned farmland we have left here is limited, and it has not been exempt from the real estate crisis that's affected the rest of the country. In most cases, farmland is more expensive than other types of real estate. And unfortunately, it's in short supply.

You can't blame renewable developers for trying to get the best possible land (at the cheapest price) for their projects. It's not just about the quality of land or the price, but the red tape that might be lying in the way of development, making construction or operation more expensive after the land has been purchased or leased. You'll see more developers flocking to states like California, Florida, New York, and North Carolina than you do to Alaska or North Dakota simply because of different regulations and different incentives, with some states being much friendlier to renewable development than others.

And although the need for suitable land to farm is most pressing for the individual farmer, farming communities extend well beyond the small bubble that is the individual farm. Our sheep have benefited dramatically from agri-energy, to be sure, but our broader community has benefited as well.

Farming towns are notoriously some of the poorest in the United States. Agri-energy allows more money to stay local than perhaps any other formula for doing business. It allows for energy and food independence in ways that fossil fuel energy simply does not. Community solar, a common model for solar farms that are developed on agricultural land, is a great example. In this model, customers can take more control of their energy costs, with community members able to tap into the energy that's being produced right in their communities and receive a credit on their monthly electricity bill.

There are many other solar models, including utility-scale solar, that generate electricity that is shipped out of the county or even the state. Nevertheless, community solar presents an opportunity fossil fuel generation never has and never could: It opens up the renewable energy market to people who want to invest in cleaner energy but don't have the land or resources to do so.

While the benefits of renewable energy for the environment tend to be quite clearly publicized, they can be tougher to quantify for agri-energy—although they become obvious the moment you set foot on a solar site that's being used for agri-energy. Many assume that the benefits are limited to the reduced carbon emissions that come from making the switch from fossil fuels to renewables, but they go far beyond that. It's not even as simply quantified as being able to use the land for more than one function. Agri-energy offers much, much more in terms of environmental sustainability.

For example, as I'll explore in more detail throughout this book, agri-energy can help retain topsoil and improve soil health. It can boost pollinator numbers. It can even help populations of certain birds and mammals, like ground-nesting birds, rebound and, in many cases, thrive.

We talk a lot about what's called prime farmland and lose sleep over our concerns that solar and wind are snatching up all the prime farmland that exists in this country, but we talk very little about what that farmland actually is. Agri-energy has the unique ability to create farmland that is truly "prime"—land that is healthy now and will continue to be healthy many years into the future. And since agri-energy can even help solar panels perform more effectively, it's also helping with that emissions debacle in more ways than we could ever have possibly imagined.

They say that what's good for the goose is good for the gander. In short, agri-energy is a holistic approach that isn't just good for the goose. It isn't just good for the gander. It's good for the whole gaggle, and then some.

The Future of Energy

Agri-energy development is happening at a breakneck pace—faster than anybody can keep up with. At the end of 2023, the United States had 4,185 solar PV facilities capable of producing more than one megawatt of electricity each.[6] Because the productivity of these facilities is measured solely by energy output rather than acreage, determining the size of these by land area is challenging, to say nothing of how many properties are actually being farmed for food and not just used for energy production. And on the international scale, from Japan to Belgium, Germany to Malaysia, few corners of the globe have been untouched by agri-energy.

Some data *has* been collected on the number of agrivoltaic farms (farms that combine solar panels with agriculture)—it's estimated that there are 567 agrivoltaic projects being conducted on more than sixty-two thousand acres in the United States—but these numbers are likely convoluted. Current agricultural census data in the United States doesn't weed out which farms are "agrivoltaic" or "dual-use" farms and which aren't, and many studies include *only* projects that are being used for experimental or research purposes as part of their final tally.[7]

That's one reason why I try to use the term *agri-energy* as much as possible in this book. My goal in doing so is to highlight a broader term that encompasses any kind of setup, whether that's using renewables to power your own farm (like the Menards), getting paid to graze a leased solar site (like us), or grazing under solar panels or turbines you personally own.

Regardless of what you call it or how it's being measured, agri-energy is happening, and it's happening fast. Agri-energy, in all its forms and under any and all its assorted monikers, is giving farmers a new crop to sell long after the farmer's market has shuttered for the season.

It's providing us with a way to diversify our offerings even further—and in a way that allows us to be more independent than we ever thought possible.

For too long, the conversation around renewable energy has been too partisan. There's no solution, according to many people, that prioritizes both the environment and agriculture. In this book, however, we'll walk through the benefits of agri-energy from environmental, economic, agricultural, and societal perspectives. You'll learn more about how agri-energy is unfolding around the world. I'll explain how these solutions, though in their infancy, are already proving to be a massive boon for farmers and clean energy developers alike.

If you're interested in exploring agri-energy for yourself, whether that's as a developer, a farmer, or even just someone who feels strongly about the topic, I'll give you some advice on how to get started. I'll cover everything from how to land your first grazing contract to questions that need to be asked if you're a developer.

But my real goal in writing this book is to show you how things are changing in the world of agriculture. Here, we'll see how agri-energy can help farmers make changes that not only benefit their individual operations, but the planet as a whole.

It's a big topic, something I naively didn't really realize when I first started writing this book. My initial plan, to talk about how some sheep grazing under solar panels could be great for farmers, was nice and simple. As I began to peel back the layers of this very complicated onion, however, I realized there was so much to the story than a few sheep under solar panels. It was beef cattle under tracker panels. Dairy cows under wind turbines. Tilapia in Hawaii. Pigs in the Finger Lakes.

Agri-energy is going to be big, bigger than we ever could have imagined. But for Josh and me, it was, first and foremost, an economic lifeline. It helped us go from barely keeping our heads above water to building a successful business that we were, and continue to be, proud of.

CHAPTER 1

A Cash Crop

The farmer has to be an optimist or he wouldn't still be a farmer.
—Will Rogers

LET'S TALK "FARM-ENOMICS." When Josh and I first started our small family farm, we were selling lamb for $11 a pound. To the average consumer, that sounds like highway robbery. Had you asked me five years before we started raising sheep, I probably would have agreed, turning up my nose at the $11 local lamb chops in favor of the less expensive cuts from Australia because it couldn't possibly be that much better than the "cheap stuff."

Now that I produce my own food (and take pride in producing it for others), I recognize the many merits of locally sourced products over the cheap stuff, from improving rural economies to reducing carbon emissions (an unfortunate result of trucking food many thousands of miles to its final destination on your plate) to supporting humane animal agriculture to the value of knowing the farmer who's raising your food. Local food is certainly worth it, and once I started farming, I realized that $11 a pound isn't price-gouging, as many would claim. It's simply covering the cost of doing business. Hay, vet bills, and milk replacer don't come cheap.

Yet to many consumers, cheaper is better. That is not said with the intention of blaming or shaming. We're all on a budget, and if you need to feed your family on $50 a week, $11 probably *is* too much to pay for a cut of lamb that will provide maybe half a meal for a family of four. That many families can't afford the price of groceries is a serious problem, but it's not one that can be solved by slashing prices charged by local farmers (and perhaps may be indicative of another problem entirely unrelated to food, as our global food system and commodity subsidies have made American food quite cheap; in 2022, we spent an average of 11 percent of our disposable income on food, but we spent more than three times that amount on food in 1919[1]).

Today, the price difference between what you see local farmers charging and what you see charged at the grocery store is simply a matter of small farmers needing to charge enough to break even, let alone to make a profit. Before Josh and I discovered agri-energy, the immediate goal for us wasn't even to make money—it was just to figure out how to lose less of it. We had thousands of dollars of lamb, chicken, and pork sitting in our freezers, and it wasn't going anywhere fast. We needed the inventory to grow the farm, but the stagnant inventory was killing us.

The losses continued to pile up as we researched new ways to market our products, with most of our efforts inhibited, sadly, by regulations imposed by the US Department of Agriculture (USDA) and other governing bodies that make it next to impossible to sell meat to grocery stores in New York without a relationship with Tyson, Cargill, or Smithfield. We had a loyal customer base to whom we marketed direct-to-consumer pork and chicken, but it wasn't enough. We couldn't sell the vast quantities of product like those major corporations (nor did we necessarily want to), and we also didn't want to hike our prices for our loyal local customers. We needed an alternative solution.

Farmers Deserve to Make a Living Wage, but They Seldom Do

Like most farmers, Josh and I consider ourselves to be good problem solvers, but our luck was running out—and so were our coffers. "You don't farm to get rich," our friends and family would tell us, our concerns warranting little more than a dismissive shrug at the dinner table. "That's why you guys have other jobs," they'd say.

Yet you don't tell a banker that he should have another job to complement what he's already doing all day long in the office. You don't tell an attorney that he shouldn't factor the cost of labor into his hourly fee because "he loves what he does." I'm amazed at how often I'm told, even by other farmers themselves, that the goal of farming full-time is not to make a profit.

Farming is an occupation just like any other. You could argue that many small-scale farmers or homesteaders are doing it in the name of self-sufficiency, and that's a completely separate argument, one I won't disagree with. As far as forward-facing farms go (that is, those that are selling to the general public in any capacity), they are *businesses*. And just like any other business owner, farmers deserve to get paid, and they deserve to get paid a fair wage.

Sadly, that's not usually the case. The only farmers that are doing alright are the ones who are subsidizing themselves with off-farm jobs or are buoyed by substantial government subsidies. In an interview with *USA Today*, Tom Cunningham, a farmer leasing to wind, said that many farmers refer to wind turbines as their "second wives," because all too often, farm wives have to work in town to make ends meet.[2] That was equally true on my farm, where both Josh and I have worked multiple jobs to support the farm.

When we're talking about income from farming, it helps to have a clear understanding of the numbers and terminology. First, median off-farm income in the United States in 2023 was $79,900, whereas the median total household income was $97,984.[3] (Per the USDA, "The median is the income level at which half of all households have lower incomes and half have higher incomes. Because farm income and off-farm income are not distributed identically for every farm, median total income will generally not equal the sum of median off-farm and median farm incomes.") The median income from farming for households is a lot higher, around $167,550.[4]

Commercial farms are defined by the USDA as farms with $350,000 or more in gross cash farm income, "regardless of the principal operator's primary occupation."[5] The USDA further defines "small farms" as any farms making a gross farm income of less than $250,000. Technically, any farm can be a "small commercial farm" as long as it generates at least $10,000. In other words, as long as your farm produces at least $10,000 worth of, say, tomatoes, you can be considered a small commercial farm, even if you never sell those tomatoes. "Noncommercial" farms are those that have enough land or livestock to generate at least $1,000 in sales, regardless of whether or not they actually sell that much. The vast majority of American farms (91 percent) fall into this category, but large farms (generating $250,000 or more in gross farm income) account for 85 percent of all agricultural production.[6]

Farms in the United States are getting bigger, but they aren't necessarily getting better. Large commercial farms are often referred to as agribusinesses rather than farms because the true focus is on production and a commitment to shareholders rather than on the more traditional, pastoral elements of true agriculture.

Some of the income disparity cited above has to do with the type of crop being produced. Rice, tobacco, peanuts, and cotton provide the lion's share of income for the high earners, with dairy, cash grains and oilseeds, and other "high-value crops" coming in after that. Livestock are at the very bottom. Sheep don't even make enough of a dent in the average farmer's income to make the list and instead are lumped in the general "livestock" category, not broken down into their own categories like beef cattle, hogs, and poultry. People aren't getting rich off raising sheep, at least not in the United States. The same can be said of other noncommodity crops like fruits and vegetables.

There are many complex reasons for this noteworthy schism in US agriculture, this stark division between the massive Smithfield barns housing thousands of sows and the part-time construction worker/farmer raising a hundred or so hogs in the back forty. One of the most obvious is the principle of the economy of scale. When a farm increases production, it can lower its costs of doing business by spreading them out among all the individual products, but that requires significant capital investment in labor, equipment, and supplies, a financial investment that most small farmers simply can't afford to make even when they take on thousands of dollars of debt. It also requires a certain level of Machiavellianism. We like to think that corruption and a general disregard for workers' rights ended after Upton Sinclair published *The Jungle*, but unfortunately, things only seem to have gotten worse. Though certainly not the case with all large, commercial farms, it's safe to say that it's not the small-scale blueberry farmer who's exploiting contract workers and paying below-poverty wages to undocumented workers, but instead, the concentrated animal feeding operations, or CAFOs.

Small Farms, Large Farms, and Subsidies

Again, the distinction between "agriculture" and "agribusiness" is important, especially as it relates to income. The chief executive officer of Tyson Foods earned a total of $12.014 million in 2022, up 33 percent from 2021.[7] To many, bigger is better; large commercial farms with three thousand beef cattle can produce and distribute much more beef than the small farm with thirty animals—and for far less expense because all those costs are spread out (and, likely, because there's far less concern given to the experience of the individual animal from birth to death, and therefore, again, less cost).

In an economy of scale, the relationship between expenses and profits isn't necessarily a linear one. It's easier to make money if you have lots of animals, but to raise those animals (and to raise them the right way, with regard for the life of the animal and the lives of the people who care for those animals) requires a lot of capital.

Large commercial farms are the ones that have the means to supply big food companies (like Tyson or Cargill) with the raw product or are owned by those large food companies outright. You typically won't find the small farms in your community selling to the big packinghouses, simply because the barriers to entry are too steep. They can't produce enough volume at a low enough cost to make it worth the effort.

Another issue that comes into play is subsidies. Although there's technically no exclusionary clause barring small farms (those grossing less than $250,000) from applying for subsidies, they're certainly off the table for noncommercial residence farms, since those farms aren't producing enough salable product to be considered viable businesses.

Instead, the bigger problem has to do with the type of product being subsidized.

This book isn't about farm subsidies, so I won't go into extensive detail here. But you need to know that, as taxpayers, we fund a system that spends billions of dollars each year on farm businesses and agriculture. These subsidies are marketed as a way to protect farmers from fluctuations in prices and revenues while also providing cost reductions (subsidizing) through things like loans, research, export sales, and insurance. Crop insurance, disaster aid, price loss coverage, and agriculture risk coverage are all examples of farm subsidies. What makes farm subsidies potentially more nefarious than other types of subsidies, however, is that they can distort planting decisions, incentivize overproduction, and increase inflation.

Farm subsidies disproportionately benefit the wealthiest of the highest-earning large commercial farms described above. One study found that 60 percent of subsidies from crop insurance, price loss coverage, and agricultural risk coverage (three of the largest farm subsidy programs) go to the largest 10 percent of farms.[8] USDA published data showing that 23 percent of farms with yearly revenues of less than $100,000 receive subsidies, whereas 69 percent of farms above that threshold do.[9]

The whispered truth that everyone ignores is that although farm subsidies are funding agriculture, it's not in the way we assume. Crop subsidies don't trickle down to the average farmer down the street from you, at least not in large amounts, unless that farmer is growing a subsidized crop at a large enough scale or unless that farmer is receiving some sort of state or federal aid in the form of a grant.

The issue of crop subsidies has long been contentious, with some people arguing that they're necessary to buoy farms throughout turbulent environmental or economic times. But they also inflate our food supply to an unnecessarily high level, and when supply is high and demand doesn't increase proportionally, prices tank and the farmer receives less and less.

Although subsidies can be a lifeline, I don't think I've ever talked to a farmer who views receipt of subsidies as a point of pride. I personally want a business that's thriving because I've found a way to make it thrive. I want a business with a reputation for producing an outstanding product, one my customers can afford and enjoy feeding their families. I want a business, not a subsidy machine.

My logic here also applies to grants and loans. I'm not antigrant. Grants from any funder are valuable resources for farmers to get up and running. But to say they're solutions for struggling farms is a fallacy. And often they don't amount to much. In 2018, the New York State

New Farmers Grant Fund, for example, offered a maximum of $50,000 to assist farmers with expanding their agricultural production, at a time when the average cost to build a barn was more than $75,000.[10] Tell me, how are you going to sustain your farm and all those infrastructure investments once the initial payment has run out?

I may just be speaking for myself, but I don't think farmers want more subsidies or more grants. Rather, we want a way to make a living doing what we love. And while our voices might not be the loudest, they're certainly the majority.

Josh and I run a small family farm, and our focus is on the community, not on increasing global sales or the interests of shareholders. For the most part, the vast majority of people who farm are people just like us. They're people who produce a gross annual income of less than $250,000. Together, we represent more than 90 percent of farms in the United States, the largest as measured by our population, but unfortunately, not by our bank accounts.[11]

That's especially true here in the Northeast. Here, we're more likely to see small commercial or residence farms rather than the large commercial behemoths that dominate the monocrop landscape in the Midwest (including the now-infamous CAFOs).

All in all, the income disparity between the largest commercial farms and the smallest operations can be best summed up by the phrase, "big ag or gig ag." You either do it on a massive scale, or you do it as a side hustle. There's no in-between.

But for many of us, the in-between is a gray area we no longer want to reside in. We don't want to run our farm as a side hustle. We don't want to sell out to a larger corporation. We want to have a successful farm, on our own terms. Maybe it won't make us rich, but if it can pay the bills, that's all we truly need.

When you have the nerve to utter a statement like that in the presence of an old dairy farmer in upstate New York, you'll find yourself laughed at. We certainly did. I'm sure the same is true anywhere else in the country, too. But if there's one thing farmers are, it's stubborn. We're stubborn to a fault. It takes a lot more than getting laughed off a hayfield to get us out of the game for good.

A Pessimistic Outlook for the Most Optimistic Folks

Despite all our grit and perseverance, things just aren't panning out for those of us trying to make a living in the unforgiving world of agriculture, especially small-scale or regenerative agriculture. Compared to other occupations, farmers as a whole are most likely to die by suicide, at a rate that is three and a half times that of the general population.[12] From a loss of pride in not being able to keep their farms running well to increased farm debt and reduced prices for commodities, there are many reasons behind this sad stat. Still, I've noticed two brighter takeaways here about farmers.

The first is that we must be optimistic. The grain prices will go down. It will rain. That ewe will recover from her broken leg. If we're lucky, our wishful thinking and prayers are answered. Things do get better. There's no choice here. We just have to be optimistic.

A lot of times, things do get better. You reach a new market with your products. You sell a few more beef shares. Grain prices to feed your hogs drop a little. But things never get better *enough*.

The other thing I've learned is that all small-time farmers have a love for the land and a love for what we do in common. We're not getting rich, but we're not in the game because we want to get rich. We're doing it because it's a labor of love, a love we want nothing more than to pass down to the next generation.

I didn't fully appreciate this feeling until I had my son. In his first few weeks, as I walked around the farm with him in my arms, I realized that this chunk of land wasn't just where we lived or where we worked.

It was *us*. Every inch of that place, every speck of dirt, held meaning. The greenhouse where we planted tomatoes, where the air hung heavy and thick with midsummer humidity. The first barn we built, where our first lambs and piglets were born, where swallows nested in the rafters and twittered good morning, and where my son later earned his first set of stings from a pair of angry yellowjackets. The bumpy, rutted-up mud road winding back into the forest, where we'd chased rogue pigs in the summer and watched deer nibble on bits of spilled grain in the winter. That's what drives us as farmers. It's admittedly a relaxing and rejuvenating thing to hike through the forest, to stop and listen to the birds sing, to hear the gentle sigh of the trees as the wind brushes through their branches and moves them back and forth.

But there's nothing quite like helping a ewe deliver a stuck lamb. There's nothing like seeing that lamb, who you thought had died, take in its first deep, unsteady breath, then rise to meet its mother.

There's nothing like walking out into a field dotted with jet-black cattle, watching as the sun comes up behind them, warming and illuminating their backs. There's nothing like being more than just a passive bystander or a casual witness to everything Earth has to offer, but instead, interacting with it, fully human and fully alive.

There is nothing like farming.

Farming itself is a beautiful thing. But the farming *business*? That's the stuff of nightmares. As of 2021, the average price of an acre of farmland in New York was more than $3,200.[13] It takes much more than an acre to raise even a few head of sheep. And that's just the acreage—bare, unimproved acreage.

Add in irrigation, fencing, feed for the animals in the winter, veterinary expenses, and everything else that goes into running a farm, and you're into trust fund territory, meaning that to have any chance of building a farm of any size, you'll need a healthy and generous trust fund to tap.

Josh and I didn't have a bottomless bank account; instead, we had debt. With our twenty-two acres, we quickly found ourselves tapped out on pasture. We knew we needed to increase the number of animals we were raising to meet the local demand of our customers, but we simply didn't have the space to do so. We also believe strongly in the core principles behind regenerative agriculture, and that requires good land.

We raise multiple species of animals and rotate them to new spaces often. Thus, we rely very little on commercial feed and even less on the medications and supplemental grain and expensive housing facilities that CAFO agriculture necessitates.

Our entire marketing plan and operating principles are based on our animals' need for lots of space, green grass, and sunshine. But with hundreds of animals and no place to put them, we needed another solution.

When Farming Is in Your DNA, but Money Isn't

When Josh and I were starting out, we researched grants and loans for the so-called first-generation farmer. I personally hate the term *first-generation farmer*. I think it's a misnomer—we all have farming in our DNA. Farming is a memory handed down from generations, one that remains running rich in your blood just as naturally as the instinct to chew, to walk, to run. Anybody can farm—but not anybody can make a living doing so, something we realized far too well. While the grants and loans would have been helpful in the short term, it was a Band-Aid that wouldn't do much to solve the long-term issue.

Just about every farmer in our area was in a similar situation, but that was small comfort. The only advantage other farmers in the region had was that most were *not* first-generation farmers. They'd been bequeathed large tracts of land, old (yet reliable) equipment, and breeding herds with decent genetics. We had a John Deere we were financing ourselves, twenty-two acres (much of it being wet, wooded ground), and a large flock of hodgepodge sheep that we couldn't even afford to have professionally sheared anymore. We DIYed everything.

We just couldn't DIY enough to make a profit.

While it's not comforting to know that others are in the same boat, it's the truth. Farming is an occupation with a notoriously stubborn glass ceiling; as hard as it is to succeed as a small farmer, it's even harder to get started, especially without a family history in farming.

Land access is a problem, but so is access to equipment. A new tractor can easily cost between $25,000 and $100,000, to say nothing of the implements required to use it effectively.

Then there's the knowledge gap. No amount of college education, no textbook, will prepare you for the realities faced on the farm. You have to learn simply by putting your feet directly into the fire and doing it, often failing, time and time again, and catching yourself on fire, time and time again.

To say it's challenging to get started in a career as a farmer, particularly a first-generation farmer, is a great understatement. Since there's no real monetary incentive to get into farming, there's no great reason (besides pure passion) to get into this field in the first place. Our numbers are dwindling by the day. About one-third of all US farmers are older than sixty-five. The average age of the US farmer is around fifty-eight.[14] From 1991 to 2020, the percentage of people who work in agriculture dropped by 18 percent worldwide.[15]

Only one in four farmers is a beginning farmer with less than ten years of experience, for which the average age is still high at forty-six.[16] New farms, like ours, tend to be smaller than average in acreage and in production value. George Giroux, the farmer who owns the first solar site we grazed and who sells us our winter supply of hay, frequently laments, "I just wish we could get more young people in farming." I can't blame him. But for a young person, getting into the farming business is anything but attractive. The same factors that are making it impossible for young Americans to own their own homes are also driving them out of farming. Land is too expensive, and there's not nearly enough of it to go around.

A Solution for New and Underrepresented Farmers: Model 1.5

Short of taking on a second or third job or selling off the entire farm and abandoning a generational treasure trove, renewable energy contracts are a way to help farmers make ends meet. By farming the developer's land, newer farmers can bring home a nice-sized paycheck without having to break their backs in the milking parlor.

Agri-energy has been revolutionary for me and Josh as we begin our career, providing us with access to land that we wouldn't ordinarily have. And we aren't the only ones.

During a phone call in the spring of 2024, Byron Kominek of Jack's Solar Garden told me that while agriculture has an inherent issue of diversity, equity, and inclusion, agri-energy has the potential to help smooth out some of those rough edges, opening doors to folks who have traditionally been unrepresented or underrepresented in the agriculture community. One of the biggest barriers for beginning farmers is accessing land, something that's true for any first-generation farmer, but it is especially problematic for farmers who belong to minority or immigrant communities.

Around 1910, ownership of farmland by Black farmers peaked at around sixteen million to nineteen million acres. It has since dropped to fewer than three million acres today, with Black farmers representing just over 1 percent of all American farmers.[17]

There are many reasons for this low figure. One is the issue of heirs' property, which occurs when a landowner dies without any estate planning to transfer the land to someone else after their death. The first generation of Black landowners did not have equitable access to the legal system. Without proper estate planning, the land continues to change hands as the years go on, but with only the original landowner's name on the deed and no clear documentation of who should get what. Proving ownership becomes difficult and expensive, and often, the land is lost.

Although this example is specific to the Black community, land access is problematic for many minority or underrepresented groups. Allowing aspiring farmers—perhaps ones who don't even have access to their own land to build a home on, let alone run livestock or grow crops—to farm on leased solar or wind land could be revolutionary, a historic move that could very well give US agriculture a more diverse (and much needed) facelift.

When we talk about the challenges faced by farmers, one of the most substantial is land access. Tied to that is the security that comes with knowing you have access to a plot of land to farm for the long haul. Agri-energy offers security, and that, in many ways, is more valuable than just money.

Diversification of products and services plays a big role, but having a reliable tract of land to farm on does, too. It's not just about finding ways to do more; rather, it's about being able to sleep at night knowing that you will be able to continue doing it because the land is being leased for several decades and you've been given the ability to farm it. Even as a first-generation farmer. Even as an immigrant.

That's true both of farmers who are engaging in agri-energy on land that is not theirs as well as those who are farming on their own land. David Specca, a researcher at Rutgers University, told me over Zoom that with agri-energy, farmers leasing their land to solar can make "more money than they can ever make by just farming." And that's something we never truly thought was possible—until now.

The Dollars and Cents of It: Model 1 and Model 3

We're not just talking about large farms, either. The more property a farmer has, and the better the location, the more turbines or panels can be installed. But, as mentioned earlier, wind farms can bring in anywhere from $8,000 to $80,000 per year for the farmer,[18] not a small sum by any means. Individually, wind leases can be paid in a variety of ways: a flat fee from $4,000 to $10,000 per turbine, a payment of 2 to 4 percent of gross revenue, or a set dollar amount based on megawatt of capacity.[19] The larger the turbine—and the more turbines there are—the larger the payments. A wind project needs roughly sixty acres of land per megawatt, but only about 3 percent is occupied by turbines; the rest is access roads, substations, and most importantly, buffer zones to preserve wind flow.[20]

The same goes for solar. In 2022, solar lease rates averaged $250 to $2,500 per year per acre.[21] The typical site requires ten to twenty acres of solar at a minimum, so farmers often receive lease payments of $40,000 or more. That's reliable, long-term income that farmers can count on—income that's immune to the changing tides of policy changes and fluctuating commodity prices.

It's not just farmers who are getting out of farming and want their land to produce a secondary income that this model can benefit, either. Many farmers are negotiating land leases with solar developers while at the same time having conversations about how they can continue to farm the land themselves.

Tony LaPierre owns Rusty Creek Farm in Champlain, New York. As a longtime leader within the Farm Bureau, he's frequently advocated for the need to secure the future of farms for younger generations, citing challenges like missing safety nets to keep farms solvent and poor pricing systems that make any kind of financial stability an uphill battle.[22]

He first started thinking about putting in a solar farm on his own land several years ago, telling me over the phone, "We needed a way to diversify and bring in revenue with assets we already had."

For farmers, the biggest asset is often land, but figuring out exactly how to make the most of it can be a tough decision.

"All the stars have to align," he said. "We had other pieces we wanted to use that weren't as productive, but [the solar company] had to put the solar on the better farmland." So Tony and his family dedicated a fifty-five-acre plot of land to solar, including thirty acres for the arrays along with buffers (and some areas that are still considered croppable along the outside).

He's making these decisions not just for the future of his farm as he can see it, but for his family's future. "There used to be twelve farms on my road," he told me. "I'm the only one left." Tony's adult son, Alec, runs the farm alongside his father. Despite having a background in mechanical engineering, farming is where Alec's passions lie, and Tony wants to do everything he can to help his son pursue them. Converting some of the land into solar is the best way to "get his stars to align on his own terms," as he might say, without having to wait for milk prices to come back up (which they won't) or land prices to fall (which they won't).

"Things are changing so fast," he told me. But he's confident that this step—a step to reclaim some autonomy in an industry that seems hellbent on taking it away—is the right step forward.

After speaking to Tony, I interviewed Rutgers researcher David Specca because I was interested in learning more about the technical details behind agri-energy, namely, how can we farm under solar in the most efficient, simplest way possible? Though my conversation with Specca started purely as a technical one highlighting the different applications of different types of panels, it showed me another benefit of agri-energy for farmers: the ability to access land in a more stable, secure, and reliable fashion compared to conventional agriculture.

Specca's team researches vertical bifacial panels, which allow farmers to go about business as usual on their farms. These panels are fixed in an upright position and offer a clearance of about two feet on the bottom with twenty to forty feet between rows. Farmers could potentially still harvest a hay crop, grow vegetables, or even graze animals (including

Two beef cattle grazing near the agrivoltaics panels at the Cook Animal Farm site. The Animal Farm installation, one of three sites of the Rutgers Agrivoltaics Program, consists of vertical bifacial panels. It is currently used to conduct research regarding large animal grazing and movement patterns in agrivoltaics systems. Credit: Rutgers Agrivoltaics Program, https://agrivoltaics.rutgers.edu/

cattle, who could be fenced off these sorts of panels with strands of electric wire).

Other styles of panels, like single-axis trackers, move with the sun throughout the day or can be "parked" in fixed positions. Farmers can then double up, generating money from lease payments while continuing to farm beneath the panels.

Referring to farmers who install their own panels and farm under them, our model 3 of agri-energy, Specca admits that there's a trade-off, since productivity will understandably be somewhat lower under solar panels than if the farmers were growing their crops in open fields. He told me that "they won't get that kind of revenue per acre if they lease it to agrivoltaics, but it will allow both to be done. It's additional income you can always count on." With that in mind, Tony, too, is hoping to incorporate agri-energy in some capacity once the solar panels go live, though he hasn't quite decided what that might look like.

Tony isn't the only farmer who sees promise in agri-energy and its on-farm applications. Nor is this phenomenon only happening on the old cow pastures of upstate New York.

Amanda Stoffels owns a farm in Keller, Texas, offering grass-finished lamb raised predominantly on solar sites. The Stoffels family got into solar grazing more or less by accident.

Along with five other families, the family made the decision to lease hundreds of acres to Lightsource bp. "We didn't want to walk away from the land," Amanda told me in a call, "but we did want the opportunity for solar." She feared that they'd have to move after leasing, trading the lifestyle they loved dearly for financial stability. Previously, they'd raised grass-fed beef on their farm, selling direct to consumers, but found it difficult to make a living. It was tough to get their mostly urban customers to buy a full side of beef when they had limited freezer space in their city homes (a similar problem my farm has faced).

After leasing, Amanda was ecstatic when she was presented by Lightsource bp with the opportunity to graze the site with sheep.

Amanda, who homeschools her children, wanted to be able to generate an income while also having the flexibility to raise her family. "I can still be working and not have a nine to five," she remarked.

For the Stoffels family, it all started with just twelve bottle lambs "to get my kids involved," she laughed. At the time, her children were fourteen, twelve, and ten years old. Today, solar grazing is part of their family fabric, with many more sheep serving as the thread that binds. In fact, during our phone conversation, she was driving to the solar site to check the sheep while one of her children worked on homework in the front seat of the truck.

"The blessings that have come out of dual purpose are huge," she told me.

The Stoffels farm is in the growing stage and they plan to add more sheep, but what struck me most was that Amanda, like so many of us,

Sheep grazing a solar site in Ennis, Texas. Credit: Stoffels Family Farm

turned to solar grazing simply as a way to support her family with the lifestyle they desired.

"It's bringing together the modern-day renewables with the old-fashioned, Biblical sheep raising," she said. It blends the newest professions and the oldest, nurturing, innovating, and building a legacy for generations to come. The Stoffels, like the LaPierres, are thinking about how the practices they implement today will affect the land and the people who occupy it fifty, one hundred, two hundred years from now.

They aren't thinking about how their viewsheds might be disturbed, but about how all the individual puzzle pieces come together to create a stable present along with a stable future.

Perhaps more so than money or any other factor, it's this kind of stability that farmers crave the most. If a lack of stable land access presents a major hurdle to farmers, particularly new or young ones, agri-energy, then, presents the ultimate solution.

The Giroux family has taken a slightly different path and has chosen to lease out land that they are not currently farming (our model 1). George and Marcel Giroux, two brothers in their seventies, sell us our hay and are repaid in cash (and the belly laughs they get every time they see Josh and me do something stupid as we learn how to farm, which, frankly, is quite often).

They put in one of the first solar farms in our area (the first we were ever hired to graze) with Delaware River Solar and Kendall Sustainable Infrastructure (later, it was turned over to GreenSpark Solar to manage the operations and maintenance, or O&M). The brothers, as mentioned earlier, suggested the idea of solar grazing to Josh before their project was even fully connected to the grid.

Solar grazing was still very new then, in 2019, around the time when I wrote that first article about solar grazing, and nobody was doing it in our neck of the woods. But George and Marcel recognized the need to think creatively, especially when it meant that they'd be taking some of their best land out of production. Quite simply, it broke their hearts to watch their fields go fallow. If we could continue to farm it by proxy, it would be a win-win.

"We bought this farm forty years ago," George told me as he, Marcel, and I sat in their shop one chilly May morning. "I had just turned thirty, and we paid a quarter of a million dollars with 7 percent interest. People complain about 7 percent interest now." But those were the times, he reminded me, and even though interest rates were high, land prices were not. George and Marcel farmed hay and raised dairy cows on that land for four decades before considering a change.

"We would do it all again," they said practically in unison, and as they both grinned boyishly, it was easy to see the brotherly bond between them.

They didn't stop with that first site. Pleased with how they've profited off the first, they're now working on a second lease agreement with another energy company on their other plot of land, about two hundred and fifty acres in total. They'd also like to see that grazed.

"A lot of people will tell us, 'You're taking good farmland out of production,'" George said. "I always say, 'But you didn't buy it, and you're not the one paying my pension.'"

Homegrown Power: Model 2

As we think about how to make farming profitable, another important problem faced by farmers should be highlighted: rising costs across the board, and not just of land.

It's no secret that inflation rates have exploded recently, and the cost of living has risen accordingly, too. While many of our expenses are out of our control as farmers, energy costs are something that do, believe it or not, remain within the scope of control. In 2023 alone, retail residential electricity prices in the United States grew year over year by 6.3 percent, the highest growth registered since 2000.[23] They're expected to continue to rise, at least until our grid has caught up to current demands (if that leveling out ever does happen—we are an electricity-hungry society obsessed with gadgets and gizmos, to say the least) or until the costs of adding renewables to the system have become amortized.

In the meantime, agri-energy is something that can be used on farms to *reduce* expenses rather than simply *increase* profit or *decrease* loss. It can be used as part of a larger system that's all about efficiency.

Connie and Gary Menard, owners of Happy Haven Farm in Mooers, New York, are no strangers to hard work. They've owned a dairy and beef operation for several decades, and despite working long hours doing some of the toughest work in the world, they're never too busy or too tired to lend another farmer a hand.

During the height of the pandemic, we called Connie in a panic about a ewe who was refusing to bond with her lamb. Connie matter-of-factly walked us through some suggestions of what to do, even though she'd never actually raised sheep before.

The Menards don't milk cows anymore, but when they did, one of their biggest incentives in adding solar to their farm was to increase the farm's production without also increasing its energy bills. They were doing everything they could to make *more* money, but they needed a way to stop *losing* it.

"Every year, our power went up and up," Connie said, "but Gary was *obsessed* with solar panels." When a company came knocking trying to sell them solar, the Menards quickly decided to install twelve kilowatts of panels.

Once the panels were installed in 2006, they could add more lighting, better motors, and other equipment drawing on electricity—thus reducing their labor and boosting their production—all without increasing their costs. Today, they produce about one-third of their own power with the solar panels and can also participate in net metering, a process that allows residential customers who generate their own electricity to sell the electricity back into the grid. Some states have strict net metering laws; others offer these programs voluntarily. The rules, as such, vary depending on what state you live in and sometimes on what service provider you have.

If you generate more electricity than your home uses during the daylight hours, net metering allows the electricity to run backward to provide a credit against the electricity that's consumed at night (or during other periods when the electricity use exceeds the system's output—in the Menards' case, when they were milking). The energy that is sent back to the grid then helps serve the energy needs of local customers, further "localizing" the energy process.[24]

Unfortunately, some utilities view net metering policies, regardless of the energy source, as lost revenue opportunities and do not allow it. Paul Gipe, a renewable energy advocate, wrote in his book *Wind Energy for the Rest of Us: A Comprehensive Guide to Wind Power and How to Use It,* "There are often onerous restrictions on net metering: who can use it, the size of the system permitted, and the size of the total program."[25]

So although net metering isn't always an option for every family, like it is for the Menards, it can significantly reduce the strain on distribution systems and prevent losses in transmission and distribution.

The Menards also benefit from selling renewable energy credits. These credits represent the "green" value of electricity and are sold separately from the electricity that solar panels produce. To meet sustainability requirements mandated by each state, utilities must buy a certain number of credits each year, and doing so allows the utility company to "hire" people like the Menards to produce electricity for the company.[26]

The payback, the Menards told me, was worth it. "It's a win-win," Connie told me.

The Menards qualified for both federal and state grants for solar installations. Once the money was in, the installation process was fast, taking less than a month, Gary told me. But the grant-writing process was intensive. "They wanted to know everything—down to what kind of underwear we wore!" Connie joked. Everything else was seamless. "We didn't need to do anything beyond what we'd need to do if we were building anything else on the farm, like a barn," she said. They needed to have a building permit, but since they were installing the panels on their own land, they didn't have to jump through too many regulatory hoops. The Menards installed single-axis trackers and appreciate the way they work seamlessly with the landscape.

"We didn't really consider rooftop panels," Connie remarked, for a number of reasons. The biggest was that the roof just didn't have good southern exposure. Another issue was maintenance. Connie and Gary were concerned about damage to the roof and potential additional maintenance demands. Putting the panels on the ground was much easier.

In addition to the grants, which covered about $100,000 of the total project costs (the Menards were responsible for about $40,000, which has since been paid off), they have enjoyed a significant tax break. "This is very much an individual thing," Connie told me, "because we have a farm and we do qualify for other credits and deductions, of course. But we haven't owed New York State taxes since we installed the panels."

New York offers a personal tax credit for systems installed at permanent residences. The credit is equal to 25 percent of a qualified solar energy system and is limited to $5,000 per year. It can be combined with the 30 percent federal tax credit.[27]

Depending on where you live, you can qualify for a tax credit in the year in which you install the panels as well as for exemptions or credits throughout the life of the panels. In some places, these credits are in addition to net metering. The South Carolina Solar Tax Credit is one of the most generous, offering a credit of 25 percent of the cost of a system, up to $35,000 or 50 percent of the taxpayer's overall tax liability for the year, plus property tax exemptions and the ability to tap into a net metering program.[28]

The most challenging part of the solar installation, according to Connie and Gary, hasn't been the solar part at all. Rather, it's been working with the local utility company, New York State Electric and Gas.

"They have a license to steal," she told me. In many states, rising energy costs are due, at least in part, to the monopoly that utilities have on the market. That happens here, in New York state, as well as in places like California and Hawaii. When utilities aren't forced by market competition to lower their prices, improve their infrastructure, or in any other way remain liable to the general public, they simply don't—and with dire consequences for the consumer.

In many states, utility monopolies still make it challenging for consumers, whether farmers or not, to lower their energy prices. But when farmers can take back some control by installing on-farm renewables, there is now a solution.

Despite any challenges associated with installation, the Menards still say they "made out like a bandit" when it comes to solar. They are considering adding more panels to power their house, in addition to the ones already powering the barn.

Solar isn't the only resource that allows farmers to lower their energy costs. Small wind generators, ranging from four hundred watts to one hundred kilowatts or more, can meet the needs of an entire farm or be used for individual operations (just like solar was used in the Menards' case to power the dairy barn). In the Midwest, many farms use electric wind generators to pump water for cattle.[29]

Although the problem of utility monopolies is a relatively modern one, on-farm renewable usage is not, by any means, a novel concept. In fact, it was in Denmark's farming communities where wind energy famously got its origins.

After reading about the experiences farmers abroad have had with wind and solar installations on their farms, I reached out to renewable energy advocate Gipe for more information. Gipe has worked tirelessly to promote community-based renewable energy systems. He was named person of the year by the American Energy Association in 1988 and has garnered numerous other accolades for his work, which spans more than four decades.

Despite his lengthy résumé and undoubtedly packed calendar, he still found time to chat with me one blustery March afternoon. During our video call, Gipe told me of the farmers in Denmark. "They were the ones using it, so farmers would get together and buy the windmills. The windmills would be placed on the land where they lived and worked," he said.

As of 2022, Denmark generated more than half of its electricity from wind energy.[30] In *Wind Energy for the Rest of Us*, Gipe wrote that "90% of all the wind generation capacity installed on land in Denmark has been developed by windmill guilds or what we call in the English-speaking world, cooperatives."[31] Denmark's done a wonderful job of making its citizens more energy-independent and also of creating microcommunities around its energy assets. The introduction of wind made farmers in Denmark more autonomous, emancipating Danish peasants from feudal serfdom and effectively raising their standard of living.

For a time, things were headed in this direction in the United States, too. From the late 1800s all the way up until World War II, farmers in America used wind power to help them pump water, grind grain, and even generate their own electricity. In 1936, however, the Rural Electrification Act extended electrical service to rural America, and much of the demand for wind went away.[32] That on-farm self-sufficiency of harnessing a natural resource to generate power without having to rely on anyone else began to disappear.

Fortunately, the clean energy revolution is seeing a slight resurgence in on-farm wind. According to the Union of Concerned Scientists, "In Texas and the West, for example, many ranchers use wind generators to pump water for cattle. Electric wind generators are much more efficient and reliable than the old water-pumping fan-bladed windmills. They may also be cheaper than extending power lines and are more convenient and cheaper than diesel generators."[33]

In the United States, modern energy assets aren't often owned by private landowners or groups of farmers, but instead by massive corporations. We've lost much of our sense of self-sufficiency and a desire to seek community solutions. It's not a group of farmers who own and operate a wind farm, but a faceless entity. If we come back to it, though, we come back to the community—and to agriculture.

Think about why we call them solar "farms" and wind "farms." It's because they're producing a brand new cash crop—energy—but that's not all. As Gipe wrote, "Wind cognoscenti adopted the term in the late 1970s because wind generation and farming depend upon seasonal cycles, the turbines are planted in rows like fields of corn ... and there is a literary association between the rural areas where turbines are often sited and with harvesting a renewable crop."[34]

What better way to honor Mother Nature than to get even more of those natural, seasonal rhythms moving in harmony on your farm?

Farmers are often praised for their quick thinking, particularly as it relates to solving emergencies with a bit of baling twine or duct tape, but seldom for their creativity. Tony LaPierre's solar farm is still under construction, but he's already cooking up more ideas. "Can we do solar grazing?" he mused aloud to me. "Put in some apiaries with clover?" For him, solar is just another crop—and he's curious about how he can maximize his yields by considering multiple "crops." Diversification—and creativity—are key.

Thinking Outside the Box

LaPierre, the Girouxs, and the Menards have the proclivity for thinking outside the box that farmers need to stay successful through all these changing tides. Many farmers scoff at the idea of on-farm renewables, arguing that the technologies are too unreliable and not very cost-effective. Yet these aren't one-size-fits-all solutions; they can be retrofitted to meet whatever your farm needs. You've just got to be willing to explore some fresh (and potentially scary) new concepts and think about how they might fit your needs.

For farmers, those needs tend to fall into two categories: powering equipment (like milking parlors) and pumping water. Gipe recommends a hybrid system that meets your goals with minimal cost. "In many areas of the world," he wrote, "wind and solar resources complement each other: winter winds balancing summer sun."[35]

In the often-humid Northeast, installing renewables solely for the purpose of irrigation doesn't make much sense, simply because we just don't pump a lot of water. The story elsewhere is different, though. Farm windmills still commonly pump water for livestock on the Great Plains. As a farmer, you could easily use a small or medium-sized wind turbine to help you pump water mechanically or to produce electricity to run a large well motor.

The beauty of installing on-farm renewables is twofold: It allows the farmer to become energy-dependent, not playing the part of David to the Goliath utility companies, and it allows farmers to make the best possible use of their land and resources. It also saves more of that hard-earned money.

Although still considered an "alternative" prospect in the United States, such systems have been in place in Europe for decades. In the Netherlands, for example, it's common to see sheep grazing beneath wind turbines along dikes or fields planted with crops right up to the base of wind turbines.

When we spoke via video chat in March 2024, Gipe laughed out loud in an expression of continued disbelief and nostalgia when he recalled to me one of his earliest visits to a wind farm abroad that played host to more than sixty turbines.

Looking up at them, he had no idea how they would possibly be serviced: There weren't any roads leading up to the turbines, as typically seen on projects in the United States. (Even with road access included in siting, however, it's important to mention that wind only uses about 1 percent of the land. The rest can still be farmed.)

On this site, though, without any road access, every single piece was cropped. How could that possibly be done?

It was simple. When the turbines needed to be serviced, which wasn't often, the workers laid down metal plates to allow them to travel from the main road to the turbines. Again we see that unique agrarian proclivity for thinking outside the box, and we witness the marriage of agriculture and renewable energy at its finest.

There are a lot of advocates for such systems, something Alex DePillis of the Vermont Agency of Agriculture, Food, and Markets described to me as "farm-integrated renewable energy—made on the farm, used on the farm."

DePillis noted that many forms of renewables have superfans who advocate solely for one type of renewable without acknowledging the benefits or applications of another. While it's certainly easier to dedicate your research and advocacy efforts toward just one type of system, it's probably not wise to do so.

An example is biochar, a charcoal-like substance produced by heating dry organic matter (like wood or crop residues) that has exploded in popularity over the last few years, particularly for on-farm use. However, it's nothing new. This recalcitrant carbon has been used for many years as a soil amendment. It has the potential to hang around for hundreds of years and can not only improve soil health and boost pH but also remediate polluted soil.[36]

"Biochar is great," DePillis remarked to me. "But specific biochar does specific things. We need to ask what's in it."

It's not a blanket solution, but it has diverse applications. Many farmers and gardeners already use biochar in compost to fix carbon and nitrogen, as well as to reduce ammonia emissions in chicken houses. Others are experimenting with biochar (as well as wood ash) in manure pits.

This trend has caught so much traction that in 2024, the USDA's Natural Resources Conservation Service introduced a new practice called the Soil Carbon Amendment that proposed guidelines for funding biochar applications through the Environmental Quality Incentives program. It offered funding to agricultural producers who wished to improve soil health via biochar application, with exact amounts varying by state. Although not meant to cover the full cost of applying soil carbon amendments, the program allows for up to 90 percent reimbursement in some cases, with funding reviewed annually.[37]

Another technology with plenty of superfans is the on-farm digester, which can help manage nutrients and reduce odors (and generate some extra income for the farm). These digesters, also known as anaerobic digestion systems, collect biogas from the waste and separate out the manure into usable components. According to the Environmental Protection Agency, the biogas can then be used as fuel in "engine-generator sets; directly as a medium-BTU fuel in on-site or adjacent furnaces, chillers, kilns, boilers or other fuel needs; upgraded for use in vehicles or distribution through natural gas pipelines; or flared."[38]

In the crudest terms, digesters turn poop into power. Typically, they're used on pig, dairy, and poultry farms, but many facilities will also accept outside food waste.

Anaerobic digestion systems don't make sense for every farm; it all depends on the size of the farm, what type of livestock are being raised, and how the manure is handled (and how often). It takes a lot of poop, in other words, to generate enough energy to make these systems worth it, and some critics have said that these digesters (also referred to as methane digesters) are really only feasible for large commercial farms. Yet, there always outliers; in Denmark, where there are "more pigs than people," Gipe reminded me, biogas makes sense.

Heat can also be captured in on-farm digesters, and heat is something Stacie Peterson feels doesn't get enough attention.

Stacie manages the energy programs at the National Center for Appropriate Technology, or NCAT, and has an environmental engineering background. She's also a poet and an author—the true definition of a Renaissance woman. Recently, she was also named the executive director of the American Solar Grazing Association.

Stacie noted that the potential for using solar thermal in the dairy industry has been neglected. She cited Winston Cone Optics as a company that manufactures solar thermal systems to offer farmers viable alternatives to fossil fuels.[39] The hot "solar water" produced by these systems could then be used to clean pens or equipment or to preheat water going into a conventional water heater. Water heating can account for up to 25 percent of an ordinary family's energy costs and up to 40 percent of the energy used in a typical dairy operation, and a solar water heating system has the potential to cut those costs in half.[40]

Solar thermal is based on a principle most of us understand: Leave something in the sun, and it gets hot. If you put some kind of glass cover over it, it's going to get *really* hot. Modern solar thermal technologies are a little more complex than that (and can be scaled to help heat water everywhere, even in hospitals and hotels), but the idea is more or less the same. Solar crop dryers are another commonly used technology.

There's a lot of debate in the renewable energy world about which technologies work best, where, and for whom, but most people recognize the value of hybrid systems. Gipe wrote, of remote farms, "With advances in solar and wind technology, it just doesn't make sense today to design an off-the-grid system using only wind or only solar. Hybrids offer greater reliability than either technology alone because the remote power system isn't dependent on any one source."[41]

There are multiple solutions, and none of them are necessarily better than others. "While solar can be an excellent opportunity to generate income and reduce electricity costs, there may be more cost-effective efficiency improvements that should be considered a priority," the Guide to Farming Friendly Solar states. "Depending on location, a farm might find that wind generation is possible."[42]

In many states, governments are offering incentives for farmers who want to give these ideas a try. In Massachusetts, for example, farmers have access to incentives for roof-mounted solar arrays (which can be installed on barns, greenhouses, farmhouses, or other buildings), canopy solar arrays installed over walkways or parking areas, agricultural dual-use arrays that allow agricultural activity (like grazing) to continue underneath, and ground-mounted solar arrays that exist solely to meet on-farm electricity needs.[43] (In chapter 7, I'll go into more detail about the considerations farmers need to take into account if they're thinking about signing leases to energy companies or about installing their own systems to boost on-farm efficiency.)

Renewables can and do offer big, tangible payouts to farmers, both in terms of additional revenue *and* additional efficiency. It's not just about how to bring money *in*, but how to stop so much of it from going *out*.

"Solar on a small fraction of a farm operation can substantially increase overall farm profitability and economic resilience," wrote Dr. Arjun Makhijani in an analysis of solar and agriculture specific to the state of Maryland. "Reliable profits from solar on 2% to 10% of a farm operation can significantly and reliably improve farm finances.... Lease revenues range from $500 to $2000 per acre.... Ownership profits can be $5,000 per acre or more" (the latter being if net metering is permitted and at what rate).[44]

Ultimately, it's all about figuring out what works best for your farm and how you can extract the maximum benefit possible, whatever that might look like.

The "Magic" of Diversification

Diversification in farming is nothing new, and its benefits have been recognized for quite some time. For one, it provides insurance against the unexpected: the drought that wipes out the almond trees while sparing the amaranth, the influenza that kills the chickens while leaving the sheep unscathed.

It provides a buffer against market volatility. Milk prices tank, but you still have beef and pork to sell.

It also provides novelty. Very few of us enjoy performing the same tasks, day in and day out, serving as assembly-line workers on our own farms. So, diversification provides a sense of newness that helps keep each day fresh and, admittedly, fresh sets of challenges that need to be overcome and new knowledge bases that need to be acquired.

Unfortunately, since monocrop agriculture became more prominent (a shift that progressed rapidly around 1945), diversification has not been at the forefront of most farmers' minds. But in all fairness, specialization, too, can offer its own set of benefits. If you only grow corn, you only need equipment to plant, grow, and harvest corn. You need to market your product only to a set group of buyers. You only need to understand one supply chain. You can be more efficient and, as the logic follows, more profitable and productive.

But monocultures work well only in theory and only in the short term. I'll talk later in this book (namely, in chapters 4 and 5) about the risks monocultures pose to our environments (and our economies), but for now, remember that nature itself is not set up to operate with all its wheels turning independently. Every aspect of nature, from the soil to the butterflies to the large ungulates, are meant to work in a delicate, intertwining highway system that feeds every other part of the system. Everything is part of a much larger machine.

Monocultures don't work in agriculture, which is perhaps one of the biggest reasons modern American farms are failing. No longer can we rely on antiquated skill sets and theories that push us to specialize, specialize, specialize. The derisive phrase "Jack of all trades, master of none" isn't very friendly to people who choose to diversify. However, if you want to survive as milk prices tank and fuel prices soar, you must become that Jack.

When we think of diversifying in agriculture, windmills and solar panels probably don't come to mind. But renewable energy is presenting an opportunity for farmers to diversify in ways they never dreamed possible. Rather than serving as a barrier to agricultural development (and overall agricultural success), they can, in fact, serve as a springboard, helping the farmer increase profits or branch out into new ventures.

The first time I met Norm Davis was at the 2021 Clinton County Fair. Fast-forward three years, and Norm, along with his son Chad and daughter-in-law Amelia, became close friends of ours. When I sat down to talk to Norm on a frigid day in January 2024, he was very reluctant to be interviewed. "I don't really know anything about solar," he kept telling Chad. "I don't know what she wants me to tell her."

But I wanted to talk to Norm because I've always thought that his farm, in particular, is the prime example of how diversification—and thinking outside the box—is what we need more of in agriculture.

I also believed he had a story that needed to be told. In these high-brow, theoretical conversations we have about renewable energy and agriculture, we tend to focus a lot on statistics and dollar amounts. The money is indeed important. But what's behind the bank account is always a real face, a person with a family and a history and a story that drove them to the point they're at today.

Norm and his family moved from New Hampshire to our town in the 1970s. Norm wanted one hundred acres of tillable ground, his mother wanted a big brick house, and his father wanted a sugar bush.

"It's debatable whether we really got all that or not," Norm chuckled as he thumbed through old photo albums and reminisced over the family's checklist. "My dad came over here in the dead of winter and just didn't realize how many stones were in the ground."

The soil on Norm's farm is classic Clinton County soil. It's rocky and dense, hard to work, with a lot of clay. But his family *made* it work. They started by raising Dairy Herd Improvement Association–registered Jerseys, but eventually Norm sold the dairy cows. "I figured there were easier ways to go broke," he laughed. They transitioned into beef cows, maple syrup production, and, most recently, a sawmill and box-building business.

"You have to reinvent yourself about every three years," Norm told me, a testament to the versatility and adaptability of farmers as a whole. At the time, a lot of small farms were going belly-up. Norm could have left the farm and gotten an off-farm job, but his wife wanted no part of that, preferring him to be close by during the day.

Instead, he built a box business, manufacturing custom pallets in his sawmill for local businesses while continuing to maintain the small farm producing beef and maple syrup. That worked well for him for many years. He didn't feel the need to reinvent for quite some time—that is, until the solar companies started sending letters.

Norm's property, as he puts it, is "power line central." The property is adjacent to large double transmission lines, making it a prime spot for solar developers. The first company to approach him paid him $9,000 as an option payment, something developers do when trying to figure out if a site will be a good fit for their plans. That payment was much larger than average. (I later spoke to Ken Lehman of Kendall Sustainable Infrastructure, who explained that option payments are generally not large because so much can go wrong during planning.)

Option payments are essentially prenegotiated leases. Large solar companies will often canvas several properties at once and give option payments to them all as they work out logistics. They cast a large net and hope they can reel in the right kind of fish.

But as plans change (a large business might decide it's no longer interested in tapping into the project as a source of energy, or the grid might not have the capacity to handle the power that the project would input), these option payments frequently don't lead to long-term leases. If a solar developer doles out ten option payments, it's not uncommon for only one or two to actually come to fruition, if that.

For Norm, that's what happened with the first company: The project never continued down the pipeline. Nevertheless, that first option payment was a boon. With the money from the solar company, he made a substantial investment back into the productivity and longevity of his farm.

The Davis family's story is far from unusual. Signing up with a solar (or wind) company to lease your land offers an immediate payout. Solar leases are usually twenty to thirty years long. Wind leases are thirty to forty years. That's income that can be planned on, income that doesn't require you to hedge your bets.

You know what you can't plan on? Income from a dairy herd when factors beyond your control dictate milk supply or when you're producing record amounts of milk and milk prices tank. Norm summed it up perfectly when he told me, "If you've got it in your head that you're going to run a small business, pick a business where you set the prices."

In farming, solar leases offer a way for business owners like Norm, and like us, to finally do just that. The trick is getting everyone else on board.

When planned solar or wind projects fail to come to fruition, it's sometimes due to shipping delays for building materials or holdups in projects being approved by the state. But more often than not, they're delayed or even canceled outright because the community doesn't want them there.

It's easy to reject a faceless entity, a solar farm built on your neighbor's property and absorbing your entire viewshed, or a wind turbine casting shadows on all the nearby fields. Those are ugly, industrial things, put in place by out-of-towners who don't know your community well at all or have its best interests in mind.

But what about when those installations directly benefit local farmers? What about the trickle-down effect that happens when money is being spent locally and power is being generated in your own town to electrify your own homes and businesses? That's where the benefits of agri-energy truly begin to shine. But you'll have to look closely at the details in order to see all the moving parts.

CHAPTER 2

Energizing Communities

*Someone is sitting in the shade today because someone
planted a tree a long time ago.*
—Warren Buffett

NOT LONG AGO, JOSH AND I took a drive to the small town of Potsdam,
New York, to deliver lamb to a restaurant. Our vehicle shielded us from
the twenty-mile-an-hour wind and subzero temperatures that brisk February day, but the drive was monotonous. There are many dairy farms
scattered along the route, some of them hauling milk daily to co-ops
locally and in Vermont.

There are also plenty of wind turbines, standing out starkly against
the agrarian landscape. Just as stark are the signs ironically opposing
their existence, producing just as much of a blight on the landscape (if
not more) as the turbines.

Those signs, some of them homemade, some professional, bear
messages like "TOO BIG, TOO CLOSE," "NO WIND TUR-
BINES," and "600 FEET TOO TALL"—all in caps, all angry. Needless to say, the siting of wind farms in upstate New York, as it has done

throughout much of the rest of the country, has generated quite a bit of controversy.

In 2011, then-governor Andrew Cuomo signed into law the Power New York Act, which established a unified siting review process for any major electric-generating facilities or ones with an electricity-generating capacity of 25 megawatts or more.[1] As part of this review, wind farms must go through an extensive permitting process and get input from local residents. That local input isn't always positive.

Consider the highly publicized story of an energy project in two small towns just east of where we were driving. In 2017, Avangrid Renewables proposed the North Ridge Wind Farm in Parishville and Hopkinton, located in St. Lawrence County. The plan was to place ten turbines in Parishville and another thirty in Hopkinton, mostly on fallow farmland. They would generate an estimated one hundred megawatts of energy (enough to power twenty-five thousand homes) and extend a much-needed financial lifeline to the area.[2]

At the time, St. Lawrence County had the state's third-highest unemployment rate (5.8 percent).[3] Despite the passage of time, things haven't improved much for the county; in 2023, the median household income was $56,872, with a 20.4 percent poverty rate.[4] That's well above the national average at the time of 11.1 percent.[5] Unfortunately, St. Lawrence County is far from an outlier in northern New York. Nearby Franklin County had a poverty rate of 17.9 percent for the same census period.[6]

It was once possible to make a decent living as a dairy farmer in upstate New York, but those days are no longer. The populations of St. Lawrence and Franklin Counties have dropped, the latter by nearly 8 percent between 2010 and 2020.[7] Neighboring counties have seen similar drops. It just takes one afternoon of driving through one of these towns to see the impact. Malls are empty and sprawling, shopping carts abandoned by their doors. Now-banned plastic trash bags drift around the weed-infested parking lots like tumbleweeds. "For Sale" signs are just about as common on lawns as dandelions. "Help Wanted" signs hang from nearly every shop window.

If you want people to live somewhere, you need to make sure they have a way to make a living. And traditional occupations like farming and manufacturing just aren't cutting it anymore.

The newly proposed wind farm described above would pump a significant chunk of change (to the tune of three-quarters of a million dollars per year) into local coffers. This money would then be divided up among school districts, towns, and the county. The property owners would receive a combined $500,000 annually for the use of their land.[8] Some residents could earn hundreds of thousands of dollars over the life of the wind farm. The company offered annual payouts to the local government of $38 million over thirty years, an example of a payment in lieu of taxes (PILOT).[9]

The project went through in Hopkinton, but negotiations eventually stalled out in nearby Parishville. There, opponents argued that the turbines would "change the character of the land," marring its natural beauty and creating more problems down the road. Because of this opposition, the project was never completed in full. Some Parishville residents rejoiced, while others mourned the loss of a significant revenue generator.

This case is not an outlier by any means. Historically, renewables of all kinds have faced much opposition. Wind garners a lot of attention, and solar isn't far behind. Why?

The most widely publicized concern is wildlife deaths, which I'll address in detail in chapter 4. For now, suffice it to say that this problem has been wildly exaggerated.

Aside from animal welfare, many people don't love the aesthetics of the more than three-hundred-foot-tall goliaths. Personally, I don't mind the look of a wind turbine, especially from several miles away, when the motion of the turbines looks like a graceful, choreographed dance in the sky. I certainly think they're more attractive than massive coal-fired power plants, vomiting their plumes of black smoke into the sky.

Beyond aesthetics, some argue that the towers (even the smaller ones) simply cast too much shade. The turbine blades cast a moving silhouette on nearby homes, something known as shadow flicker, which can be annoying and distracting for those nearby. Some people have even argued that shadow flicker can negatively impact individuals with other health issues (such as children with epilepsy). In reality, there's limited data on whether shadow flicker can cause or exacerbate health problems.[10]

Another complaint is that wind turbines are loud. Under full load—meaning when it's the windiest and the turbines are working the hardest—noise levels can reach up to 105 decibels.[11] However, that's at the turbine hub, which is one hundred meters in the air. You're not going to get close to that area unless you're a technician performing work on the system (when the system will likely be powered down anyway).

When Josh worked for WEST (Western Ecosystems Technology), a Wyoming-based company that studies the environmental impacts of wind farms, he was often working directly beneath the turbines. He was shocked that the noise of his car idling nearby was much louder than the turbine.

The closest a wind turbine is placed to a home is typically three hundred meters.[12] There, the turbine will have a sound pressure level of forty to forty-three decibels. That's quieter than the average dishwasher.[13]

So, is a wind turbine really any worse than any other building?

It depends on who you ask. In rural communities where renewables are being implemented at a rapid pace, everyone has a different opinion. Some of those are a little odd, to say the least. Two of my favorite myths are that wind turbine noise caused birth defects in Portuguese horses and that the low frequencies of the turbines can cause cancer. While I won't say these situations are totally impossible (the point of science, after all, is to continuously question and discover), there have been zero

scientific studies to date showing a direct causal link between wind turbines and either birth defects or cancer in any species.

And then there are the videos of the wind turbines breaking, burning, and falling down. This does indeed happen. I've spent a lot of time
watching these videos on YouTube. While it's easy to go down that rab-
bit hole, the good news is that these breakdowns are exceedingly rare. A
2014 study found that, of the then-forty-thousand wind turbines in the
United States, there had been fewer than forty of these incidents, with
almost none of them considered severe.[14]

Pieces and parts of wind turbines do break, but no more than any
other major piece of machinery. The same can't be said about coal-fired
power plants, which operate at just 33 percent efficiency.[15] Here in the
United States, we don't have great information on breakdown rates, but
in Australia, a 2018 study found that gas and coal power plants broke
down *once every two and a half days*.[16] We just don't talk about that.
Instead, we focus on the sensational—the shattered pieces of wind turbine blades catapulting through the air.

These horror stories do have real consequences: Partly because of
overblown fears, wind turbines can impact property values. Research in
2014 from the London School of Economics showed that wind farms
could cut as much as 12 percent off the value of the homes within a
two-kilometer radius.[17] Interestingly, residential solar does the opposite:
It has a positive impact on home values, increasing a home's resale value
by up to $5,911 for each kilowatt of solar panels installed.[18]

Still, solar doesn't escape scrutiny, and some of the concerns are valid.
It's incredibly problematic that universal recycling programs have yet to
be developed for solar. Even more concerning is that solar panels often
rely on the mining of rare earth minerals from rural, impoverished communities in other countries, where child and slave labor are not unheard of.

Yet we tend to draw upon these examples only when it's most convenient or most sensational. Nobody wants to talk about the other ugly

truths of our supply chain, like the horrific labor conditions in fast-fashion factories overseas or the same inhumane mining conditions that generate the batteries for our smartphones or tablets. Instead, we hold steady on our convictions that renewable energy is wrong for these reasons and these reasons alone, failing to recognize that these problems are inherent throughout the entire global supply chain, and not just in the clean energy industry.

There are lots of advantages to be found in renewables that simply can't be found in other industries. For one, the average lifespan of a photovoltaic panel is twenty-five to forty years (compare that to just a few years for that battery-hungry iPhone you're toting around).[19]

The lifespan of a solar panel is comparable to the life-span of a coal-fired power plant (forty years), but the difference here is that about 74 percent of all US coal plants are more than thirty years old. Many are being, or have already been, decommissioned. Those materials have to go somewhere, too. Recycling, then, becomes just as pressing of an issue for the fossil fuel industry as it is for renewables, but the deadline is coming up even faster.[20]

Michael Noble is the retired director of Fresh Energy, an organization that shapes policy toward cleaner energy. As he told me in a call, "The only limiting factor of renewable energy in America is people's willingness to live with it."

After all, humans are, ultimately, the controlling variable.

As we've seen, renewables are a smart choice for landowners, especially those who have much to lose if they don't find another way to make the most of their land. They can keep farming on the land they love. And in many cases, they don't have to pursue that second or third job off the farm.

But what about everybody who lives near that farmer? What about the people who don't own the land that's being leased but still must deal with the negative implications of what's happening on that land? This is where we begin our conversation on NIMBYism (*not in my backyard*) and why it's having massive implications for everyone, regardless of which side of the argument you're on.

Farmers Are People, Too

Before delving into the benefits of agri-energy for communities, it's worth remembering that farmers are members of the community, people who have just as much of a right to its resources, freedoms, and decision-making process as anyone else. That may seem obvious, but unfortunately, nonfarmers don't always remember that simple fact.

I realized this dichotomy in June 2023 when Josh and I spoke about our experience as solar graziers at the ANCA Clean Energy Conference in Utica, New York. Toward the end of the day, we sat in on a conversation about agricultural land and how to best improve community buy-in for clean energy projects.

One woman stood up and said, "I just don't think any farmland should be turned into solar."

"So where should it go?" we asked her. (The irony that the woman was attending a clean energy conference was not lost on us in the slightest.)

"On rooftops," she said. "Or brownfields."

What many people don't realize is that it costs a lot more money to install panels on roofs than to plant them across a field. It costs almost three times as much per watt, in fact.[21] And while rooftop solar admittedly doesn't compete with land, there are other drawbacks to consider. Solar panel fires are rare, but when they happen, they burn hot and are dangerous for firefighters to extinguish. On an independently sited solar farm that's set away from other structures, the policy from the solar farm owner is often to just let the fire burn itself out to keep the firefighters safe. The only thing at risk here is the panels, and they're insured. But what would happen if panels started a massive fire on top of an apartment building?

In addition, rooftop panels are harder to install and harder to maintain than ground panels, particularly on older buildings that might not be set up for them.

That's not to say that rooftop solar never makes sense. In many cases, it's a smart choice. IKEA, for example, has solar on 90 percent of its US locations.[22]

Quite frankly, there doesn't need to be a single approach. Use rooftop solar where it makes sense and rely instead on ground-mounted solar where it doesn't.

In reality, there are thousands of acres of farmland in the United States that are being foreclosed upon or are lying fallow because farmers either can't, don't want to, or, most likely, can't afford to farm them. And because it's their land, it's their decision about what should be done with it.

"This is their retirement," Josh explained to the woman at the conference, thinking of the Girouxs. "These farmers—so many of them didn't put money into a 401(k) to fall back on when they got older. They need to do something with the acreage so they can afford to retire."

This woman held her ground. The farmer should make that sacrifice so people could continue to eat.

"I have an idea," Josh said. "Why don't you donate your 401(k) to help keep these farms afloat, then?"

She sat down.

This begs the question: Would you give up your life savings to keep a farm afloat? Would you sacrifice everything you've worked for in your life—and perhaps everything your parents and their parents worked for—just to save a view? If the answer is no, that's NIMBYism at its finest.

You like seeing those farm fields across the street from where you work every day. But do you want to quit your day job and go half a million dollars in debt (if not more) to buy the land and work it? The answer, again, is probably no.

We're now past the point in this country where we can keep expecting the farmer to shoulder the entire burden. We have a collective problem, so we need to start looking for a collective solution. That solution is agri-energy.

Tax Breaks and Community Gains: The Hidden Value of Renewables

You might wonder how you could possibly benefit from a massive wind farm in your community if you aren't the farmer receiving the lease check. That was a major source of contention for the St. Lawrence County wind farms, a key battle cry of those in the NIMBY camp. Yes, a wind farm produces affordable electricity, but often those rates aren't immediately available to locals because the power doesn't always stay local. This situation can lead to resentment if locals don't see direct profits.

Denmark, leading the way in wind energy, recognized early on that buy-in from locals was an essential piece of the puzzle in large-scale wind implementation. As a result, Denmark developed a "buy-legal" system in which a developer is required to offer at least 20 percent of the project shares to residents. This system has now been adopted for Denmark's on- and offshore wind installations.[23]

Former New York Governor Andrew Cuomo proposed a similar initiative: a "host communities benefit program" to deliver incentives to communities that host renewable energy facilities.[24] This statewide initiative would give residents more transparency on a project and allow them more buy-in. It would also reduce backroom dealmaking (something residents were skeptical about, worried that the buy-and-sell nature of solar and wind development would result in a finished project that they had not themselves initially agreed to). This program was a big step in building buy-in for renewable installation around the state.

Like any other business, renewable installers are required to pay their fair share. In many cases, this increase in tax revenue leads to large increases in local revenues to school districts and other tax-driven organizations. In fact, wind projects alone deliver an estimated $2 billion in state and local tax payments and land lease payments each year on average, something that helps reduce the resident tax burden.[25]

Each state differs in how it deals with these taxes, with some providing more community incentives for renewable installations than others. Certain states, like Kansas, exempt wind projects from property taxes for the first ten years of operation.[26] Some companies make PILOT payments to the counties that are hosting the projects, but often, school districts are left out of the deal. In some states, any revenue generated from the project is fully captured by the state and redistributed, meaning that the school district where the wind farm is actually located might not get much.

Locals often have the option to buy in. Community solar projects make residential electric rates much more affordable for the average resident. You don't even have to have an array installed on your own property; simply sign on the dotted line for community solar, and you'll see an automatic reduction in your electricity rates each month.

From reduced burden on already stressed community coffers and resources to significant financial benefit for farmers and land lessees, renewables make sense. The key is to make sure everybody gets a piece of the pie. When locals can invest in a project and have a say (and share) in what goes on, everybody is happy—or at least, content.

Will Harris of White Oak Pastures is known for his commitment to regenerative agriculture and has been a solar grazier since 2019. When we spoke over a video call in 2024, he told me that he had about two thousand head of sheep on a Silicon Ranch solar farm in Georgia but expected the numbers to rise. Originally, he admitted, he didn't like the idea of solar. It would eat up a large tract of neighboring land, and as someone who had invested many years into building soil health, he didn't think fondly of the idea of spraying herbicides or mowing the vegetation on a solar farm. In fact, Harris is so passionate about the environmental health of his farm and the surrounding area that he's poured millions of dollars over decades into rebuilding the soil and restoring his farm's ecological health, making the hard switch from conventional farming practices to regenerative ones over the period of several years. In fact, he wrote a book on it, *A Bold Return to Giving a Damn.*[27]

Once he got over the initial shock of the idea of solar, the wheels began to turn. He only had a few sheep at the time. His family had always preferred cattle instead; he told me that his father referred to sheep as "pasture maggots." But Harris saw the potential for sheep to manage the vegetation at solar sites, recognizing that this strategy could provide a valuable service to the solar company while also providing his own business with an additional revenue stream. Most important for Harris is that it would help him become a better "economic ally" for the community while allowing him to continue to support his ecological goals.

Harris hasn't been the only one to benefit. In fact, even though he's still just breaking even on the solar grazing deal (because he's reinvesting the money he's made into continuing to build up his flock), it's had a huge trickle-down effect on the local community. White Oak Pastures is the largest private employer in his county, and his employees earn significantly higher wages than the county average. Many of those employees are involved in raising, transporting, and slaughtering sheep, a direct result of the solar farm business. He's also started grazing cattle on his solar sites, another revenue stream. He told me, "Solar grazing is profitable. It's definitely not a get rich quick deal, but it's a business."

Think about it: farming, a business like any other.

What Harris showed me, without having to explain it directly, was that farming, though meant to be a (at least semi-) profitable business, is one of a kind in that it has stewardship—of the community, of the land—at its core. There is perhaps no other industry in which the professional tasked with driving it forward is also equally responsible for the health and vigor of the surrounding environment and of its people. Harris isn't involved in solar grazing to get rich. His primary goal is to support the land. Through solar grazing, he's able to afford to operate his business in a way that helps the land and the community.

We need to stop thinking about the "way it's always been" and start thinking about the "way it could be." Money might be a big driver for these projects, but it's not the only benefit. My conversation with Harris made me realize that this relationship between agriculture and renewable energy goes beyond dollars and cents. The benefits spill into the environment, local tax revenue and job creation, improved crop production, pollinator health, increased energy independence, and much, much more.

As the conversation continues, we need to think about these variables as systems, about agriculture and renewable energy holistically. They are cogs in the same wheel and not simply opposing forces, or A versus B.

To enact meaningful change in our communities and for our environments, we need to start addressing issues head-on. We need to start by defining what the word *community* means to us in the first place, and for most people, that's something that's exceptionally hard to do.

NIMBYism and Renewables

We've witnessed a huge cultural shift since the start of this century. People want to be advocates for what they think is the right thing, and that's wonderful. But what *is* the right thing? Often, we hammer hard on one cause, not thinking about how that ideology fits into the big picture.

We forget that nothing exists in isolation, that nothing functions in a vacuum. It's easy to decry the expansion of renewable energy into our communities, but you can't do that without thinking about the communities currently playing host to your energy demands.

In one of my conversations with Michael Noble, a man who has spent more than thirty years in advocacy and policy for the clean energy industry, he said something that really stuck with me, something that I've seen to be true in my own experience living in a community battling with the "ethics" of renewables. He said that there are three core groups of people here: the people who are opposed to renewable energy at all costs, preferring instead to rely on the same old, same old of fossil fuels (this seems to be the smallest group); the renewable energy diehards (we need to be zero-emissions *or else*); and the people who think we need a little bit of everything.

I'm in the third group. Michael Noble told me he thinks that's where most other farmers are, too, but he's noticed something else. "Culturally, where people are producers, they like the idea of turbines. They like the idea of producing something," he told me. "On the other hand, when you have a community that's comprised mostly of consumers— people who want to use the land for hobby farms, viewsheds, housing developments, et cetera—they don't like them."

It goes back to that idea of NIMBYism. Ironically, many of the same people who oppose renewables in their own communities are the same ones who share social media posts and lobby legislators with their concerns about the environment. They buy organic produce at the grocery store and recycle every scrap of aluminum foil each week. These people aren't antienvironmentalists. They're the opposite. They just don't accept that for there to be clean energy, there must be a place to produce it.

The acronym NIMBY is often used to describe opposition to solar and wind development, but it's not only used in that sense. It can also be used to describe opposition to things like housing developments (especially affordable housing), homeless shelters, bike lanes, incinerators, and sewer treatment systems. Paul Gipe, in *Wind Energy for the Rest of Us*, argues that NIMBY is "just another manifestation of trying to pass the social costs of energy choices … on to other, and often less politically powerful, groups."[28]

The key idea here is that you paid a lot for your land and you shouldn't have to have your viewshed disrupted. There are other reasons for NIMBYism, too, such as fearing harm to locally owned small businesses, environmental pollution, light pollution, a strain on public resources and schools, and a disproportionate benefit to nonlocals. NIMBYism isn't all bad. In fact, it was a national sense of NIMBYism that led to the wide-scale adoption of wind energy technologies in Denmark in the 1970s.

Around that time, Sweden was completing the Barsebäck Nuclear Power Plant project, which was meant to bring renewable energy to thousands of Swedish households, but would also bring risk. Though the risks of nuclear catastrophe are incredibly low (about one chance in a billion for every year of operation[29]), they tend to be far-reaching. A nuclear meltdown in Sweden would surely impact neighboring Denmark. The Danes didn't want anything to do with that and lobbied for the development of wind energy as the favored renewable in their country instead. They knew wind better than any other renewable and thus gave birth to a "renewable energy revolution," according to Gipe.[30]

There's a long and storied history behind the idea of "energy colonialism." It's happening now in Africa, where more than six hundred million people lack access to electricity because fossil fuel investment is directed toward infrastructure for export rather than remaining local.[31] But it also happens closer to home.

We would rather not have solar panels and wind turbines in our backyards because we'd rather not think about where our energy comes from, just like we'd rather not think about where our food comes from. Let the poor people deal with that. It's not our concern. But when it comes to manifestations of NIMBYism in real life, many of the concerns that cause it can be solved in part by agri-energy.

Gipe wrote, "The Dutch farmers have long said, 'your own pigs don't stink.' That is, if you have a stake in something, whether it's raising pigs or operating a wind turbine, you're more tolerant of its annoyances."[32] So how can we make our pigs less stinky? "Buying" community support, through good neighbor payments and other direct monetary incentives, is one way.

Another is allowing commercial wind or solar sites to be farmed by the leasing farmer or a third party, or by helping farmers develop their own independent renewable energy systems on their own farms. All these build community buy-in and help weave a more comprehensive, cohesive picture of how renewables can be used to bolster the greater good and keep food production, as well as community morale, high.

Reducing Community Pushback

When we talk about ways to reduce the "stinky pigs" in our communities, as Gipe would call them, one of the most common ways is through good neighbor agreements or their equivalents. For example, in Linn County, Iowa, developers have agreed to increased setbacks and required landscaping around solar installations.[33] Governments can also require developers to complete a scorecard that grants points for things like integrating additional battery storage. For many communities, though, that's simply not enough.

To go one step further, developers offer sweet incentives not just to the landowner or the town planning officials, but to the property's neighbors. A good neighbor agreement often exists as a lease, typically a wind lease, that provides payments (often anywhere from $3,000 to $7,000 per year) to landowners who are close to solar or wind developments.[34]

It's more common for this to happen with wind leases than for solar leases, for obvious reasons—you aren't going to be able to plant a few hedges around a wind turbine and conceal it from the view of passersby. It's easy to see where these payments, which don't require any work on the part of the neighbors, might be attractive.

Other "good neighbor" benefits that developers implement aren't quite as direct as writing a check to neighbors but still offer the same sort of advantages. For example, for a project to qualify for planning permission, Nebraska's Rural Community-Based Energy Development Act requires that 33 percent of the gross power purchase agreement payments from a wind project over the contract period must go to the qualified owners or local community.[35]

Alliant Energy in Iowa offers another example, going so far as to shift the location of solar farms and pay out good neighbor incentives to neighboring landowners to encourage communication and goodwill about the projects.[36] Linda Garrett with the American Farmland Trust admitted to me in a video call that it's not always feasible for developments to be placed on land with zero agricultural impact and zero community impact. "It's not like prime land comes in these nice square boxes," she said. "But impact payments can really help reduce tension and opposition between neighbors."

But even when solar or wind *is* placed on farmland, there are other ways developers go about "buying" community support. Norm Davis told me that, for his proposed solar project, the developers have already asked him what he thought the town needed the most. This kind of outreach is not uncommon. Often, solar companies will invest money back into the community to boost support for their projects, doing things like building playgrounds or parks for residents to enjoy.

"We didn't really need another playground," Norm said. "But our fire department did need some help." The ink hasn't yet dried on Norm's contracts with the solar company, but he was confident that, if the project goes through, it will be incredibly beneficial for everyone. "Not too many people have really complained," he said.

And what would there be to complain about? As Norm and Chad repeatedly told me, it's *their* land. Most of the solar farm won't even be visible from the road. And, though they're admittedly an eyesore, the transmission lines that will carry the future power produced on that solar farm have already been there for decades, so they aren't anything new.

Plus, when their project is built, Norm and his son Chad said, they'd like to have it grazed by our sheep. Norm has a soft spot for sheep. He once owned twenty Hampshire sheep—"about twenty too many," joked Chad. Despite the jab, both Chad and Norm like the idea of the land remaining agricultural even after it's been converted into solar arrays. Jobs for sheep, jobs for people.

Speaking of jobs, most states—including New York, Vermont, Georgia, California, Washington, Oregon, Illinois, Minnesota, and Ohio—have renewable jobs that now vastly outnumber those in coal and gas.[37] Wind generation alone employed more than twice as many people as coal power generation in 2022.[38] Admittedly, about half of these new jobs in the solar industry (and about 30 percent in wind) were in construction, which are roles that are often temporary. Yet if we take those jobs out of the equation (and let's not forget that many of the jobs in fossil fuel generation are *also* temporary), we find that renewable job creation in 2022 still rose above the industry average—even though renewables currently account for only about 21 percent of our domestic energy supply in 2023.[39]

Again, not all investments in renewable energy result in the generation of *local* jobs. Many exist in factories afar, in manufacturing panels or batteries or blades, in trucking, or in other aspects of the industry, often many miles away. But, by comparison, in 2019, clean energy jobs outnumbered jobs in the fossil fuel sector three to one.[40] The US Bureau of Labor Statistics estimates that the two fastest-growing jobs in the

United States by 2028 will be solar installers (expected to grow by 105 percent) and wind technicians (96 percent).[41]

While the jobs in installation might not last forever, facilities still need to be managed and parts still need to be made. Renewables generate more energy than what's used in their production, and systems can last as long as twenty to forty years (depending on the energy source and materials used).[42] These long-term gains can serve a community well into the future.

Another common argument is that any benefit renewables provide to local economies is negated because developments receive significant government subsidies. Indeed, renewable subsidies doubled between 2016 and 2022, reaching $15.6 billion.[43] For comparison, however, note that the federal government also doles about $20 billion to the fossil fuel industry each year.[44] And, as Gipe wrote, "We are spending enormous sums to import fossil fuels—money that is lost to our economy, money that enriches others, not North Americans."[45] There's nothing inherently wrong with using US money to build up other countries or communities. But in the context of limiting subsidies, that argument really doesn't hold water, at least not when you're comparing the amounts paid out for renewables versus fossil fuels.

We need to think more carefully about the interconnection of those fibers—about the externalities of fossil fuels and outsourcing food production and how they come back to affect the fabric of our close-to-home communities.

We're All Cogs in the Same Machine

So much of the NIMBYism seen regarding renewable energy can also be found in the world of agriculture. We would much rather buy our food from the grocery store than grow it ourselves. You could argue that much of this is due to a lack of time, resources, or knowledge on how to do so, and that's also true. But so much of it has to do instead with an unwillingness to face the brutality of life, the trade-offs that must occur as part of nature, the sacrifices that need to be made so one can eat. These sacrifices are so often taken by the farmer.

Every single thing that lands on your fork is the direct result of something else dying. It's not a matter of *wanting* to kill. It's a matter of *needing* to eat. We live in a culture that is far removed from what it takes to produce food. Today, just a small percentage of our population produces the nation's food, yet it seems as though every single person has an opinion about how that food should be produced. It's just like everyone has an opinion about where their electricity should come from; that opinion, more often than not, is that electricity should not be coming from their own backyards.

I can't tell you how many times I've been told by someone how "cute" our animals are. They aren't wrong. There's nothing more precious than a baby lamb scampering around in the pasture, jumping up on its mother's back, playing its own version of ovine peek-a-boo with the rest of the flock. I don't care how jaded or coldhearted you are. You're *going* to smile.

But that comment almost always comes with the second piece, the one that frustrates me to no end, no matter how kindly it's uttered: "I don't know how you can stand to kill them." I never have much to say in response. It's not because I don't have a lot that I *want* to say. When it comes time for an animal to be slaughtered, it's not something I take lightly. I'm not excited about butchering chickens. It's not how I would choose to spend a free Saturday. But when you farm, you recognize that there are opposing forces, and you recognize the fragility and immutability of life.

When the mature lambs are sent to the slaughterhouse in the late fall, the ewes back on the farm are pregnant with the next group to be born in just a few short months. The cycle repeats. The energy we lose from the animals who are no longer living will be recycled, in the form of meat that feeds our body and their bones feeding the compost that then feeds our plants. It's all cyclical. It may not be pleasant to kill an animal, but it is part of the human experience, if we choose to live the truest version of the human experience.

Whenever I'm asked this question, my knee-jerk response (that I always force myself not to actually voice) is, "Are you a vegetarian then?" The answer, likely, would almost always be, "No, of course not." So, the question is: Why do we consider it socially acceptable to pluck packages of chicken breasts from the coolers at the grocery store? How is that less cruel to the animal than taking that life yourself? It's not a matter of having the "personal strength" or "callousness" to slaughter an animal. It's about perspective. It's about recognizing that nothing exists in a state of pure perfection or isolation. It is all a give and take. For one thing to happen, another must occur.

Farming is ugly, like nature itself. It can be breathtakingly beautiful, but it is also functional. Everything in an ecosystem serves a purpose. We're all cogs turning in part of a much larger machine. For one creature to eat, another must die. That's a fact that needs to be recognized, no matter how harsh it might sound, for each of us to truly recognize the role we play within our own community and ecosystem.

For the larger machine to function well, we need to think about whether our actions are self-serving or are serving the larger community. We need to think about how our actions are affecting each and every other cog in that machine. Nothing is permanent, ourselves included. It is time to think about how the actions we're taking now will eventually flow downhill to affect other communities in the future—whatever those communities might look like.

Strengthening Food Independence and Community

I don't necessarily believe that every single person needs to grow or raise all their own food. I don't think that's practical for many people, nor do I think it's prudent. However, we do need to provide more support for the farmers who are attempting to do more, to produce more, with fewer resources. As we move into the future, we need to see, in particular, a resurgence in small-scale production, infrastructure, and on-farm processing. Our goal should be not necessarily doing more, but doing more with what we already have.

Agri-energy has the potential to help us do more on limited acreage, and it's not something that works well just with livestock. In fact, growing fruit, grain, and vegetable crops under solar panels is another viable option that's worth exploring.

Perhaps the most pressing argument made against crop production under solar is that it reduces the yields of the panels (in some cases, they need to be spaced farther apart to allow room for planting equipment) while also reducing the yields of the crops (you just aren't going to fit as many spinach or broccoli plants in a solar field), as Rutgers University researcher David Specca mentioned to me.

But we're talking about quality, not necessarily quantity. With agri-energy, you might reduce your crop yields, but in doing so, you also allow that farmer to continue to produce the crop while receiving a more stable financial benefit from the panels (which produce energy even in a drought or amid an infestation of slugs). In this regard, it's important to view both systems as a whole rather than viewing each in isolation. How can you maximize the output of both systems, agriculture and renewables, *combined*, instead of just focusing on that x acres of broccoli and that x acres of solar?

In places like Hawaii, where land prices have soared, this land use factor is a monumental one for communities that want to remain farming. It serves as a classic example of how agri-energy can help communities maintain their energy and food independence, keeping the production of both localized and, in this case, more affordable.

Hawaii aims to draw 100 percent of its energy from renewable sources by 2045.[46] About 1.93 million acres in Hawaii is zoned for agriculture, but precious little is used for growing anything. Farmland is being lost at a rapid pace (largely due to the skyrocketing cost of buying land there).[47]

Dual-use presents the ideal scenario because it offers an avenue for climate-resilient farming—the shading from solar panels is advantageous in Hawaii's hot climate—while boosting local food security. The state is heavily reliant on imported food (importing up to 90 percent of its food supply[48]) despite its favorable climate, simply because land is sold at such a premium there. Though much more pronounced, the issue faced by Hawaiian farmers is the same one faced by farmers on the mainland: Nobody can afford to farm, even if they want to.

We are up against a monumental challenge. As of 2025, the global population has crept up over eight billion and is projected to be close to ten billion by 2050. There are major concerns over whether we'll have enough land to produce food to feed all those ten billion people (let alone enough energy to produce that food or provide electricity or fuel for our cars). The United Nations Food and Agriculture Organization (conservatively) projects that food production will need to increase by 70 percent by 2050 to meet the demands of our growing population.[49]

Just as concerning is that food is not produced uniformly around the world, but instead, only in isolated pockets. Just 1 percent of Americans are responsible for producing the food that the people of the United States eat as well as the food that we export.[50]

The minority is producing food for the majority, and much of that food is being trucked and shipped and flown all over the world. Farming accounts for less than 1 percent of the US gross national product.[51] Meanwhile, in 2024, agricultural imports amounted to roughly $213 billion.[52]

It's true that many of the foods we consume can't be grown on American soil, or at least not without major modifications to the environment. You can't grow tomatoes outside in January in Vermont, and there are very few places in the United States where you can grow bananas or pineapples or avocados at all. But much of the food that could reasonably be produced here isn't. Why are we importing so much honey ($794 million per year) and broccoli (195.9 million pounds from Mexico alone)?[53] Why is it cheaper to buy lamb from New Zealand than it is from the farm down the road?

It's all basic economics. The US dollar is stronger in many parts of the world from where we import our food than it is at home. The food is also being produced at scale, in some cases with looser labor and industry regulations. Often, production costs are lower than they are in the United States. As for food produced here, but at scale, consumer tax dollars keep corn and soy prices low while other government subsidies funnel into the mass production of animal feed.

Let's talk, on the other hand, about potential agri-energy crops. In the United States, we produce around 129 million pounds of lamb.[54] However, we import around 305 million pounds of it, mostly from Australia (about 75 percent) and New Zealand (24 percent), with this meat typically less expensive than what's produced domestically.[55]

Or consider spinach. The United States is the world's second-largest producer of spinach, growing 960,600 pounds per year (most of which is grown in California and Arizona and heavily irrigated; agrivoltaics presents another huge advantage here, which I'll touch on later).[56] We export about $134.1 million of that, but we also import around $101.8 million of spinach.[57] Most of that is from Mexico, with some also from China, which accounts for about 90 percent of the world's spinach crop.[58]

If we are *already* so successful at growing spinach, why not keep the food supply local? It's based, again, on the premise of an economy of scale. Exporting often leads to higher profit margins, particularly for larger companies. The laws that govern farms in the United States are set up to accommodate large farms, not small ones.[59] For large commercial farms especially, you can make more money by shipping than by direct marketing—not to mention that subsidies make it more attractive to grow crops like corn and soy than they do spinach or broccoli.

Historically, the United States has exported more agricultural goods by value than what it imports, but the balance has started to tip in recent years, contributing to a "negative trade balance," per the US Department of Agriculture.[60] The biggest issue here is that much of the exports we are shipping out aren't necessarily ready-to-eat food products. In 2023, more than half of our exports were in the form of grains and livestock feeds, oilseeds, and products, while a much smaller percentage were dedicated to horticultural products like fruits and vegetables.[61] Cattle, corn, and soy are our top three products, and those are three very land hungry commodities. We certainly are not getting the most bang for our food production buck when it comes to land use, especially considering that most of the corn and soy grown here are used for ultraprocessed foods (which require more land, labor, and energy to produce), ethanol, or livestock feed.

Beyond creating trade deficits, our habit of using US land for export crops while relying on imports for the food we eat has serious implications for food security. What happens when the imports we rely on stop, whether that's due to global wars, scarcity, or climate disasters? When COVID-19 caught us all off guard, these issues came to the forefront as the pandemic brought our supply chains to a screeching halt, but they had been bubbling under the surface for quite some time. Though the rates of food security did dip somewhat between 2020 and 2021, they weren't regarded as being "statistically significant," likely because many households were buoyed by federal and state subsidies.[62]

Some communities, however, suffered far more than others. Despite national averages that indicated rising food insecurity, households with children actually became *more* secure, likely due to support from the schools (many bussed meals directly to students), along with the expansion of pandemic EBT benefits and the Child Tax Credit.[63] Adults living alone, particularly women living alone, became less food secure as many of the credits did not extend to child-free households.

And despite what the rates said otherwise, the reality was a depressing one. Still working then as a high school English teacher, I found it devastating to hear stories of families in our community struggling to feed their families. Meanwhile, the national news was flooded with images of farmers plowing under fields of fresh vegetables, euthanizing pigs and chickens, and dumping thousands of gallons of milk. There was plenty of product, but no transportation system to get it where it needed to go.

What kind of world do we live in where those two scenes can be juxtaposed together?

If there were ever an example of NIMBYism as it relates to food, this is it. We outsource the vast majority of our food production to other countries so it can be out of sight and out of mind, but it's not until our food distribution networks are damaged or halted that we notice the problems of this outsourcing. The COVID-19 pandemic brought this fact to light for so many, and it's something that reverberates throughout our food supply chain.

In 2020, the US Department of Agriculture created the Coronavirus Food Assistance Program to provide relief for farmers, sending a portion of that food and those funds to stock the shelves of food banks. But this temporary Band-Aid doesn't do anything to resolve the major issues we have with our supply chain.

Our world is supposedly more connected than ever before, yet we're also more *dis*connected than we've ever been. The American Farm Bureau Federation estimates that only 6 percent of all US farms supply food locally. The rest ship products out to supply grocery stores and the food-service industry.[64]

A food-independent America is not impossible. Based on recent studies, 90 percent of Americans could be fed entirely by food that's grown or raised within one hundred miles of their homes, but that will require a rethinking of the way we use land and how we do business.[65] There are many issues at play here, but very few of them have to do with consumer preference. We have never had an issue convincing our local customers of the benefits of eating local food; in fact, when Josh and I expanded our farm sales significantly in the spring and summer of 2020, we couldn't keep up with the demand. We kept saying if we had a hundred more acres, we'd be able to grow our business exponentially.

But land comes at a premium, and most first-generation farmers don't have access to the land that would allow them to stay in business and feed the community. It's not about whether we have the *ability* to become a food-independent United States. It's just that we need to rethink what, where, and how we are growing that food. We have the way and just need the will.

Opening up access to land on solar farms, in particular, is groundbreaking for livestock producers like Josh and me, who can now use that land to graze sheep or cattle, or even for vegetable producers looking to grow crops. With solar companies willing now more than ever before to experiment with new forms of production, it really does present a win-win opportunity, especially if you think about food independence and helping those who want to rely more on local food do just that.

Plus, you're helping a farmer open up additional streams of revenue *in addition* to additional tracts of land. When a farmer can farm without significant financial barriers, food can stay local—and create a more resilient local food supply for the community.

Energy Independence and Rethinking Community

Energy, like food, is also better for communities if it is kept local. Instead, all our energy is currently produced on roughly 74.5 million acres (about the size of Arizona), or roughly 3 percent of all land in the US. About two-thirds of that is used to grow corn and soy for biofuel (typically, ethanol).[66] The United States is, in fact, the world's largest exporter of ethanol. On the other hand, the US could supply all its electricity with solar alone on just 0.4 percent (ten million acres) of the country's land area.[67] That's without even taking advantage of rooftop solar.

If the country were to transition forty million acres of ethanol fuel to solar (ideally dual use solar), it could meet 100 percent of its electricity needs while at the same time also powering a nationwide fleet of electric vehicles.[68] Solar panels produce roughly two hundred times more energy per acre than corn[69] (and there's a solid argument here that corn isn't even that much of an efficient so-called biofuel anyway, since it produces 24 percent more emissions than gasoline through its resource-greedy land use, processing, and combustion[70]).

A solar farm might affect your view. But wouldn't it be worth it, at least a little bit, if that view disruption meant that a farmer was using it to keep his lights on in the barn during calving season or to power his milking parlor, or to water his tomatoes? Or even if—all agricultural production aside—a farmer was using it to supplement their nonexistent 401(k) so that they could finally, *finally*, retire at the age of eighty-two? Or perhaps even if that solar farm was helping make energy costs more affordable for the elderly couple who lives down the road from you and is now able to tap into community solar?

Just as the United States needs to build food security, it is also imperative to build energy security. Gipe wrote, "We need to envision an electricity system that is sustainable, meets the needs of people today as well as those of tomorrow, and is built upon sufficiency for all, equitably distributed. We need to envision a system that enhances the quality of life for all, rich and poor alike."[71]

Phal Mantha knows that better than most. He works at Ridge to Reefs as the director of agriculture and sustainability. As the name implies, Ridge to Reefs tackles pollution in a "land to sea" perspective, focusing on green infrastructure in places like the Chesapeake Bay, Puerto Rico, Palau, American Samoa, and Hawaii.

When we spoke over Zoom in 2024, our conversation started with a lengthy tangent about some of the work Phal has done in Hawaii. As an aside, he mentioned that the state has a massive problem with pollution from hog farms and is home to eighty-three thousand cesspools (holding tanks that store untreated waste). It has more cesspools than any other state, with a fifth of them located less than a kilometer from the shore. The state mandated that all these cesspools be removed by 2050, but this process won't occur instantaneously.[72]

Cesspools aren't inherently problematic, but in Hawaii, where sea levels are rising and intense storms are happening more often, the sewage is polluting aquifers and traveling through springs back to the ocean. For example, researchers found that bacteria levels in the ocean in front of Puako, a town on the Big Island, exceeded state health standards in 81 percent of the locations sampled.[73] Hawaii also has double the rate of MRSA infections than the national average.[74] "I have a friend who's a scuba diver," Phal told me, "and he won't go diving anymore."

What happens on the land has a huge impact on what happens in the water, Phal reminds me. That's part of why he's made it his mission to help improve environments in both places—and from a holistic, innovative, and nature-based perspective.

Phal didn't grow up on the coast, but instead in landlocked Michigan, where he studied agronomy and started his career as a first-generation farmer, managing several farms (including some on the Big Island). At one point, back on the mainland, he ran a farm to produce fresh farm-to-table offerings for a hotel group. Around this time, he was introduced to Paul Sturm, founder of Ridge to Reefs.

In 2017, when Hurricane Maria struck Puerto Rico, Paul reached out to Phal to see if he would be interested in helping the farmers there as part of the relief efforts. Phal agreed to travel to Puerto Rico immediately and used two weeks of personal time off. A donor lent them a private jet, which they filled with four water filtration systems and other equipment, including gravity-powered lights, drinking water, chain saws and extra chains, gas, and bar oil. "The pilot wasn't too impressed," Phal said, about their unconventional carry-on luggage.

When they arrived in Puerto Rico, Phal was stunned by what he saw. "It looked like a bomb had gone off," he said. People were drinking from rivers and sewage outflows. There was no power, no fuel, no communication, no food.

Actually, there technically *was* food—unharvested crops left in the fields—but the farmers couldn't do anything with it because the weather was too hot and humid. Ironically, even though many of the crops had survived the floods, the farmers had no water to wash those vegetables; the water system, which runs on electricity, had no backup power. The packing facilities and refrigeration units were also now defunct. There was no reason to cut the crops because they couldn't be washed or stored and would go bad within a couple days of being harvested.

Acting quickly to stop the bleed, Phal and his team worked to install solar panels on roofs and implemented a CoolBot system to create hasty refrigeration units; these systems use any window air-conditioning unit to create a pseudo walk-in cooler in any room, even one made out of scrap lumber. Through $150,000 raised through a GoFundMe drive, they worked on building out systems that would help the farmers where they were hurting the most. The team set up cisterns for rainwater harvesting and built gravity-powered wash and pack stations, where farmers could capture the rain, store it in a cistern, and then use it to clean produce in a three-sink setup. The farmers could now capture rainwater and have it on tap if they lost power.

When we think about implementing renewables, it's important to consider our vulnerabilities to climate change disasters. We need to think about our communities and how well they'll be able to handle emergencies, particularly when the government isn't able, or isn't willing, to step in and help.

As Phal saw in Puerto Rico, the results of complacency can be devastating. We need to start paying close attention to the impacts of climate change, even if it's not yet affecting our communities close to home. "The public," he said, referring to climate change, "is bearing the negative externalities."

Again, we're starting to see the negative externalities of fossil fuels come to light, and it's not just about the pollution of the atmosphere. It's also about how they create an overreliance, a false sense of security, on the systems and grids that hold our lives together.

For too long, we've ignored the massive blackouts that have occurred in places like Puerto Rico (including those in the aftermath of hurricanes and other disasters) because here on the mainland, things tend to get back up and running fairly quickly. Energy emergencies on islands tend to be just a blip in the news cycle.

As our global environment changes, however, we're starting to see the instability of our foreign energy reliance coming to light. Today, it's become clearer than ever that we need to localize our energy.

The United States is the fifth largest importer of electricity in the world (to say nothing of the country's other energy needs).[75] Upon taking office in 2025, President Donald Trump announced a set of sweeping tariffs that would apply, among other things, a 25 percent tariff on goods imported to the United States from Canada. (Of the electricity we import, about 90 percent comes from Canada alone.[76]) In response, Ontario Premier Doug Ford slapped a 25 percent surcharge on all electricity sent to the United States from the province, with many other provinces expected to follow suit.[77]

In the United States, we're about to see our electric bills soar. We're about to discover what the people living in Hawaii and Puerto Rico have always known: You can't depend on someone else for your electricity.

Phal told me, "Grid connections make sense in the continental US, where electric rates are relatively low, but in Hawaii, they're 50 cents per kilowatt hour. In Puerto Rico, they're 45 cents." Those places are nearing five times the national average on electricity costs, which, as Phal emphasizes, clearly demonstrates that "not all places are created equally." Here, we're about to see our prices reach, or perhaps even surpass, those paid by folks on the islands.

Beyond highlighting the issues that exist within our energy system (an energy system that's highly dependent on other countries), the current economic and political climate in the United States highlights another important fact: We can't apply blanket solutions under the foolhardy assumption that just because something doesn't work well in your community, it won't work well elsewhere.

It makes good sense to rely on renewables in Hawaii or Puerto Rico, and it has for a long time. In those locations, energy costs are high, and energy independence is a top priority. The phrase "being an island unto oneself" applies quite literally here. When you live on an island, you're isolated. You need to be able to fend for yourself. Renewables make sense because they localize the energy process. And they're about to start making more sense for the rest of the country, too.

As our electricity rates climb higher, and as our trade agreements with other countries deteriorate, we need to think about how we can do more with what we have here. We have sun. We have wind. We have the land to install renewable energy systems.

It's time to stop outsourcing our energy production to other countries, just like it's time to stop outsourcing our food production. It may be ugly to have a solar panel in your backyard or a wind turbine blocking your view of the farmer's field, but wouldn't you rather have a community that's resilient against whatever nature, international trade agreements, or the next global pandemic throws your way?

We need to rethink the definition of community. We need to think more clearly about how we can bring energy production back into the hands of Americans, and I'm not talking about building more power plants.

What Does "Community" Mean to You?

"The value of human life is probably undervalued," Gipe told me. "Power plants are cheap to build. But they don't pay for the wind, water, and air pollution. They also require *fuel*." It's primarily in the United States where we harbor such vehement opposition to renewables. Much of that opposition is because our power plants are currently cheap. They're old, they're built, and they're paid for. Yet they still require fuel, and that fuel is *not* paid for, nor is it cheap.

Even with all those factors considered, most of us still tend to be okay with that. After all, as mentioned before, our energy needs are still being met, but the difference is that the production remains out of sight and out of mind. We like not having to think about it. But what about when climate change causes a disaster in *your* town? What then? We don't think about the community benefits of renewables (or of local agriculture, for that matter) because most of us have a very loose definition of what community actually is and then don't think too much about our energy production until problems hit *very* close to home.

If I were to ask you who your community is, who are the people you regard as your community, what would your answer be? Is it only your closest family and friends? Perhaps just the people who live on your street? In your town? Your county? Your state? Is it the people who go to church with you, who vote the same way as you, the families whose children attend school with your own? Is it the people who live within a hundred miles of you? Your fellow Americans? Humans?

When we think about the community benefits of renewables, we need to have a clear idea of who it is these projects are benefiting. I've heard so many complaints, time and again, that the power produced in one area is being sent to another area, from a rural area into a city. "Why does our land have to get used up so that *they* get power?" I'm asked.

I understand the frustration, especially when you see a plot of land that's been farmed since your grandfather was a small child being turned into something else. I won't argue that it's easy to deal with change, especially when that change doesn't seem to be benefiting you directly. But let's not forget the conversation about externalities. The energy produced at that commercial solar farm might not be juicing up your own electronics. You might not be driving an electric vehicle. You might be perfectly fine driving a gas-powered pickup truck to work and using fossil fuels to heat your home.

I don't drive an electric car. I drive a gas-powered pickup. Our tractor runs on diesel. We're tied into the community solar program in our community, but we also heat our home with fuel oil because we can't yet afford more renewable alternatives. You need to do what's right for you. But let's not ignore what's best for everyone else and make broad strokes about what will or will not work based on your own lived experience and your own priorities.

In Hawaii, a conversion to renewables makes a lot of sense. The ability for Hawaiians to generate power with wind or solar not only helps them save money but fosters a sense of energy independence. This energy independence is what provides a buffer against risk. We know, just by looking at what happened in Puerto Rico, that we can't keep relying on the way things have always been. We need to build stronger, more climate-resilient communities in whichever ways make the most sense for those communities.

Renewables can also promote more on-farm energy independence. Gary and Connie Menard of Happy Haven Farm in Mooers, New York, mentioned in chapter 1, save thousands of dollars on their energy costs with solar each year. But there are many other ways we can reduce our reliance on the grid and bolster our defenses for when the worst happens.

One way is to use on-farm resources like biochar. The tradition of using it as a farm amendment goes back many years and spans continents.

In the Amazon rainforest, Phal says, the soil was originally clay, and most of the materials had leached out. The indigenous people there followed a slash-and-char method that incorporated organic matter back into the soils in an early application of biochar.

Now, Phal also studies the ways we can use biochar on farms, something he's been passionate about for years. (Phal first met Paul Sturm when he stumbled upon his work when researching where to buy biochar to increase his farm's plant yields.) Hurricane Maria later led Ridge to Reefs to develop an innovative wastewater treatment method that used wood chips, biochar, and native and invasive plants to clean wastewater before being dispatched into the leach field. As you can see, Phal's a champion for thinking creatively about how to best implement renewables and technologies on the farm.

An autonomous electric tractor is another example of creative renewable applications. Phal told me, "Small-scale family farms that don't need a lot of acreage for vegetables—these would work nicely here. You can have a solar shed to charge your own tractor. For soil preparation and harvesting, all equipment could be renewable." He also cited renewable heating and cooling systems for livestock, anaerobic digesters to harvest methane, and other technologies that could make life on the farm easier, more affordable, and, most importantly, more independent.

H2arvester, founded in the Netherlands, is another new, circular energy system that promises to revolutionize renewable energy, too—without the loss of crop production. They are solar cars arranged in a matrix of solar panels that move autonomously across fields.[78] The cars can be rotated with grazing or even driven over ditches. With these systems, farmers can balance their production while generating energy (hydrogen as well as heat, as the output from the panels is converted to green hydrogen and stored). Or the energy can be sold to third parties.

"You can't beat decentralized systems," Phal argues. "We *can* have circular economies and regenerative societies. We need to think cradle to cradle versus cradle to grave." In other words, we need to think not only about which actions and which decisions will benefit *us*, but everything that will come *after* us.

Reweaving the Community: The Connection Between Fiber and Local Economies

It's not just in food and energy where these issues of sovereignty versus supply chain become apparent, but also in products like textiles. Wool is a good example of this dichotomy. We may have the capacity to produce more of our own nonfood products like wool domestically, but we don't.

Very little wool is imported into the United States. Although we import more than $250 million in wool, animal hair, and horsehair yarn per year, that only accounts for 0.44 percent of the total global consumption of wool.[79]

Domestically, we produce more than $45 million dollars' worth of shorn wool per year, or roughly 11.54 million pounds of cleaned wool.[80] Prior to about 2018, the wool industry was doing alright. The largest buyer of wool was the US Department of Defense (which remains the top buyer, capturing up to 20 percent of the total market for uniforms and bedding), but much was also exported. China alone took 59 percent of all American wool.[81] Then, trade relations between the United States and China fell apart, leading to an exchange of penalty tariffs on a number of products, including wool. COVID-19 dealt another blow, shuttering droves of textile production facilities in China as well as the rest of the world.

There are now stocks of unsold wool sitting in factories, and nobody quite knows exactly what to do with it. It's no secret that Americans have become enamored with lighter, cheaper textiles like polyester, cotton, nylon, and rayon. Polyester is the most widely produced fiber, making up more than half of the global market (polyester is made of petroleum-based chemicals).[82] Wool costs more, but it lasts longer and can be produced locally. More than 97 percent of all apparel sold in the United States is made overseas.[83] That's problematic for a number of reasons, with labor conditions and environmental issues at the top of the list. For sheep farmers who produce wool, agri-energy may be the ideal solution.

Nick Armentrout, who now lives in Maine, spent much of his early career in Idaho and Wyoming. He got his feet wet working with sheep on Western ranches, though he considers his expertise to be more in the draft horse domain.

Nick started working with a wool clothing company in 2008 with the goal of creating a US-sourced wool textile. First owned by Tom Chappell, founder of Tom's of Maine (the toothpaste company), Ramblers Way works with ranchers in the West to procure 18.5-micron wool, a superfine wool also known as 100s grade. The wool is milled and woven in the US and then processed into a fabric that's cut and sewn in Massachusetts.[84]

To Nick, agrivoltaics and agri-energy present an opportunity to localize not just food but also fiber. "We need to maximize the good, not just the yield," he said, and look at the other benefits of grazing on solar besides just x pounds of wool or y pounds of lamb. How is grazing helping with soil stabilization? How is it supporting the economy?

The United States is not a top-ten wool producer. Far from it. And there's not a lot of wool being produced on solar farms—yet. Nick said he thinks that there's a lot of room for (wooly) growth since only about 25 percent of solar sheep contribute to the wool crop. Wool is unique because it contains a high amount of carbon, so using renewable energy to remedy the climate crisis by stacking these many benefits is important. He admits that the market for US wool isn't great but said that we need to think outside the box. "It's hard for wool to compete," he said. "The lucrative markets that do exist are for superfine wool, next-to-skin fabrics." Coarser wools also have immense value for things like carpets and rugs or even for wool fertilizer pellets, however. Wool is high in nitrogen and releases nutrients slowly. It can also reduce watering needs and repel pests like slugs. Today, some companies even specialize in turning unprocessed, raw wool into pellets.

"Wool follows where the processing is available," Nick told me. "There's so much just sitting in warehouses because the market is poor." What's really changing the market for wool is renewables. "You have a user who's mandated to find ways to stabilize the soil," he said, referring to developers. "They must find community support, collaboration, and partnership." Here, agriculture and renewables could, yet again, create the perfect marriage.

We need to think carefully about the effect our dollars are having, big or small. Agri-energy allows us to bring energy and food independence back to our communities and to our farms. It helps us reclaim some sense of connection with our communities, and that holds true regardless of whether you consider your community to be just you, your partner, and your kids or you and the entire country or even you and all the other humans on the planet.

We have always been proud of the work we do as solar graziers because it helps us close many of the loops in our systems. Our lambs are born on our farm. Their mothers are fed hay all winter purchased from the farmers who lease the solar farm that we then graze the sheep on in the summer. When they're mature, they're sent to a local processing facility. The meat is then sold to a local restaurant and local stores (along with direct to our local customers). There's a beautiful sense of synergy in all these systems relying on each other. That's what the idea of eco-modernism, which advocates for technological development to protect nature, gets wrong. We don't need to reinvent the wheel. We just need to use our wheels *together* instead of turning them in a different direction while trying to get to exactly the same place.

When we think about how we can produce more of our food, fiber, and other products locally, we reduce the friction that's generated in the debate over renewables versus agriculture, something that clearly doesn't need to be an either-or situation in the first place. Often, we return to the issue of cost. We get so caught up in figuring out what the "ideal scenario" is that we lose sight of the "best-case scenario for right now." There's some risk involved in committing a section of a solar site to crops, or to cows, or to whatever it might be. But think of the opportunities.

There's a lot of studying, researching, and compiling pros and cons lists for agri-energy. I get it—there's a lot of money wrapped up in these projects, and a lot at stake.

But there's also a lot at stake if we don't start taking action. It might be something we aren't able to quantify with research or with balance sheets. It might just be something you have to experience. Jack's Solar Garden in Colorado generates power for three hundred homes while also teaching farmers how to grow vegetables beneath solar panels. The primary goal of the farm is selling energy—with the biggest subscriber being a local cannabis company. It also donates 2 percent of its power production to low-income households through the Boulder County Housing Authority.[85]

At Jack's Solar Garden, visitors can see the microclimates that are created under solar arrays. They can see how the vegetation is impacted and even how the system impacts people working beneath the panels. Without a doubt, it's the most comprehensive and largest agrivoltaics research site in the nation, providing valuable data on the impact of agrivoltaics for crop production while also donating thousands of pounds of produce to local nonprofit organizations.

You can't quantify those benefits easily when you write them down on paper. But I'd bet a visit to that food bank on delivery day would give you all the proof of success you need.

Energizing Communities

Agri-energy, when done correctly, can keep the money and the food in the community. It can also keep the energy local.

Unfortunately, renewables, like energy in general, still create pockets of opportunity for some while disenfranchising others. Minnesota sets a great example of how to avoid issues of "energy colonialism," or, as Alex DePillis put it, "ghettoization."

In Minnesota, there's lots of wind on farmland. Here, Paul Gipe told me, agreements stipulate that lease payments must stay with the resident of the land, not necessarily the owner. This requirement reduces concerns about wealthy out-of-towners buying up land so that they can reap the benefits of paychecks from "Big Wind" without having to deal with the viewsheds because they then move away and rent the property out.

Developers are trying to get ahead of this worry, looking at ways they can garner community support before a project is even built. How can they reinvest back into a community—besides just through PILOT programs and job creation?

For starters, transitioning to renewables can save towns and businesses money on their electric bills that can be returned to local communities. Renewable projects are often used to power schools, hospitals, large businesses, and the like. I taught English at a high school that now has a small solar farm behind it. The energy created by those panels goes directly to the school to help manage costs and reduce spikes for electricity that happen in the open market. Other than providing the land, the solar farm cost nothing to the school.[86]

This trickle-down effect here often doesn't occur in larger economies but is more likely to be found in small communities where community solar projects are built. In the private sector, for example, a business owner who can save money by tapping into community solar can give raises to their employees, or a city with a solar farm can reallocate money that would have otherwise been spent on out-of-state energy to build affordable housing for its constituents.

Solar and wind farms are repeatedly criticized for shirking tax responsibilities, but in many cases, they are simply taking advantage of local legislation that may benefit individuals as well as companies. As an example, New York law allows residential solar owners to file for a fifteen-year exemption from real property taxation from the increase in value resulting from the installation of a system.[87]

Here and in other states, property owners pay real property taxes based on the combined assessed value of their land as well as any improvements made to the land. Real property that's leased by a developer is subjected to special assessments and special district taxes, such as water and sewer fees.

Discounts, terms, and conditions are typically negotiated by an industrial development agency (IDA). IDAs are local authorities that, among other things, give mortgage, sales, and property tax breaks to developers and other businesses that will bring jobs to an area and boost its economy. An IDA's board usually comprises half a dozen or so unpaid members, typically community members appointed by a county legislator.

There's some criticism that IDAs dole out millions in tax breaks to wind and solar developers—enough to make their projects financially viable when they wouldn't be otherwise—but the flip side is that IDAs also hand out billions in tax breaks to fossil fuel projects.

Generally, an IDA will require a project to promote "economic welfare" and create jobs for the communities, so not just solar and wind developments are negotiated by IDAs. Everything from Amazon warehouses to fast-food restaurants and distribution facilities take advantage of them. The majority of all IDA tax breaks go to manufacturing facilities; in 2021, 1,064 out of 4,342 total projects in New York State funded by IDA tax breaks were in manufacturing, versus just 85 in clean energy.[88]

When an application for a tax break is approved, the IDA will execute a payment in lieu of taxes agreement. Through a PILOT agreement, a developer or company must make payments to "affected tax jurisdictions," including the school districts, counties, cities, villages, and towns, instead of paying property taxes. These agreements tend to last for ten to thirty years; after this period, the property is no longer considered tax exempt, and the property is subject to property taxes.

Through PILOT programs, developers don't directly pay taxes, but these programs can create significant tax revenue for cities, counties, and school districts. "Community solar customers, which may include municipalities, businesses, and residents, save money on their utility bills. Taxing jurisdictions can benefit from PILOT payments, negotiated by IDAs. At the same time, given the passive nature of a solar array, a solar project does not create increased demands on municipal services and infrastructure," according to the New York Solar Guidebook.[89]

Even with a PILOT agreement, in most cases a developer will still need to pay special district taxes for fire and ambulance.

In New York, communities have the option of opting out of the tax exemption under the state's Real Property Tax Law.[90] A community can choose to make the added value of a solar panel system fully taxable, but often choose to *not* opt out and go for PILOT agreements instead. PILOT programs do tend to be more beneficial for communities that are interested in setting up community solar farms than communities that are not.

Many developers also often choose to invest money back into the community, spending hundreds of thousands of dollars on facilities like playgrounds or on other philanthropic projects. That's to say nothing of job creation.

Community solar allows local residents to tap back into the energy that's being produced, with less of a concern about the energy being farmed out. Community solar projects are typically in the two- to five-megawatt range and allow anyone, including renters, to purchase a fraction of the electricity generated by the system, receiving credits for the electricity on their monthly utility bills. "Community solar," solar developer Elie Schecter explained to me, "opens up the marketplace to people who couldn't install their own solar."

On our farm, we only save about $200 per year by leveraging community solar. Still, I like knowing that our community is diversifying its energy sources and making it a little more resilient to disruptions in the centralized grid.

Energy independence aside, there's still a prevalent, and valid, argument that many of these good-faith efforts by renewable developers to build and bolster community support are strictly in the name of good public relations. I won't argue that. As a business (of any kind), trying to find new ways to make yourself look good is the name of the game. As long as you're not trying to make yourself look good in the name of doing *more harm*, I don't necessarily see a problem with it.

When agriculture is added into the mix, the benefits compound. Living in a colder region of the country, our grazing season is limited. We usually have sheep on-site from April to November. The rest of the year, we must feed our animals hay since the grass simply is not growing enough to sustain a flock. We purchase our hay (and the grain we feed to pregnant ewes) from other local farmers. We frequent a local veterinarian, and we have our tractor serviced at a local shop. When our lambs are ready for harvest, they are sent to a local slaughterhouse and the meat is sold to a local restaurant, both of which hire local employees. It's almost impossible to quantify the benefit that agri-energy has on communities because the benefit is so far-reaching, creating an inter-connected web with tangled threads and seemingly no end.

As Phal showed me, shit always flows downhill. Whether it's sewage flowing into the Pacific from the mountains of Hawaii or the trickle-down effect that energy developments have on local communities and economies, we need to make sure we're not sending our shit to our neighbors. We need to make sure we're keeping everyone's best interests in mind—and that requires some thought and deliberate action.

A solar farm might not make quite as much money by combining its operations with grazing or crop production. A wind farm might not make quite as much money by investing in community projects to build support. But the net benefit will be much higher when everybody's needs are accounted for.

Indeed, Phal put it best: "We need to manage our crap correctly."

CHAPTER 3

Developing a Renewable Future

If everyone is moving forward together, then success takes care of itself.
—Henry Ford

ON NOVEMBER 1, 2023, I sat on a barstool in a diner in Kingston, New York, sipping a cup of black coffee while I waited for Marguerite Wells, executive director of the Alliance for Clean Energy, to arrive. Marguerite owns Two Mothers Farm in Ithaca, New York, with her spouse, Lexie Hain, who works for Lightsource bp as director of agrivoltaics and land management. We had a meeting scheduled that day with a downstate senator and had planned to meet at the diner next door to huddle up beforehand.

During my drive to Kingston, my mind was consumed with thoughts of how this meeting might have the potential to really change the narrative around solar grazing. Michelle Hinchey, a New York state senator for the Forty-First Senate District, is also the chair of the Committee on Agriculture. After reading about some bills Hinchey had been involved in and reading some of her public statements, I had the feeling that she, a Democrat, would be pretty easy to convince. After all, what

Democrat doesn't love renewables? It's practically a wrung-out stereo-type by this point.

Yet Marguerite had repeatedly told me that Hinchey believed other-wise. The meeting had been pushed off many times because the senator wasn't terribly keen on the idea of agrivoltaics.

I had found that hard to believe. Clearly, Hinchey just hadn't talked to the right people yet. Naively, I had a hard time seeing any of the negatives of either solar grazing or agrivoltaics. Lots of people had issues with solar, but what complaint could there possibly be when you could marry solar *and* agriculture? I was confident that we would be able to win her over. Hinchey had a reputation for being sympathetic to farm-ers, and Marguerite and I were both farmers, so it should be an easy sell, I told myself.

After Marguerite met me at the diner, we walked next door to Hinchey's offices. There, we were ushered into a conference room to meet the senator. Hinchey sat at the head of the table and began talking tirelessly about her work with farmers. By this, she meant that she'd vis-ited a few. She cited four or five examples, all in Dutchess and Columbia Counties or on Long Island.

In all fairness, Hinchey represents District 41, which is in the Hud-son Valley of New York State and incorporates almost all of Dutchess County, including the city and town of Poughkeepsie, and the western half of Putnam County. Yet as she was the chair of the Committee on Agriculture for the entire state, it is my opinion that Hinchey's site visits shouldn't be limited to a one-hundred-mile radius of her district. These far-reaching, systemic problems affect every corner of every state, and you can't make policies that impact that entire state's systems (and the ag industry at large) without knowing the different challenges that are faced throughout.

Perhaps the biggest problem is that Hinchey's view on solar develop-ment and agriculture (like the views of so many others in decision-making capacities) follows a very formulaic, one-size-fits-all approach. It doesn't examine the unique attributes and needs of each individual community up close before forming the full narrative. It looks at one piece of the puzzle, not at the entirety. And when you're trying to create systems that are independent and self-supporting, and economies that are fully circular, you simply can't do that. You can't look at individual farms in isolation or take a sampling from just a handful of farms geographically close to your headquarters. If we want to create a system that can produce its own food and its own energy without relying on expensive imports or unstable supply chains, then we need to look at how everything works together rather than lumping everyone into the same category.

Hinchey's stance is that farmland should not be used for solar, at least not without doing extensive amounts of research. In January 2024, she announced that the Smart Integrated Tools for Energy Development Act (known as the SITED Act) was signed into law. It requires the state to develop a Clean Energy Mapping Tool to "allow communities to identify the lands best suited for renewable energy siting and designate preferred sites on the map for renewable energy developers to search." It also has provisions to "help communities better understand" the benefits of hosting renewables.[1]

Other states are following similar paths. Colorado, for example, passed the Agrivoltaics Research and Development Funding Act, which authorized "funding in the form of grants for new or ongoing research and demonstration projects studying the use of agrivoltaics."[2] Massachusetts has a comparable program, the MA Act Driving Clean Energy and Offshore Wind, that "allows agricultural and horticultural land to be used to site solar panels and establishes a commission to study the deployment of these 'dual use sites' while minimizing ecosystem and agricultural impacts."[3] At the federal level, the US Department of Energy has funded more than $15 million in research on how agrivoltaics might be able to work around the country.[4]

As of writing this, however, very few states offer clear-cut incentives for developers to actually follow through with agri-energy projects, at least beyond the research stage. Maryland offers property tax exemptions for community solar agrivoltaics, but it has strict standards, requiring at least 50 percent of the energy generated to be provided to low- to moderate-income consumers at a discount of at least 20 percent less than local utility electric rates. If not used for agrivoltaics, the site must be located on a rooftop, brownfield, landfill, or clean fill.[5] Massachusetts offers incentives as well, including feed-in tariff adders of six cents per kilowatt-hour for agrivoltaic projects through the Solar Massachusetts Renewable Target (SMART) program, but again, these incentives and their accompanying laws tend to be rather prescriptive.[6]

I'm all for more research and a better understanding of how agri-energy works and where it works best. I'm also in favor of any policies, whether at the state or federal level, that incentivize developers to do the right thing and plan for agri-energy from the outset of a project. To be clear, getting developers on board early can be challenging, as there are countless policies governing siting and multiple considerations and strategies to be taken into consideration.

However, we need to be careful about making regulations so prescriptive that it's hard for agriculture to happen naturally. I've visited many solar sites where sheep wouldn't be the best choice but where another crop, like broccoli or even cattle, would be better. By writing laws that are overly rigid or place too much of an emphasis on the research stage rather than the action stage, we're making it more difficult for our future selves. We need to have some fluidity in how sites are managed for agri-energy, and, most importantly, we need to stop holding up the process out of a fear of the "money-hungry" developer.

Do developers want to make their projects as cost-effective as possible? Absolutely. It's a business. Businesses need to make profitable decisions, or there's no point running the business. And are there bad actors who would compromise environmental health in favor of a cheaper project? No doubt. But I've never talked to a developer who's said, "Our goal is to put this solar farm in the middle of this protected wetland because we think we can get the land really cheap."

The reason so-called prime farmland is often selected for solar developments is because it offers the perfect blend of resources: close to major byways (meaning access to transmission lines), decent soil (not too wet or rocky, which can pose problems when setting posts), and the right amount of sun exposure to make things profitable. Often, there's simply no alternative to farmland, even if a developer would rather put a project elsewhere.

"Why not just put all those panels on roofs?" I'm often asked. Rooftop siting is great, but it's going to be tough to find enough warehouse roofs to meet our clean energy goals (not to mention the other problems associated with rooftop siting, as I discussed in chapter 2).

If all we do is say solar "really should" go on rooftops or brownfields first, we'll be talking in circles. There's just not enough space until we start considering farmland, and since so much of it is lying fallow (or projected to be fallow soon, or even redeveloped into residential or commercial lots), why aren't we exploring alternatives that might work everywhere with a bit of tinkering and customization?

Making it harder to develop solar and wind on farmland won't reduce the number of projects that need to be sited on farmland. It's just going to slow the process down and make it take longer for struggling landowners to be able to tap into another revenue stream they desperately need. Or, more likely, it's going to mean that the land goes into something else, like storage units or big-box stores.

Hinchey has said in formal statements, and indeed, has repeated this mantra again in our face-to-face meeting, "We cannot exchange an energy crisis for a food crisis."[7] We're already having a food crisis. It's just that nobody wants to talk about it. Farmers can't afford to farm, consumers can't afford to buy the dwindling amount of food that *is* produced in the United States, and nobody wants to farm because it's a business that rarely looks good on the balance sheets.

Before we can explore the benefits of agri-energy for the renewable energy industry (and the climate at large), we need to talk about the current state of renewables, as well as what the process looks like for developing a solar or wind project in the first place. Let's start with some hard facts.

The Current State of Our Energy Affairs

In 2022, the coal industry emitted around 970 tonnes of greenhouse gas emissions per gigawatt hour. Closely behind was oil, at 720 tonnes, and then natural gas, at 440 tonnes. For renewables, biomass was only 78 to 230 tonnes, hydropower was 24, solar was 53, wind was 11, and nuclear was 6.[8]

The differences in emissions are stark.

Harnessing the power of natural resources like the sun, wind, and water has dramatically transformed the landscape of energy production. And as we've seen with examples of European farmers, it's really nothing new.

How do solar panels actually work? The simplest explanation is that they capture sunlight and convert it into electricity through photovoltaic (PV) systems or through solar thermal systems.

Much like solar, wind energy offers a clean and inexhaustible source of power. Wind turbines generate electricity by converting the kinetic energy from wind into mechanical power. The life-cycle emissions of wind power are remarkably low, with studies showing that wind energy has a carbon footprint of 99 percent less than coal-fired power plants.[9] Offshore wind farms, benefiting from stronger and more consistent winds, can achieve even higher reductions.[10]

Shifting away from fossil fuels and toward renewables is imperative to slow climate change, and the time has long passed to debate the necessity of doing just that. It's time for us to do something. But as Teddy Roosevelt said, "In any moment of decision, the best thing you can do is the right thing, the next best thing is the wrong thing, and the worst thing you can do is nothing."[11]

In all fairness, we haven't totally been sitting idle. Since the 2016 Paris Agreement, the US government has passed several accords in the effort to do *some*thing. The 2022 Inflation Reduction Act, passed under the Biden administration, contained $369 billion to boost clean energy and cut emissions, mostly from the electric power sector due to wind and solar growth.[12]

In twelve states, wind and solar are expected to make up more than 80 percent of electricity generation by 2035, with New Mexico, Vermont, Wyoming, and Virginia expecting to generate 90 percent of their electricity capacity from wind and solar by 2035.[13] Offshore wind is expected to take the lead in Massachusetts and New Jersey, while utility-scale solar will lead the way in twenty-eight states (including Alabama, Arizona, Florida, Georgia, Ohio, and Nevada).

Again, individualization is key here. There's no single best solution to supplying our energy needs. Solar panels might not make sense on *this* slice of farmland, but they might work wonders across the road.

A Natural Solution for Renewable Energy's Manmade Challenges

When referring to solar development, Dr. Anna Clare Monlezun told me, "We're altering nature's patterns, but what does that mean?" Also, does it matter?

Humans are often critiqued for altering nature, and that's not something I'll dispute. "Scaling the current renewable energy technology, like solar, wind, hydro, and biomass, would be tantamount to ecocide," wrote Derrick Jensen, Lierre Keith, and Max Wilbert in the book *Bright Green Lies*. "Consider that 12 percent of the continental United States would have to be covered in wind farms to meet current electricity demands. But electricity is only one-sixth of the nation's energy consumption. To provide for the U.S.A.'s total energy consumption, fully 72 percent of the continent would have to be devoted to wind farms. In reality, solar and wind development threaten to destroy as much land globally as expansion of urban sprawl, oil and gas, coal, and mining combined by 2050."[14]

The problem with the above statement (as well as other statements in *Bright Green Lies* that I won't get into here) is that its authors aren't looking at the full scope of the issue.

To begin with, Anna Clare's words remind me that humans are inherently part of nature's patterns. We often view ourselves as something "outside" of nature, something that "uses" nature, but humans are just as much a part of the natural world as anything else. It's one of our communities, something we need to take into consideration as a whole and not just an individual part, as I discussed in chapter 2.

Unfortunately, unlike other players in the natural environment, we tend to want to exploit it more. Converting to wind, solar, and other renewables is going to take a vast amount of land—but the major fallacy in *Bright Green Lies* is the assumption that this land will be virgin, untouched land that's currently unaffected by humans at all. What about the millions of acres of corn being grown for ethanol? What about the working farmland that can be converted into solar or wind and then can continue to be cultivated to feed our people?

For all the destruction human beings have wrought on the planet, we're still just as much a part of this planet as the songbirds and the sharks. We deserve a place on this planet, too. But we do need to be more creative about the ways we're using that land, because right now, we're destroying our natural resources faster than any other organism ever has, and even that's probably the largest understatement you'll ever hear.

As you can see by the statistics cited above, renewable energy is the way to go if we want to curb carbon emissions. But we don't need to completely get rid of fossil fuels—that's not practical, at least not yet. And we certainly don't need to make our questions of land use an "if-then-but" conversation. We can do it all.

As I've stated before, it's not just about the benefit to the environment. Per the United Nations, renewables "offer a way out of import dependency, allowing countries to diversify their economies and protect them from the unpredictable price swings of fossil fuels, while driving inclusive economic growth, new jobs, and poverty alleviation."[15]

Paul Gipe told me, "Most of the cost from a power plant is the fuel. They also don't pay for the wind, water, and air pollution." In any conversation about economics, there are seldom visible and rarely talked about externalities. These are the consequences of an activity, whether it's farming or energy production or something else entirely, that produces a cost or a benefit for one party that is incurred or received by another. Externalities can be negative or positive, but when we talk about the pollution from fossil fuel plants, they are primarily negative.

Our aging fossil fuel plants might be currently cheap to run since they only require inputs (the fuel). Renewable plants, on the other hand, are still being built, and therefore the costs of construction make them marginally more expensive.

Yet the outputs are incredibly costly. Fossil fuels produce hazardous air pollutants, including sulfur dioxide, particulate matter, mercury, and carbon monoxide. They're contributing to ocean acidification, which makes it harder for sea life to thrive. Oil spills and fracking fluids lead to water pollution, contaminating our drinking water with arsenic, lead, chlorine, and more. Air pollution from burning fossil fuels contributes to health issues like heart disease, asthma, and cancer.[16]

In 2018 alone, 350,000 deaths were attributed to fossil fuel–related pollution, with the highest number occurring in the major mining states, like Ohio, Pennsylvania, and West Virginia.[17] "The value of human life is probably undervalued here," Gipe admitted to me in another huge understatement. The problem is that these externalities can't easily be quantified on a profit and loss statement. You can't add up the costs, so in our nearsighted economic eyes, they just don't exist.

The problems are just now beginning to come into focus. The old power plants produce cheap energy because they've already been paid for. But we have to keep feeding the fossil fuel machine, constantly, every single day, and as our appetite for energy increases, it's costing more and more to feed it. We're eventually going to run out of it. As our supply chains grow less reliable and environmental (and human) health begins to decline worldwide, we're finally opening our eyes to the inherent problems of the current energy system.

"Nothing is free in this world," Dr. Serkan Ates of Oregon State University told me over Zoom. "There's no good solution in terms of energy production."

From a purely dollars and cents perspective, renewables still present a better option. Between 2010 and 2020, the cost of electricity from solar power fell by 85 percent and onshore wind by 56 percent. Yes, we need to invest trillions into renewable energy—about $4.5 trillion before 2030. But $7 trillion was spent on subsidizing the fossil fuel industry in 2022 alone (not counting the health and environmental damages that can't be priced and quantified).[18]

We have the potential to *save* trillions by investing in renewables—and create a more localized, independent, and resilient economy as a result.

There's no doubt that switching to renewables presents massive challenges. There's not a lot of suitable land, and the land that *is* available is expensive. (It could be argued, however, that we're exaggerating the amount of space that's actually needed if an efficient land use model is used; when I spoke to him, Gipe argued that wind takes less than 1 percent of the land that's allotted for a project, especially if you're planting crops right up to the base of a tower.)

You could also contest that the materials used to create these new renewables aren't efficient. Solar is repeatedly criticized for its use of heavy metals. Most solar panels installed in the United States are constructed with silicon, which is made from sand and quartz and is not harmful. Silicon is also used in toys, countertops, and glassware. But you've likely seen the fearmongering posts that spread like wildfire on social media—the ones that depict solar panels after hailstorms, their components heavily damaged, glass lying everywhere. This exposure has launched a nationwide concern about heavy metals "leaching" into the soil and harming human health.[19]

According to the Solar Energy Industries Association, "Even if the panels did contain harmful levels of toxic substances" (which they don't), "'leakage' is not possible." Most solar panels are laminated between two sheets of sealed transparent plastic, then covered in tempered glass, then filtered with another layer of glass or plastic, and then sealed in an aluminum frame. "Even if the glass breaks and is left untouched or unrecycled, it would take decades to extract any type of substance from the broken panels," the association contends.[20]

Solar panels are not immune to natural disasters any more than any other technology. Coal piles can freeze. Nuclear power plants can melt down. Wind turbines can catch on fire. But it's not in the best interest of a solar company to install technology that's going to have extensive amounts of downtime or inefficiencies; if a solar panel were to act in this way, it would lose the company money. From a profits-and-production perspective alone, it doesn't make good financial sense. This myth, therefore, doesn't hold water.

Another concern is that solar panels are going to contribute dramatically to our "global garbage" problem. Yet the panels, according to developer Ken

Lehman, are typically not buried or thrown out when they reach the end of their life-span. "Most panels get reused at other sites," he told me in an interview. "The only thing that can't be stripped back out is the silicon wafer." He said that there's no variation in efficiency when temperatures dip below freezing. Most panels are now also hailproof, rated to withstand hail up to 0.98 inches falling at 50 miles per hour.[21]

Ken's firm, Kendall Sustainable Infrastructure, is headquartered in Boston and has been building solar for ten years. About 80 percent of this solar, according to Ken, is located on former or current farmland. About 50 to 60 percent of the company's portfolio is community solar, generating a bill credit for consumers who choose to connect. The other half goes to municipalities, generally schools, universities, hospitals, and other large businesses looking to "greenify" their electric supply.

There's a goliath misconception about solar developers in the United States, namely that they're only in the business to get rich. That's probably true about some subset of this population (and I've certainly encountered some who care solely about the balance sheets), but for the majority, there's an altruistic driver behind their work.

Ken is an example of the latter. If ever there was someone interested in making a quick buck, he's not it. He's fully invested in ensuring that projects are not only profitable but also provide some lasting benefit to the community. And he doesn't spend all his time behind a desk; he gets up close and personal. In fact, a few summers ago, Ken and his family visited our farm to meet the sheep. It was at a time when solar grazing wasn't quite as in vogue as it is now, and Ken took a big gamble by advocating to get us on our first solar site.

Prior to meeting Ken, we had our own hesitations about working with developers, viewing our communications back and forth with them as little more than a necessary evil. We knew we had to forge those connections if we wanted to get on solar, but we assumed that we had to market our grazing services purely from a dollars and cents perspective because why on earth would a developer care about anything else *besides* money?

Our early bias against Ken and other developers was simply a mirror of what we'd seen reflected back to us from our community. We thought everybody hated renewable energy (and anybody trying to sell it) because it was new, strange, different. Renewable energy is the outsider people love to hate, and it's easier to jump on the groupthink bandwagon than to accept new ideas into the fold, into the community. But when Ken arrived on our farm (with his entire family along for the visit), we were proved wrong, and in a massive way.

The time has come for us to start opening the door to the stranger, to approach these conversations with a bit more openness to the idea of change. Our farms and the people who farm them simply can't afford otherwise. And while the ideas of renewable energy and agriculture might seem inherently at odds with each other, the truth is that, with agri-energy, they are anything but.

Ken and other developers or investment firms are interested in making money because, after all, they are running businesses. As a farmer, I want to make money, too. I want to be able to put food on the table for my family, to keep the lights on. It is possible for both things to be true—to have a desire to do good things while also making a living doing them. Ken showed us that. He also proved to us his interest in making sure solar was a solution for the long haul, not just a way to make a quick buck, as I'd so incorrectly assumed.

The truth is that renewable energy technologies are far from just a fad. There's a lot of money to be made in implementing these technologies, but these solutions are going to last long into the future, perhaps longer than our aging fossil fuel plants, and likely at a lower cost to taxpayers, too—especially when agriculture is brought into the mix.

Between 2009 and 2021, the cost of renewables like solar and wind declined by as much as 90 percent.[22] Even when we consider storage and network costs, solar and wind are seeing steep price declines as the technologies continue to evolve. The result is that it opens the door to innovation, to thinking creatively about how we can protect the environment even more as we switch to these renewable energy solutions.

For example, instead of steel for solar mounting, the Germany-based company Agro Solar Europe GmbH developed a yet-to-be-released mounting structure made out of organic materials for use in agrivoltaic facilities. It uses materials like wood fiber, flax, and carbon to create racking systems (which look a lot like trees) to support agricultural PV systems. It reduces natural material use by 90 percent and is 90 percent lighter than a steel structure. It has a "particularly high load bearing capacity."[23]

Other companies have developed wood-based PV racking systems that are cost-competitive and can be used as trellis supports and even for irrigation (ideal for growing crops like cucumbers, peas, pumpkins, and strawberries on solar while also cutting down on steel costs).[24]

It might cost more, whether it's in effort or in actual dollars, to create PV systems that allow cows to graze beneath them or tomatoes to produce decent yields underneath. But think about the net benefit to the economy—to the community—to the environment. As Josh Bennett, formerly of EDF Renewables, told me, "Hand a challenge to an ag community, and they'll figure it out."

The Makings of a Great Negotiation

Both in terms of energy and food production, we need to find a way to make the most of the dwindling space we have available to support the increasing population. But how do we do it?

The secret lies in negotiation. In a good negotiation, no party is 100 percent satisfied. Nobody walks away thinking they got a good deal. The key is getting the deal you can accept with (ideally) only moderate discomfort.

More than thirty states have set goals requiring anywhere between 2 and 100 percent of their energy to be from renewable sources by either 2030 or 2035, with fifteen states setting targets of 100 percent by 2050.[25] If we're going to meet those goals, it's time to sit down at the negotiating table and come up with an arrangement we can all be happy with.

Solar developers are now leveraging the power of the American farmer, inviting farmers to take a seat at the table and, it is hoped, show the rest of the community that what's being served up isn't so bad. Kevin Campbell, another developer for EDF Renewables, said that a deep mistrust and misunderstanding of the industry is one of the biggest challenges he faces. "I wish everyone got to see a solar facility," he told me. "People are on edge and they think the worst.... They go through a lot of effort to make people believe what they believe. But what's the other side of the coin?"

People like Kevin spend a lot of time speaking with communities here in New York, where community buy-in is an essential part of the planning process. The problem is that community members don't always like what Kevin's selling, so his efforts to educate often fall on deaf ears. "People don't want to hear from us," he said, "because we're directly benefiting from the project, so we 'can't be speaking the truth.'"

But sheep may be able to help people listen a little better.

Kevin's first site with sheep was in 2016, when he was developing a project in Ottawa, Canada.

"We started noticing some issues with the project," he recalled. There was rolling terrain that would make it tough to mow, and the biggest cost of solar, he said, is often vegetation management, or what he calls "farming around obstacles."

The company encountered major opposition in the community. Nobody wanted to see this "productive farmland" turned into a solar farm, and a meeting was held in opposition. There, Kevin broached the idea of incorporating sheep to a farmer, who was adamant that sheep would never work.

Shortly after, Kevin was approached by different farmers, Chris Moore and Lyndsey Smith of Shady Creek Lamb Company. This initial conversation evolved into one of EDF's first pilot projects with sheep. Since then, Shady Creek has run hundreds of sheep on EDF sites.[26]

Talk about quite literally eating your words—or, rather, the sheep eating them.

Arnprior Solar Project, Ontario, Canada. Credit: EDF Renewables

Sheep—and other forms of agri-energy—have rapidly become one of clean energy's biggest marketing tools, helping combat some of the misinformation that circulates about the industry. This, according to Kevin, is his biggest Achilles' heel (the irony of this statement is that when we spoke, Kevin was suffering from a ruptured Achilles and getting around on a knee scooter).

Injuries aside, Kevin's now proud of the work EDF is doing to champion sheep on solar—so proud that he's considering other agri-energy experiments: "Can we take a few cuttings of hay off solar? Graze cattle?"

People worry about taking good farmland out of production. Once you bring up sheep, though, very few people can complain.

It would seem as though any form of agri-energy on a solar site would be a no-brainer. But, as Gipe wrote, "The growth of an industry is partly about technology, but also about the market for that technology."[27]

The same holds true for agri-energy. It's not that there isn't a market yet, it's just that nobody's really sure how this market is going to function because everything is so damned new and because there are so many metaphorical cooks in the kitchen.

Developer Incentives and Hesitations

Like any recipe, many ingredients go into siting, designing, and building the ideal solar site. Although many players (plenty of cooks) are involved, that's not always a bad thing, since it means that the needs and stakes of many are being considered as part of the process.

And, also like any good recipe, advanced planning is key to make sure we get it right. "Sheep and pollinators are what we know, and what we're comfortable with," Juliet Caplinger, senior project manager at Encore Renewable Energy in Vermont, told me. "We try to find a partnership up front and design [the site] to meet the needs of the farmer."

Juliet, along with Amber Lessard, Encore's director of construction and asset management, emphasized that because siting requirements differ in just about every state, so, too, do developers' attitudes toward agrivoltaics. In some states, the requirements or incentives for implementing agrivoltaics just aren't there. Yet the costs (and risks) are still high.

It takes an innovative, daring, and slightly rule-breaking personality type to want to pursue agrivoltaics. While that will likely change as more research unfolds and more positive best-use scenarios come to light, it's still a no-man's-land. Just not for Encore.

Encore is unique because the team pursues projects with agrivoltaics even though they don't have to. Vermont, where Encore does the bulk of its business at the time of writing this book, does not offer incentives for agrivoltaics yet. But the company is still pushing hard on the issue of agri-energy on as many of its solar sites as possible.

Vermont also does not require local siting approval, as most states do. State by state, the siting process can be arduous and drawn out, requiring the approval of everybody from the town planning council and zoning board to state-level administrators like the Office of Renewable Energy Siting in New York. Each state goes about the siting process differently, with some, like Delaware, delegating siting authority to local governments and others, like Nebraska, leaving it mostly up to the state.[28]

Thus, there can be many hoops to jump through—or barely any at all. Texas, the team at Encore said, "is like the Wild Wild West," with limited, if any, permitting requirements. For other states, where local approval is not only a nice-to-have, but a must-have, parading agrivoltaics like a prize pony at a 4-H show can provide a big assist. When the opposition to a solar farm centers solely on concerns about taking good farmland out of production, agri-energy eliminates that argument and makes the idea of renewables a lot more palatable. In many cases, it can be the factor that seals the deal on a project's siting approval.

Despite higher costs of raising cattle or growing crops on solar, Encore is a company that's eager to experiment. "We're really looking forward to some pilot programs," Juliet emphasized, referring to initiatives that would allow developers and farmers to test out new ideas for producing food while maximizing land usage under solar.

We need more risk takers to make agri-energy work, but they're hard to find in an industry that's decidedly risk-averse. Alexis Pascaris of the

National Renewable Energy Laboratory told me that agri-energy "is good, for social and environmental reasons, but you just don't know how to quantify the benefits or deliver solutions."

Of the large utility solar sites in the United States, very few are currently being used for commercial agrivoltaics. The rest are considered research plots.

Many states now offer siting incentives and research funding for developers interested in implementing agrivoltaics. In June 2024, the New York State Energy Research and Development Authority announced that $5 million would be available for "demonstration projects" that colocate solar and agriculture within the state, with each individual project eligible for up to $750,000.[29]

The goal is to expand the available knowledge on how technically and financially viable solar agrivoltaic facilities can be. Interestingly, projects that solely include sheep grazing, crops for biofuel generation, pollinator-friendly ground cover, or apiary installation are not eligible— New York State is clearly interested in seeing what *else* we can do. We already know that pollinators and sheep are a good fit.

These projects are all steps in the right direction when it comes to breaking new ground and discovering the upper limits of agrivoltaics. But the *money* is still limited; in fact, the only state with bona fide financial investments for agrivoltaics is Massachusetts. Other states offer significant amounts of research funding (and again, siting priority) for agrivoltaics, but that's about it.

The reward is clearly there, something I'll continue to demonstrate throughout this book, but it's hard to quantify. In addition, since there's a perceived risk of animals damaging panels and costing the company more money, developers remain hesitant.

So, to understand exactly how agri-energy is eventually implemented on a site, we need to look at the development process from the developer's point of view. This viewpoint varies a bit depending on the company, the players, the state, and even the individual project, but each has a few key components.

Finding the Ideal Site

The first step in development is siting. I've referenced this process a few times before because figuring out where a project will be located is one of the most important decisions that will occur over the entire life cycle of a solar or wind facility. Multiple players are involved throughout the planning, design, construction, and management of a project, and the siting process isn't always limited just to one company (and certainly not to just a single individual).

"Some companies do everything end to end, but others are less likely to have all those skill sets," Ken Lehman told me. For most solar projects, the process starts with a developer, and that developer ends their involvement when the project is ready to be constructed. Generally, it's the developer who goes to the town meetings, talks to the utility, and arranges leases with landowners.

Siting is incredibly time-consuming and complex. "The perfect site gets the right amount of sun exposure," Ken explained. But problems arise if that site is near wetlands. It also needs to be close to power lines for interconnections, and that utility has to have the extra capacity for the additional energy.

The developer will typically make option payments to a landowner up front for a prenegotiated lease (these payments can be structured as a single lump sum or as a series of payments, depending on the contract terms, but are generally paid out up front in one go). The landowner doesn't have to do anything except agree not to enter into a deal with another developer.

Many large companies will canvas several properties at once, as mentioned in chapter 1. That's why so few planned projects end up being built. Often, a site will end up being a poor fit, either because it doesn't have good connectivity to the grid or because the previously negotiated leases will be too expensive to maintain in the long run. Plans also change when businesses, schools, or other large energy buyers change their minds about whether they want to be powered by the project.

Sometimes, a developer will run into hiccups with town planning boards and budgets. For instance, solar panel prices can increase without warning, causing planned project prices to skyrocket and all the other pieces to go out of whack.

Generally, lease options (with option payments) are for one to two years with the opportunity to extend. Then, if the project ends up going through, the lease option is converted into a more permanent lease of twenty to forty years (again often with an opportunity to extend).

This type of arrangement tends to upset some people. "Solar companies can typically afford to pay eight to 20 times more per acre than farmers leasing land for crops, and no regulation prohibits them from leasing the most productive, prime farmland, even when less productive land is available," wrote Kevin Conlon in the *Adirondack Daily Enterprise*.[30] (That statement is only partly true; many towns, states, and even countries have regulations that prohibit putting more than a certain percentage of farmland into solar. For example, in the town of Beekmantown, New York, you can only enroll 50 percent of your tillable land into solar. In many other cases, states include scorecards for developers to follow when siting a project and are offered priority if the development is not on prime farmland.)

What *is* true is that developers can indeed typically pay farmers much more than they would otherwise get for that land. US Department of Agriculture data shows that farmland rent in top corn- and soybean-producing areas of Illinois, Indiana, and Iowa averaged roughly $251 per acre; solar leases in these same areas can run $900 to $1,500 per acre.[31]

Remember that it's great to have prime farmland, but you also must have someone to farm it. Land's not getting any cheaper, and is it right to ask a young farmer to take out an astronomical $500,000 loan for land or to ask the older one to drop their prices low enough so that the younger farmer can afford to buy or lease it? Plus, as EDF Renewables developer Kevin Campbell notes, we need to meet our energy goals one way or another.

Now is not the time to be discussing whether land *should* go into solar. "That ship has sailed," Kevin told me. "So, you can either benefit from it in your community or let other communities benefit."

Using so-called lesser-quality farmland for solar projects is often presented as an option. According to Conlon, citing a Cornell University study, doing so would provide "82 to 85 percent of the land needed to achieve the state's energy goals."[32]

But as Linda Garrett from American Farmland Trust reminded us in chapter 2, farmland doesn't come in neat, tidy boxes. Often, the land that's not as productive as so-called prime farmland just won't work. It might not have the right kind of access to the transmission lines. It might not get the right kind of sun exposure. Even soil conditions can impact the cost. If there's a lot of rock, it will be more expensive to drive in and stabilize piles than it would be to do it on tilled ground.

Although we talk often of prime farmland, there's precious little discussion about what that actually means. There's no set definition of it, and worse, there's much dissent about what the best use of it might actually be. While some folks might argue that prime farmland is best reserved for our cash crops—which, today, are probably best defined as the ones that are heavily subsidized, like corn and soy, rather than by the traditional definition (which includes cotton and tobacco)—others might say it should be reserved for grazing livestock.

Still, until we wake up to the realization that prime farmland isn't useful unless someone is actually farming it, we'll be spinning our wheels in the pursuit of a definition and best-use case that is, ultimately, quite useless.

It's impossible to avoid prime farmland, but developers do try—for many reasons. One is for the same reason we'd like them to: They know they need to eat, too.

Plus, from a business perspective, prime farmland will almost always be more expensive than other land. It wouldn't make sense to pay more for acreage if a site would work just as well on lesser-quality farmland, so in most cases, developers won't do that if it's not absolutely necessary.

Planning a Site Early to Cut Costs and Gain Support

If a site can be planned for agri-energy before posts are even pushed into the ground, that's great, because it means that agri-energy will likely happen once the project is finished (rather than existing only as an early selling point). It also means that the construction phase of the project will include more elements to make the life of a grazier easier (and more affordable) later on.

Grazing (or other forms of agri-energy) provides a great benefit to a solar company in terms of good public relations and sometimes priority in the siting process. However, it's still an expense, and like any other expense, it needs to be accounted for early on. "Grazing is the lowest cost in SOME areas, but not all, so this all needs to be in the bid so it's accounted for from day one," Kevin Campbell told me.

That's one reason novice solar graziers may find it challenging to get themselves onto sites. You must be persistent because as Ken Lehman said, so many people just aren't aware of the benefits of solar grazing since it's not their "department," but also because it's often not a part of the original budget. It requires a change of thought and processes (and often, a lot of signatures from all the right people) to make agri-energy happen.

Planning a site proactively also benefits the farmer who wants to come in to graze; in many cases, that's the landowner himself. That was the case with North Carolina solar grazier and coordinator of the Amazing Grazing Program, Johnny Rogers.

"The biggest benefit [of solar grazing] is that we're grazing free grass," Johnny told me. "But [the solar developer] was great to work with. They even built a secondary gate. There is a water line running through, and … the company even helped pay to reroute it. They put in quick-connect hydrants so we have access to water."

This kind of advanced planning may also help reduce some of the skepticism people have about solar grazing. Because so many developers have now jumped on the agrivoltaics bandwagon, there are a fair number of concerned citizens who fear that solar grazing, when included as part of a project proposal, will become yet another form of greenwashing, used by the developer to gain access to a site and then never actually pursued.

Implementing things like water, proper fencing, specific pollinator mixes, and other infrastructure that requires an additional up-front investment on behalf of the developer helps safeguard a developer against the loud opposition who, Jonathan Barter of the American Solar Grazing Association told me in a call, view sheep as "a gimmick."

It's not just about the warm and fuzzy public relations, either, although one study found that agrivoltaics increase public support for solar by about 80 percent.[33] In some places, developers are given priority consideration from the state when it comes to getting permission to build a site. And many states, including Florida and Minnesota, already have scorecards in place that require developers to submit details about site preparation and include components on pollinators and agrivoltaics.[34] Massachusetts's SMART program gives a dual-use incentive to developers and requires certain standards, like adjusting panel height on proposed sites.[35]

Solar grazing is not without its critics, though. Byron Kominek of Jack's Solar Garden told me that the biggest issue with solar is how "public utilities choose to prioritize projects. This is where there is the most room for improvement." The evaluation criteria for a site, out of 100 percent, he remarked, often is broken down into 40 percent price, 30 percent experience, 10 percent land, and so on. But ultimately, Byron said, what it will end up coming down to is, "Do you have the money?"

To encourage agrivoltaics, "the legislature needs to make it more substantive," Byron explained. "There's often nothing in there about land stewardship—whoever is largest can offer the cheapest price." This method doesn't benefit small-scale developers, even those who want to do the best by the land—and that's where state governments can really make a difference in encouraging all the right practices on sites. "We need to think up front about how to integrate these things. It's not just about how to incentivize companies to do the right thing," he told me. But that's often what happens.

In many cases, incorporating agrivoltaics in the request for proposal language can mean the difference between a developer getting to build on that site and not being able to build on that site. It still often comes down to dollars and cents—who can do it for the lowest price—but if all other variables are equal, agrivoltaics can often be the tipping point on that scale.

This money is often big money, Elie Schecter of OurGeneration, a small solar developer, told me. It's not just Monopoly money, often costing hundreds of thousands of dollars just to "commit to the utilities," he said.

Once a developer signs an interconnection agreement, there are payments to be made, which requires all the right partners to turn the wheels at all the right times, with a whole lot of money twisted up in the meantime. OurGeneration's approach is unique, since the company develops projects and then brings in financing, allowing it to invest more in small community solar. "Finding the right partners goes a long way," said Elie. "So many big financing entities are obsessed with deploying capital, but developing community solar takes time." Community solar offers a little more predictability in this regard, but getting financed is still tricky, and there are a lot of loose ends to tie up, all before the dirt work can even start.

Building Up and Out

After planning, the next phase is design and construction, which again introduces new faces. There are owner/operators (like Kendall Sustainable Infrastructure) and companies charged with managing operations and maintenance. This phase occurs regardless of whether agri-energy is preplanned or an afterthought following siting.

In the case of the aforementioned Plattsburgh site that Ken Lehman visited on his bicycle, his company hired a third party, GreenSpark, to construct the site and also manage operations and maintenance. Green-Spark then creates agreements with various subcontractors (like us with our sheep in the case of sites that decide to pursue agri-energy or, for those who choose to mow and spray, with landscaping companies). From an agri-energy perspective, vegetation management is the most pertinent demand that must be fulfilled with subcontractors, though the company may also hire out for other tasks, like snow plowing, too.

"It's so hard to pair solar with agriculture because there are so many people and players," Ken said. For any solar farm that's built, there could be multiple companies involved (again, all those cooks in the kitchen). You may have an investment firm, like Kendall Sustainable Infrastructure, that's funding the construction of a site, then another that handles construction, and a third that handles operations and maintenance once the site is built. The sites can change hands multiple times throughout its design, build, and operation. Therefore, even if you have an initial developer or investor who expresses a profound commitment to agri-energy, that commitment and interest may not trickle down throughout the process. Like a warped game of Telephone, the message of "Agri-energy is important for this site!" can quickly turn into "Agri-what?" by the time the site is up and running.

Each player in each individual company also has to consider their own specialties and their own stakes. While agri-energy might be cheaper for the company that takes over operations and maintenance, it might be more expensive to build a site with agri-energy in mind from the outset. Even though the project would ultimately save money over the course of its thirty-year life-span by using grazing instead of mowing, it might take a bit more up-front money to get the site sheep-ready. Ken told me that to pair agriculture with solar, all the parties involved need to make sure that the added expense is justified. And because many of the benefits aren't quantifiable on balance sheets, doing a dollar-to-dollar comparison becomes tricky when you're trying to make the case for agri-energy to someone who doesn't wholeheartedly believe in its full life-cycle benefits.

In many cases, it comes down to comfort levels.

To pair agriculture with solar, Ken said, "it takes a conversation and an explanation … and strongly encouraging our [operations and main-tenance] provider to find a way to make it work…. Companies need to make sure the [added expense] is justified—just like any other business." And although the renewables industry is growing more and more com-fortable with the idea of agri-energy by the day, that hasn't always been true. Historically, it has always come down to cost.

While the narrative is, fortunately, beginning to change, keeping operations and maintenance costs low will always be important for developers, since it's one of the few variables they have control over on a site. Overall operations and maintenance "typically accounts for between 1 and 5% of a MW-class plant's total lifetime expenditure," one study spearheaded by the National Renewable Energy Laboratory (NREL) found.[36]

We know that agri-energy is better for the environment, for the community, and for the economy than mowing and herbicide use in the long run, but when it comes down to cost-cutting, it's not always the cheapest.

On average, graziers receive $300 to $500 per acre (often more) to graze. In some places, it costs less than that to mow—but not always.

Much of this also comes down to the type of vegetation that is being grown. Per the NREL study described above, "Native vegetation sites are more expensive to establish in the first 3–4 years, with expectations that the cost of maintenance eventually declines."[37] For mowing, the median cost where native vegetation was used was $121 an acre, whereas it was $113 for sheep grazing. As you read these numbers, you might be confused about why this median is so much lower than the averages cited above. This is likely, in part, because there's such a wide range of compensation amounts for sheep graziers (in the early days, many graziers were not paid at all for their services). It may also be because these figures include both implementation and maintenance of a site's vegetation or lack thereof.

To that end, sites with herbicide applications for native vegetation had the highest median cost of maintenance at $293 per acre. Another study found that on one rocky site in Texas, grazing with sheep led to cost savings of $413,774 compared to mowing (likely because of the reduced damage to the panels).[38]

Despite these cost differentials, the authors of the first study repeatedly emphasized that many factors influence whether sheep grazing is cheaper than the alternatives and that it's difficult to quantify.[39]

In most cases, it's likely to be a toss-up whether sheep grazing or mowing is cheaper, but again, we need to consider the risk of damage to panels. It's true that grazing animals *can* interact with the array and cause damage to PV modules and electrical systems. Yet in our years of grazing, we've never had that happen. There's some concern over running cattle on solar for this same reason. On the other hand, it's all too easy for a mower to kick a rock into a module or to accidentally collide with above-ground infrastructure.

Vegetation also helps to increase the production of solar panels. When a solar farm is not revegetated after construction but instead is put into gravel, the best overall energy production isn't always achieved.

Some worry that the panels create heat and can have unintended consequences for our climate patterns. Indeed, temperatures around a solar plant can be up to 7.2 degrees Fahrenheit warmer than nearby areas, fostering a heat island effect that is similar to what we see in large cities.[40] However, studies have shown that the panels only increase the temperature at night; during the day, they actually cool the environment. Also, when you put PVs in an urban setting, they don't perform as well as in rural ones. That's likely because the environment is already warmer and panels aren't as efficient when they start to overheat.[41]

I've been told that we "should just put all these solar farms in the middle of the desert. Plop these solar farms in the middle of the Mojave and they'll get all the sun they need." Yes, they will, but at a huge cost. Solar panels perform best on days where the temperature hovers between 59 and 95 degrees Fahrenheit (with a sweet spot of 77 degrees) and there's minimal cloud cover.[42]

It's actually *better* for panels to be placed in overly cold climates instead of overly hot ones. Solar cells are semiconductors, and their efficiency decreases dramatically as it gets hotter. In fact, for every 1 degree Celsius (about 1.8 degrees Fahrenheit) above 25 degrees Celsius (77 degrees Fahrenheit), a panel's efficiency drops by up to 0.5 percent.[43]

Vegetation under solar panels can dramatically improve production and reduce this loss. Such vegetation has a passive cooling effect. Scientists in the Netherlands, in fact, have found that "blue-green" PV system roofs (which use green technologies like irrigation for plant growth along with "blue features" like rainwater storage) can lower the roof's surface temperature by up to 4.64 degrees Celsius compared to conventional bitumen roofs.[44]

This lower surface temperature is due in part to the light-reflecting powers of the plants, which can cool the ground surface and reduce the exposure of the panels to heat. It's also been demonstrated that building solar panels four meters (thirteen feet) above vegetation allows for convective cooling to occur between the units and the ground.[45] Evapotranspiration provides another cooling effect.

Vegetation also works better than gravel or hardtop for erosion control, something that's required in most places. Every state is different, but most developers aim to have about 70 to 90 percent uniform coverage of vegetation at site completion with the idea that it eventually revegetates itself back to 100 percent.

Why does it matter? It comes down to site stabilization—and protecting an investment.

Imagine that you're standing in a bare dirt field in the middle of a rainstorm. There's nothing growing there. As it rains, that dirt turns to mud. Your feet become, as my son's *Little Blue Truck* books say, "sunk down deep in muck and mire." It's hard to lift your feet, let alone to maneuver yourself out of the field. You fall down.

The same goes for equipment, buildings, and so forth. If you have a post stuck in the ground and that ground becomes compromised, the post is more likely to tip or become damaged. If, however, the soil is filled with the roots of native vegetation, serving as an anchor for that soil, keeping the post in place, it is much more stable. We need vegetation to keep things secure (and keep the dirt where it's supposed to be instead of running off into our roads and waterways).

The issue with vegetation is that it grows. If the vegetation gets too high, it shades the panels.

Traditionally, operations and maintenance teams have relied on mowing to keep the grass short, but mowing is problematic, namely because it's illogical to use fossil-fuel mowers to manage the vegetation around renewables. Solar grazing is a good work-around—sheep don't run on fossil fuels. They also don't require worker's comp, and they work 24/7 (and, really, without complaining; you won't find ewes bickering in the breakroom). Plus, the design of many solar arrays can be tough for landscapers to work with; often, panels are situated low to the ground, making it impossible to get beneath them with conventional mowing equipment. That's not the case with sheep. They're happy to dip underneath the panels, provided there are some tasty morsels there for them to nibble on or even some shade to grab a quick nap.

We often find our sheep napping beneath the panels, but they're still more productive than they seem. One study found that "even in the lowest sheep grazing density, the forage below the panels was successfully maintained below 18 inches. This presents a major advantage in using sheep for vegetation management, compared to labor (and cost) intensive manual string trimming efforts in areas under the panels."[46]

Typical vegetation management also presents the risk of fire. A mower engine, for instance, can become superheated in a drought, producing sparks that can ignite into a full-fledged wildfire under panels that are further fuel for the fire.

The enduring beauty of having sheep or even cattle on-site is that there are constant boots on the ground. Most solar shepherds visit their sites at least two to three times per week to deliver water and check on the herd. They're the unofficial eyes and ears of the operations and maintenance team.

If you pay close enough attention, you can hear the coins clinking.

The monetary benefits are there for the developer, if only we consider them all, even the less obvious ones.

What Happens in the Aftermath

The last stage of development is decommissioning. What happens to a site when it is no longer operable? According to Ken Lehman, that hasn't really happened yet; the vast majority of solar sites are still functioning several decades after their construction. Those timelines will likely be extended even more as advanced technologies are put in place to extend the life-span of PV systems.

According to Kevin Campbell, "Plans are required for New York State for permitting for all sites that are twenty megawatts and up. We must provide an assurance that this will be done in five years." In plain language, this means that developers must put money aside in a security fund that will go toward the decommissioning of the site. The solar company is responsible for this payment, and it is adjusted for inflation.

Read that again. The *solar* company is responsible for decommissioning. Not the town, nor the landowner leasing the property. The solar company will be responsible for taking everything down once the facility is no longer functioning. That's yet another consideration for developers as they determine whether a site is suitable for a solar project, because (barring a sale to another company) they're responsible for it through the final curtain call.

As of this writing, thirty-two states require a decommissioning plan to be submitted with a renewables application.[47] Ken told me that "solar panels last a long time—up to thirty years, if not more—but we write decommissioning plans for thirty to forty years out."

It's not just about the site ceasing functionality and the panels being trucked away. These plans also typically require developers to have provisions that prevent "excessive earth disturbance" and to ensure site stabilization.[48]

Decommissioning means removing racking posts entirely from the ground. Removing foundations for inverters. Decompacting-compacting soils and vegetation. Even testing soil and incorporating needed amendments for farming. And again, it's the solar company—not the town and the taxpayers—that is responsible for paying for the decommissioning.

In this debate about turning farmland into renewables, we often forget that leasing farmland for wind or solar isn't the kiss of death to agriculture on that land forever. Take a look at that Dollar General across the street. What happens when that business goes belly up? I'd be willing to bet it doesn't have a decommissioning plan, meaning it will sit there, indefinitely, as weeds grow up through the sidewalk and property values nearby continue to tumble.

There's no guarantee that a solar site will go back into agriculture. But if I were to hedge my bets on one plan or the other, you can bet your bottom dollar I'd go for solar.

Coming Away from the Table Satisfied

For now, most developers are cautiously optimistic about the role agrivoltaics plays (and will continue to play) in their projects.

It will always come down to business. Although there's plenty to criticize when it comes to capitalism, the United States is a capitalistic country, and many of our major decisions will be driven by economics.

As said earlier, in a good negotiation, no party is 100 percent satisfied. Nobody walks away thinking they got a good deal. But in the world of business, nobody wants to walk into an agreement thinking they might lose something. Our job is to make all the benefits of agri-energy shine the brightest, and one way to do that is to make sure you have all the right information and knowledge at your fingertips—exactly when you need it.

InSPIRE is a tool created by the US Department of Energy to help developers figure out, based on industry averages and location data, the best path forward with agrivoltaics.[49] It lets them compare three options: solar only, agriculture only, and solar and agriculture combined. Because it's merely a financial model, not an actual forecast, InSPIRE isn't perfect, but it's a great starting place for developers who want to take the first steps toward making an informed decision.

The key is to be willing to explore these other options rather than writing them off because it's not "the way things have always been done." As Sanjib Sahoo, executive vice president of Ingram Micro, famously wrote, "In today's industry, in which change happens at a relentless pace, standing still is not an option. You must take a risk at some point."[50]

If you're going to take a risk, why not take one that benefits *the* most important industry in the world: the one that produces your food?

CHAPTER 4

Powering Healthy Landscapes

That which is not good for the bee-hive cannot be good for the bees.
—Marcus Aurelius

AGRICULTURE IS ONE OF THE BIGGEST CONTRIBUTORS to global greenhouse gas emissions, accounting for about 22 percent of all emissions in 2019.[1]

That percentage alone has given fodder to a litany of battle cries that we need to get rid of conventional agriculture and start producing all our food in factories. But it's glossing over a few key points.

First, and perhaps most important, that 22 percent does *not* account for the carbon dioxide that ecosystems can remove from the atmosphere by sequestering carbon in soils and biomass. I'm not a soil scientist by any means, but the basic explanation is that soils are, in part, composed of broken-down plant matter. They contain carbon that those plants took in when they were still alive. Particularly in colder climates, where the decomposition of these plants tends to be slower than in warm climates, the soil can store—sequester—carbon for a significant period of time, helping reduce some of the carbon dioxide that is released back into the atmosphere.

But converting grasslands and forests to heavily tilled farmland disturbs the soil structure, so a lot of that stored carbon is released in the conversion process. The problem gets worse when you factor in climate change, which makes it harder for soils to naturally store carbon.[2]

Farmers already implement some strategies to add more carbon to soil, such as planting perennial crops and cover crops (plants like beans, peas, and clover that can be plowed under as green manure to add carbon to the soil). Reducing tilling and practicing managed rotational grazing also improve soil health, offsetting some of the damage that's been done to our soil over many decades of intensive agriculture.

But to fully take advantage of this benefit of carbon sequestration, we need to rethink the way we're farming. With limited land available— and given that the warming of the planet is already leading to widespread soil carbon losses by speeding up how quickly organic matter decays—it's a tough sell.

Here's yet another area where agri-energy can help.

Carbon Sequestration: The Underground Gold Mine

Josh Bennett, formerly of EDF Renewables and now of H2 Enterprises, once asked me, "If we built a solar development on a gold mine, wouldn't we have subject matter experts involved?"

Agricultural land *is* a gold mine, but for the last hundred years or so, it hasn't been a well-managed one. For instance, the Midwest, long considered the breadbasket of the United States, is losing topsoil at an average rate of 1.9 millimeters (about 0.07 inch) per year.[3] That's roughly the thickness of a grain of rice.

A grain of rice might not seem like much, but when you add it up, year after year, that's a *lot* of missing soil.

I remember learning about the Dust Bowl when I was a child. Then, it had seemed just a past date in history, a one-time thing that we probably would never repeat—we could chalk it up to farmers with antiquated practices who didn't know any better and have since learned the errors of their ways.

To be fair, we *have* learned a lot about how to maintain healthy soils since then. Unfortunately, despite conservation practices that were put in place after the 1930s, we're still experiencing a massive rate of erosion. Let's be clear: Loss of topsoil is not a natural phenomenon, but is instead a human-caused problem. The Midwest is losing topsoil at a rate of up to a thousand times faster than preagricultural erosion rates.[4]

Many factors contribute to topsoil erosion, including wind and water. But agricultural practices are at least partially to blame. And not all agriculture is equally culpable when it comes to the loss of topsoil. Row crops that are conventionally grown with heavy amounts of tilling and pesticide and herbicide use tend to be the worst offenders. Unfortunately, switching to a no-till agricultural system requires a heavy up-front investment and sometimes requires even more chemical use in the process—meaning that it's not always a practical undertaking (nor is it always the most prudent), even for the most environmentally conscious farmer.

We need to start thinking about how to mitigate this soil loss, because it's not just a matter of aesthetics, but of food production. Erosion can cause yield reductions of up to 90 percent in some parts of the world.[5] On average, we lose about one pound of topsoil for every bushel of corn that's produced.[6] The result has been a 6 percent reduction in corn and soybean yields.[7]

Cover crops, which help hold soil in place during heavy rains, can help, as can alley cropping (planting rows of trees and shrubs in fields to hold the soil in place). But with soil erosion rates worsening—and getting worse by the day as our climate continues to change—that might not be enough.

Solar panels can make matters even worse, particularly when projects are built on sandy soil that's already vulnerable to erosion. Solar panels are far easier to install on leveled ground, which often requires mowing local vegetation or cutting down trees. Leveling can lead to further soil erosion and runoff. In 2023, the solar company Silicon Ranch was sued for completing an installation of one thousand acres of solar without installing adequate measures for erosion and sediment control.[8] When it rained, the soil at that site ran downstream into the wetlands and the nearby twenty-one-acre lake, turning it into a mud pit.

Erosion isn't just bad news for the environmentalists. It's also bad news for developers and stakeholders because instability in the soil lends itself to instability in the structures that soil is supporting—like the piles that are driven into the ground to support solar panels and their racking.

Construction of any kind can severely disrupt soil quality and make erosion worse. Opponents of renewables would argue that's a good reason to steer clear of solar, but again—here's another situation where we need to look at the bigger picture. Coal mining, for instance, often involves the removal of entire mountaintops or the excavation of vast areas, something that, as you might guess, is a big no-no when it comes to erosion. And unlike solar, where there does happen to be a work-around, there's really no work-around with coal mining.

So what exactly *is* that work-around for solar? Again, the best option for developers is to revegetate a site after construction.

Agri-Energy's Role in Stabilizing the Soil

As I mentioned in chapter 3, most places have passed regulations dictating what kind of soil stabilization work must be done before a project can get up and running, often requiring that plans include site grading and terracing, soil stabilization through revegetation, and the building of vegetated swales or retention ponds. Many stormwater and erosion control permits require about 70 to 90 percent ground cover.

Developers ensure soil quality by considering the types of vegetation that will be grown on a site, as well as where the site is located and how that vegetation is controlled to prevent shading of the panels. Spraying herbicide is perhaps the most hands-off approach to manage excess, unwanted vegetation, but herbicides can be harmful to the health of an ecosystem (particularly to pollinators) and remain in the soil for quite a long time. They can also be carried into streams by runoff rainwater or leached into the underground water supply. Often, they also become ineffective over time, with stubborn species growing back taller and more tenacious in each new year in response. Perhaps most damning is that they kill off beneficial bacteria, fungi, and other microorganisms in the soil. They harm soil structure and nutrient cycling, too, which over time means less of that valuable topsoil that we need to use to grow food.[9]

When developers consider a site, their decisions are primarily driven by transmission needs. But once it's been determined that the site *does* have good transmission access, other variables come into play. The best land for solar is flat, out of a floodplain, and, ideally, mostly clear already. Farmland is a good candidate, but more than a third of the farmland in the US Midwest alone has almost completely lost its carbon-rich topsoil as is. We can't afford to lose any more.

Without topsoil, plants can't grow. Subsoil, right beneath the topsoil, lacks nourishing qualities. When topsoil and subsoil are mixed together via rainfall and erosion, the resulting soil becomes less fertile and stable, less conducive to plant growth. Topsoil is sometimes stripped before construction begins to prepare the site for panel installation; however, developers often spread topsoil back onto a site following construction and prior to seeding. Often, they do so before construction is completely finished, with at least some seeding taking place early on in construction so that the grass can start to grow while the piles are being driven and modules are installed.

It takes a long time to get the vegetation going again, particularly compared to how quickly a site can be built. Often, it takes more than a year for the vegetation to bounce back.

Then, it needs to be managed—as I've said before, mowing and spraying aren't the best at keeping the soil healthy, soil that we've worked so hard to rebuild. Remember that solar panels create multiple microclimates, with the area beneath the panels becoming less dry and less prone to erosion than without that panel cover. Add rotational grazing into the mix, and it's a win.

Managed intensive rotational grazing is a practice that's been praised and practiced by regenerative farmers for decades. It requires farmers to move animals frequently (in some cases, daily) and to watch the pasture like a hawk, moving the animals once the vegetation has reached a specific height. We need to keep a careful eye on pasture regrowth at different times of the year; a thrice-weekly move might make sense when it's humid and the pasture's growing faster, but less frequent moves might be necessary when it's dry.

In this model, water quickly leaves the surface of the soil to penetrate through multiple layers beneath. You aren't as likely to see puddling or ponding on the ground after a heavy rainstorm. There's less erosion and runoff and more water soaking into the ground and benefiting plant roots. These plants, then, come back healthier even after being grazed. They have stronger, more robust root systems and can uptake nutrients more easily as well.

This model also helps create new topsoil. You're typically grazing at a high density in a small area for a short period of time (the biggest emphasis being on the *period* of time). The animals eat everything in the area—they don't just pick around to find their favorite species—so weeds aren't given a chance to take hold. The manure deposited on the site fertilizes the soil, with the animals' hooves packing it in. Make no mistake: If you left these animals on this site for longer than the prescribed grazing period, you'd see *more* compaction and erosion. The challenge lies in finding the sweet spot and the ideal stocking density.

It's a Goldilocks situation. Graze the animals too long, and you'll have more erosion; don't graze them long enough, and you won't be knocking the vegetation down well enough and weeds will proliferate. You've got to time it *just right* if you want to stabilize the soil and build additional topsoil. It's a labor-intensive model, but it works.

One study of rotational grazing on solar found that intensive grazing management could result in dramatic increases in soil carbon. Farms accumulated carbon at 8.0 megagrams per hectare per year and increased the water holding capacity by 34 percent.[10] After just one decade of grazing this way, soil carbon levels returned to those of native forest soils (preagriculture) and likely had decreased fertilizer and irrigation demands.

By revegetating a solar site with native vegetation, developers find that topsoil is better retained and soil health is boosted over time— even on brownfield developments. Places like old landfills and reclaimed mines have seen soil health improve after proper management following a solar installation.

An evaluation of thirty solar sites in the Midwest found that when native grasslands are restored and replace conventional monoculture crops—we're talking corn and soy—the ecosystem benefits dramatically. Projections based on eco-modeling estimate that there will be a 65 percent increase in carbon sequestration, along with better water retention, decreased erosion, and improved pollinator health.[11]

According to Russell Hedberg II, director of the Center for Land Use and Sustainability at Shippensburg University, solar farms (presumably those that are literally *farmed*) affect land no more than a regular farm does. Construction admittedly impacts the land more than anything else, but with the right approach (and the right plans in place for vegetation management postconstruction), we can easily make those nonissues.[12]

But we'll only see these results if we do things correctly. Planting native vegetation provides a big assist, but we also need to be able to properly manage that vegetation (in other words, avoid mowers and herbicides). Many solar companies now have their own in-house vegetation management teams that look at site characteristics and conduct in-depth assessments of soil fertility, organic matter, pH, micro- and macronutrients, and more. They even go as far as to look at how preseeding during construction (and following the right seeding windows based on certain soil types) can help them support stabilized soils a bit better.

As I've mentioned before, we seldom stop to talk about what so-called prime farmland actually *is*. Many municipalities maintain their own definitions of it, but on a broader scale, a pure, overarching definition doesn't exist, and for good reason. Prime farmland in Missouri will look different than prime farmland in New York or in Hawaii.

The reality is that the average person driving by a farm field doesn't know whether it's prime farmland or just farmland. They don't know whether the soil beneath the hayfield is a rich, black humus or if it's depleted dust. So yes, if we keep prime farmland as "farmland," strictly that and nothing else, we can keep farming it. But for how much longer before it's completely worn out?

A Change of Diet or a Changed System?

Prior to starting my research for this book, I wholeheartedly believed that the only livestock species that could work on solar farms was sheep. And while I love lamb, the reality is that Americans eat less than a pound of lamb per year on average, compared to 85 pounds of beef.[13]

Dr. Anna Clare Monlezun is a rancher and a researcher, grazing sheep, cattle, and horses around residential, ground-mounted solar panels on her farm in Colorado. Some of her most recent work explores the impact of cattle grazing on solar, something that, for many years, was viewed as impossible. She completely changed my mind about how I think about agri-energy. It's not just about humans, nor is it just about one species of livestock. It's about them *all*.

The major concern about cattle on solar, compared to sheep, has to do with risk. Developers are afraid to open up grazing to cattle, who are significantly larger and more bullish than sheep (just remember the etymology of that word, after all) and may be more likely to damage panels by rubbing, scratching, and other destructive behaviors.

Anna Clare is adamant that, in reality, that's typically not the case. "You definitely have to raise the panels, which can exponentially raise the capital expense," she admitted to me. But she also does not believe that cattle are nearly as destructive as we make them out to be.

She's part of a three-year study in partnership with Silicon Ranch (who trademarked a cattle-compatible solar design called the Cattle Tracker) and Colorado State University. I will describe the study in more detail later in this chapter, but ultimately, its goal is to examine the impact that cattle have on the natural and built environment: What are they doing to the soil quality? The plant species composition? The temperature? How are the cattle growing? Where are they interacting with the panels (both in terms of where, on the panels, as well as where, on their bodies)?

Most important, how can we take advantage of cattle's natural behaviors so that we can get even more out of our dual-use systems?

For so long, cattle have been the whipping boy of the climate change movement. We love our beef, but we don't love cow farts. A single cow, according to the US Environmental Protection Agency, produces between 154 to 264 pounds of methane gas per year (mostly through its belches, though I suppose also through what my kid would call its "toots").[14]

Methane is a potent greenhouse gas, hence the desire to remove it from the equation (or at least mitigate it). Highly publicized data about its dangers has led companies all around the world to invest in plant-based products that mimic meat's flavor and texture, as well as the development of certain cattle breeds that are believed to produce less methane. Some scientists even argue that feeding cattle a diet heavy in a certain type of red seaweed, *Asparagopsis taxiformis* (believed to produce less methane over time), is our golden ticket to a methane-free future (or at least one with less of it).[15]

The advice is always, "Eat less beef."

But, as Anna Clare reminded me, "Beef is America. We aren't going to change our cultural tastes fast enough." Our culture is heavily hard-wired for beef, and reducing our consumption of it is a change we're unlikely to make overnight.

Factory farming, despite all its inherent flaws, produces an absurdly large quantity of meat on limited land resources (though arguably not as much as we're led to believe, as factory farming requires large inputs of fertilizers, feed, and other variables that impose their own demands on the land). Converting a livestock farm operation to an intensive rotational grazing system is not only better for the soil, as it helps sequester carbon, but it also reduces greenhouse gas emissions, including methane, nitrous oxides, and carbon dioxide.[16]

However, rotational grazing requires space, and it requires time. Despite this, I'm not sold on the argument that it's impossible to completely eliminate factory farms because we have too many mouths to feed and not enough land to do it. By focusing our time and resources on improving soil quality, and notably pressing on with a shift away from commodity crops like corn and soy (which take up vast tracts of land while depleting the soil), we could eventually feed ourselves in a more sustainable way. And that diet could include meat.

It's likely we would still need to decrease our per capita beef consumption, even if only by a small amount. But telling people to eat less beef *right now* isn't automatically going to take care of our problems, both because we're a country that's born and bred on red meat and also because these changes take time to reveal any environmental or economic benefit. There needs to be another solution to stop the immediate bleed.

Anna Clare admits that the concept of grazing cattle under solar is still a bit contentious. It's an area that many developers are afraid to broach because, again, of fears that the cattle will destroy the panels. But multiple ranchers and researchers argue that this almost certainly wouldn't occur—as long as we respect the nature of the animal and do our best to give it what it needs. You need to take individual disposition into consideration: While your headstrong, unpredictable steer might be fine grazing at home, you might not want such a rambunctious spitfire grazing under solar. Yet for every wildcard like that, there are at least a dozen good-natured, amicable cows or feeder calves that would be perfectly suitable under solar. And, again, you would want to move these animals often to make sure they aren't given time to get bored (or hungry).

The concept of rotational grazing is nothing new, yet in recent history, we've found ourselves distanced from it. For centuries, farmers have turned their animals out to pasture and moved them on a periodic basis. The feedlot system is the contemporary model, though ironically, it's rotational grazing that's often seen as the trendy newcomer.

Several proponents argue that managing cattle in feedlots can reduce methane emissions compared to grazing, since some studies have shown that a high-grain diet produces less methane than traditional pastured diets.[17] And since the cows are less active on feedlots than they would be on pasture, they fatten more quickly and can be sent to slaughter sooner, reducing their "pollutable" life-span.[18]

However, corn farming to fatten those feedlot cows, as we've established, uses a lot of water, a lot of land, a lot of fossil fuels, and a lot of other resources (not to mention the potential health problems that can occur in cattle that are fed too much corn).

There's also the issue of soil and air quality on or around these feedlots. Nitrous oxide emissions are a significant concern here, as is runoff. The US Department of Agriculture estimates that within cattle production, about 58 percent of all emissions come from enteric emissions (those cow belches), 23 percent in feed production, and 7 percent in manure management.[19]

Switching to rotational grazing allows for the substitution of grass for the feed that needs to be planted, fertilized, grown, harvested, and, in some cases, shipped. One study found that farms practicing rotational grazing, among other sustainable agriculture practices, generated 19 percent fewer emissions than nonpracticing farms in the first two years and 35 percent fewer emissions for longer than two years (likely due to the accumulation of stored nutrients in the soil from improved manure management).[20]

This science isn't new. It's simply a return to the way things used to be done. It marks the recognition that although feedlot systems have benefits, we don't necessarily need to reinvent the wheel. We don't need to "find new space" for solar to coexist separately from agriculture. Instead, by finding ways to graze cattle under solar—returning to what was once the norm—we can feasibly do both.

"It's a novel ecosystem," Anna Clare told me, referring to the synthetic, manmade environment created under solar. "Like being on the moon."

When we think about the built environment, many of us tend to regard it with distaste. It centers on the human, and that's inherently bad, goes the train of thought, because humans should not be the focus of the planet.

It's become clear that while humans should not be the focus of the planet, they do have the potential to be the planet's greatest source of destruction. But it doesn't have to be that way—at least not if we rethink the way we're constructing our environments to best suit our needs.

We don't need to separate ourselves from nature, as the eco-modernist line of thinking goes, but, rather, find ways to better synchronize with it. Opportunities abound for us to do so on solar, but only if we put some thought into it. The solar farm of old, built on pea gravel and meticulously sprayed for weeds, is not a good example. The thriving ecosystem where ground-nesting birds thrive and sheep graze 24/7 is, though.

And the same goes for wind. In fact, Robert Margolis of the National Renewable Energy Laboratory (NREL) suggested to me that we have far more experience with wind being integrated into the built environment, and as such, it's more widely accepted as part of our rural landscapes. We've accepted small, lazily drifting turbines as a country fixture, just like diesel tractors and corner convenience stores owned by the same folks for decades.

The problem we now need to solve is how to best integrate our built environment with the natural one.

Europe has significantly more experience with blending agriculture and energy than the United States does. Compared to the United States, European nations tend to have more wind and solar integrated into the built environment—as being viewed as *part* of human and animal settlements rather than set-aside features that operate wholly unto themselves, with no coinvolvement with each other whatsoever.

They have less land space to work with in these spaces—but these spaces work. They're integrated. They're interconnected. They're more creative. And according to Margolis, "There are lots of ways *we* can be more creative."

Behaving Like Animals

Perhaps the secret to solving all these problems lies in recognizing the *animal's* true nature and then finding ways to work with it rather than simply warping our solutions and relying on new science to meet new ends. The cow is meant to be grazing fresh grass, not confined to a feedlot (where it's fed corn grown inefficiently on the many thousands of acres we could be using to produce other crops). The problem isn't one we need to solve with more innovation, with the creation of new technology. It just requires some clever, and possibly abstract, thinking about the technology we already have—and figuring out how to make everything more compatible with the methods of agriculture that worked for centuries before we decided to mess with them.

We need to go back to systems that respect an animal's inherent need to graze. The problem, again, is that doing so takes up valuable land space, space that we're already fighting about in the clean energy conversation.

Nowhere has this battle emerged more prominently than in the American West.

In the West, the US Bureau of Land Management, which owns close to 250 million acres, administers nearly eighteen thousand permits and leases to ranchers who graze their cattle and sheep (for at least part of the year) on publicly held lands. These leases generally cover a ten-year period and have been an indispensable part of traditional Western agriculture (as have the lands permitted for recreation, hunting, and mining) for decades.[21]

The idea of using public lands for energy is nothing new—today, about 23.7 million acres of federal public lands are leased for oil and gas, though less than half of those acres are producing at "economic quantities."[22] Now, the Bureau of Land Management is proposing to open 22 million acres in the Western states to solar development, using $4.3 million in funding from the Inflation Reduction Act to work with NREL and develop a proposed road map for this development.[23] The problem in this specific arrangement is that it restricts land access to families who have relied on this land to graze their cattle for many generations.

It's not just an economic or logistical battle at this point; it's a cultural one, and it's emotionally charged, to say the least. Finding a satisfactory ending to this battle requires a lot of creativity, including going back to the evolutionary drawing board.

To figure out what works best for renewables, we need to figure out what works best for the animals.

When I first started researching this book in late 2022, there were essentially two options for agri-energy that were being taken seriously: sheep and cold-weather crops (like greens and brassicas). That's no longer the case. Now, farmers raise everything from tilapia to blueberries to vanilla to pigs and even cattle under solar.

Still, sheep are pretty much regarded as the plug-and-play option for solar. They can be put on just about any site (albeit sometimes with a few quick fencing modifications) without a lot of consideration paid to design.

However, as sheep grazing on solar rises in popularity, some communities have expressed concern that this will displace local agriculture. In New York State during the spring of 2025, Senator Michelle Hinchey proposed State Senate Bill 2025-S7899, which would require all new solar sites built on existing farmland to be agrivoltaic.[24]

While that's not inherently a bad thing (I do have concerns about overprescription in agri-energy), the issue is that the bill would also outlaw the use of sheep on solar unless sheep were raised on that land prior to solar installation. While sheep were once the preeminent livestock in New York (in the 1800s, there were more sheep than people here, driven largely by a demand for wool as well as for meat), that is no longer the case.[25] Ours is a dairy-driven state, with cattle farmers taking center stage.

The rationale behind the proposed bill isn't entirely clear. However, it's my belief that it was drafted out of a fear that small, local cattle farms will be converted into solar and then grazed by out-of-state sheep graziers since there are no local sheep graziers available to meet that demand.

Again, I don't believe that the answer to this problem (which is valid) is outlawing sheep entirely. Overregulation is seldom the answer to big problems like these; rather, we must take an individualized approach that recognizes that one site will be well suited for sheep while another might be great for beef (and another shouldn't be given the agri-energy treatment at all). You can't standardize this.

Nevertheless, it speaks to a larger concern: Our economy is currently built on beef. Not lamb.

Enter cattle on solar.

The solution sounds obvious, yet it still remains that cows are not as convenient as sheep for a few reasons (one of them being the higher barrier of entry for beginning farmers, with handling equipment, facilities, and even the animals themselves costing significantly more than the equivalent costs for a sheep business).

Another concern about adding other types of (larger) ruminants has always been damage to the panels. But as Anna Clare told me, that's a nonissue.

Josh Bennett agreed, highlighting the ability of cattle to truly revolutionize the agri-energy relationship. "The quickest means of building trust is with cattle," he told me, referring to the process of building buy-in within communities where solar is being proposed. But the problem is that developers are skeptical, fearing that cattle will damage modules and chew on wires.

Before we raised cattle of our own on our farm, I always assumed that was true. When we got cattle, a hodgepodge of breeds (many of them with full or at least partial Angus genetics, a breed that's notorious for being a bit unruly), I figured we were just lucky—maybe we had some preternaturally well-behaved ones. But after talking to Josh and Anna Clare, I realize that we aren't the exception. We're the rule.

"Cattle are more attracted to forage than they are to a random steel beam," Josh said. "We just need to get over it."

What we have here, he said, are two industries that just don't trust each other. Farmers don't trust solar developers to do what's right by their farm, and developers don't trust farmers to graze animals on a solar site without damaging components.

It's time we bring farmers to the table.

Anna Clare is doing just that. She's currently grazing livestock around her own solar arrays on her farm in the West, so she has firsthand knowledge of how large animals interact with the panels. "If the animals are satisfied nutritionally," she said, referring to the wires, "they won't chew."

But it's context specific, coming down, as always, to management. She stressed the importance of low-stress stockmanship methods and rotational grazing (as well as putting out enrichment methods, like scratchers) and of stock that are calm and not easily agitated.

"We don't even fence anything off," she said, referring to her paddocks where she keeps her horses and sheep. And for cattle, she said, one strand of hot wire around the panels does the trick, something that probably wouldn't even be necessary except that she's retrofitting her grazing operations around older-style panels that are situated lower than what's ideal for cattle.

Her anecdotal experience here is strong, but she's not resting on her laurels. Per the study described earlier, she's also partnered with Will Harris of White Oak Pastures, Silicon Ranch, and the US Department of Energy to build an outdoor test lab (built to the optimal height for cattle). They're not just looking at how the cattle interact with the panels, but also how the panels interact with the cows. They're exploring critical health and welfare indicators that will tell farmers how grazing on solar impacts cattle health. Will the cattle gain weight? Lose weight? Be stressed? The study aims to measure everything from respiration to feed to carcass ratio to the thermodynamics that are created beneath the panels (again, also looking at how the cattle have the potential, or not, to damage components).

If sheep have been any indication, the results will likely be positive. One study found that sheep had more favorable outcomes under solar panels than on open pastures in terms of flock health and condition. "Sheep spend more time grazing in solar treatments than in natural rangeland pastures without solar panels or any other form of shade," wrote the authors of the study, adding that solar panels "may lead to an increase in time spent grazing in sheep."[26]

Most studies I've seen on lamb growth on solar sites haven't shown a massive increase in carcass size, meaning that "solar-powered sheep" aren't necessarily larger than ones grazed on traditional pastures. But they're keeping pace even though the variables are quite different.

When it comes to agri-energy, you'll never get the best possible farmland usage or the best possible energy yields. But you're going to maximize the good and not the yield, as sheep farmer Nick Armentrout would say. There's a trade-off.

And the trade-off may be significantly smaller than what we previously thought. One 2021 study found that although solar pastures produced "38% lower herbage than open pastures due to low pasture density in fully shaded areas under solar panels," the forage *quality* was higher. Thus, lambs raised on solar and those raised on open pastures, both grazed at the same stocking rates, had almost identical live-weight production. Lamb production, in other words, stayed the same despite less available forage due to shading.[27]

Compared to the lambs in solar pastures, lambs raised in open pastures tend to consume more water in the late spring as temperatures begin to rise. On a solar pasture, by contrast, the sheep experience less heat stress and don't need to expend as much energy to stay cool and regulate their body temperatures. This may also play a role in the dam's milk production; lambs in shaded paddocks were found to be 3.8 percent heavier at weaning than those raised in paddocks without shade.[28] Another study found higher milk yields from grazing Holstein Friesian dairy cows raised in shade in temperate pastures than those not raised in shade—again, reducing the impacts of heat stress.[29] While the pastures may not be as productive under the panels, it's clear there are significant savings elsewhere, particularly as temperatures rise. "Our net returns for grazing in solar pastures were 1.6% ... less than in open pastures, which is a small percentage when considering the potential profits from photovoltaics energy production in agrivoltaics system," one of the earlier referenced studies found.[30]

Solar panels also provide shelter for livestock in intense heat and dry spells. While the shade can sometimes be a detriment to pasture growth, that's not necessarily the case in dry weather, where panels provide yet another benefit.

Tom Warren, an Australian grazier, found that solar panels actually created their own drip lines, with condensation rolling off the panels and leading to the growth of "strips of green grass, right through the drought." The carrying capacity of his land has increased by 25 percent.[31]

Once he began grazing sheep on solar, Warren also saw a 15 percent increase in wool production. Often, shepherds report that the sheep have better-quality wool, too, with minimal burrs and dust.

Even parasite loads tend to be lower. As Erica Frenay of Shelterbelt Farm in New York explained, "Having [the sheep] off-farm over most of the growing season allowed me to interrupt parasite life cycles on the farm, and also stockpile some forage to feed the sheep on pasture later into the dormant season than in past years."[32]

Flock of sheep grazing on a Plattsburgh, New York, solar site.
Credit: J&R Pierce Family Farm

But again, we can't base an entire economy around sheep, which is why so many farmers and developers are getting creative with the types of livestock they raise on solar.

Cattle, again, are the next best choice. In one study, researchers installed a thirty-kilowatt solar panel system with panels elevated eight to ten feet above the ground so that crossbred cows could graze beneath them. Although elevating the panels increased the project cost, it allayed some concerns about cattle interacting with the arrays and causing damage. In the study, ear-tag sensors monitored the time the cows spent eating, ruminating, being active, and so on to get an idea of their overall health. The study ultimately found that "shade from an agrivoltaic system may reduce the effects of heat stress in pastured dairy cows."[33]

Best yet, the cost increase of mounting the panels above the cows was "minimal," meaning that there's a potential win-win situation here.[34]

There is, yet again, much hesitation about cows on solar because of a fear of their size. However, as Josh Bennett reminded me, beef cattle are often grazed until they're only about four hundred to six hundred pounds before being moved to a feedlot for finishing. Although utility-scale sites might be better served to proactively design sites with cattle in mind moving forward, what's to say that we couldn't retrofit, as it were, old sites by grazing young calves or feeder steers on them, just until they're too big to interact safely with the traditional panels? While this method wouldn't necessarily phase out the feedlot system (as we likely need to do), it would at least be a step in the right direction as far as maximizing our land use goes.

There's also much to be said about breed and temperament variability. Some breeds are naturally more rambunctious than others. Some are more compact. Lowline Angus typically don't get much taller than four feet tall at the shoulder, meaning that they could do just fine on a "traditional" solar site with no retrofitting needed.

Again, this is not a one-size-fits-all kind of game we're playing.

When I first learned that Caleb Scott of United Agrivoltaics was running pigs on solar farms, I had to admit that I was skeptical. United Agrivoltaics "works like a co-op," Caleb told me, helping connect solar graziers with companies in need of vegetation management all over the United States (in addition to providing other resources, like marketing, trailering, and insurance).

He first explored the idea of solar grazing in 2012, after spending several years as a landscaper tasked with conventionally mowing the areas under solar arrays. That work was tedious, time-consuming, and not very effective, he said, to say nothing of about the mower spitting rocks dangerously close to the panels. Then, he came up with an idea: sheep.

It took him three years to finalize his first contract as a solar grazier, but now, United Agrivoltaics oversees hundreds of sheep around the country.

He offers more than just sheep grazing. One of his biggest achievements of late is the work he's done with pigs. Pigs have not traditionally been seen as the poster child for solar—namely because they like to root—but the devil is truly in the details. Caleb doesn't raise the typical pig you'll see on a farm, a Yorkshire or Hampshire or Duroc. Instead, he raises Kunekunes.

Kunekune pigs on a solar site. Credit: United Agrivoltaics North America

Kunekunes are native to New Zealand and have short, upturned snouts that aren't great at rooting. These pigs don't leave as much of an impact on the soil as other pig breeds and can help clean up forage that sheep might leave behind. Kunekunes are smaller than typical pigs and are unique for another reason: They can be finished on pasture without grain, something that's not true of other breeds. Thus they open up yet another additional revenue stream for farmers.

But that's not all.

Farmers in Britain raise sheep and poultry (namely chickens, ducks, and geese) on solar farms. Caleb himself has Runner ducks alongside his pastured pigs and sheep. Even clipped-wing chickens (that can't fly up and damage the panels) can be successful additions to a solar farm, as can rabbits.

None of these were viewed as being even remotely possible just a decade ago, but now, with a bit of creativity, our solar farms are looking a lot less sterile and a lot more diverse.

Impact on Wetlands, Grassland Habitat, and Wildlife

When we first started grazing our sheep on solar in 2022, we were surprised to discover something we didn't think we'd ever have on a solar site: woodchucks. They didn't bother us much on the solar farm (aside from the holes we'd occasionally stumble into). Their presence, however, told us something much more important, a feature of solar we never expected to find. These sites can be havens for wildlife.

Just think about it. One of the biggest selling points of solar farms to us, as sheep farmers, was a selling point for other animals, too: The tall fences around the perimeter made it tough for those aforementioned predators to get inside.

We realized it wasn't just woodchucks we were seeing more of, either. There were hawks screeching overhead, mice skittering underfoot, ground-nesting birds flitting around the arrays. Some of the most beautiful and diverse landscapes I've ever set foot on just happen to be landscapes that we humans have built—here, on these solar farms. Again, we're interacting with the built environment in more natural (and more beautiful) ways than we could have ever possibly imagined.

I'm not alone in this thinking. When interviewed, Caleb said, "There's nothing more beautiful than standing out there with my sheep, overlooking the valley in a sea of blue panels. When I'm on a solar site, I see bobolinks and quail and ground-nesting birds utilizing the shade of the panels."[35]

It's not just solar, either, but wind installations that inspire us to rethink how we interact with the landscape, so long as we're willing to revisit some of our misconceptions.

It's no secret that wind has long been targeted for its impacts on wildlife, namely birds. US Geological Survey has found certain bats and birds are disproportionately affected by collisions with rotating wind turbines. One study found that nearly half of all bird species could suffer population declines as a result of wind development.[36]

My personal perspective on renewables changed abruptly in 2012, when Josh took a job with WEST (Western Ecosystems Technology), a company based out of Cheyenne, Wyoming (mentioned briefly in chapter 2). He worked as a technician monitoring the environmental impact of wind farms in northern New York. If you've ever played a game of hide-and-seek, the work Josh did for WEST will likely entertain you (perhaps only in a morbid way).

The unique spin on the game required Josh and his colleagues to take turns hiding bat and bird carcasses on wind farms, with the goal of tricking each other into missing the hidden specimen. In essence, this exercise was done to keep everyone spry—to make sure nobody was missing a single dead animal that might have met its untimely demise at the hands of one of those massive spinning blades.

The broader, high-level goal was to determine the postconstruction environmental impact of wind turbines on residential and migratory birds. Josh visited ten out of fifty regional sites daily, walking in transect grids within a two-hundred-foot radius of the turbine to search for any dead animals. Although the hide-and-seek game seemed a bit silly, it was just the dry run for the actual, more important, research they were doing. Humans just aren't that good at finding dead birds. In fact, a 2020 study found that dogs located an average of twice as many small bird fatalities as human monitors did at wind sites in California.[37] In the WEST study, each hidden bird was marked with a dark zip-tied band so the monitors could ensure that they were finding the birds they themselves had hidden (and not any real ones that had just died from a collision). The goal of the project was to answer the question we're all asking: Are wind turbines killing birds and bats?

The answer was no, at least not as much as we've been led to believe. In this particular project, wildlife was not significantly affected. Though there were some mortalities, the extent depended on precisely where the turbines were located. For the most part, these turbines surveyed by Josh and his team were not in major flyways, so any mortalities were minimal, though a slight increase in death rates during fall migration periods was indeed seen in the other dog trial study.[38]

For his respective research, Josh told me that on the ground at the base of the turbines, wildlife was remarkably healthy. Deer, turkeys, and foxes roamed freely, while the farmers who owned the land being leased to the wind company allowed their cows to graze around the concrete pads housing the turbines. In fact, the cows enjoyed lounging on the pads, which held the warmth of the sun in the early morning yet also enjoyed shade at the hottest time of the day.

Prior to this research, most numbers related to wind turbines and bird mortalities were from studies conducted in 2012 and earlier. By these estimates, about 366,000 birds were killed by wind turbines in the

United States each year.[39] Today, much of the public opposition to wind is still based on this old data.

Yet wind development (along with adequate research and technology to mitigate wildlife deaths) has increased exponentially since then. There were 60,067 megawatts of wind energy capacity in the United States in 2012 versus more than 111,800 in 2021, an 86 percent increase.[40]

Yes, 366,000 bird deaths is a lot of deaths. However, it's important to clarify that we don't zoom in on bird deaths related to *other* sources with nearly as much scorn and scrutiny as when we track those related to polarizing projects like wind turbines. For example, at least 25.5 million birds are killed each year due to collisions with power lines.[41] Between 89 million and 340 million birds are killed by cars.[42] And domestic and feral cats kill 1.3 to 4.0 billion birds per year just in the United States.[43]

Why are we so quick to demonize wind turbines? The reason is simple: Wind, like all other novel renewables, is just so easy to hate. It's not just wind that's controversial for its effect on wildlife in the public eye either. From water use and land use issues to habitat loss and pesticide use, solar installation can be equally problematic from a wildlife conservation angle. With all that said, it's important to recognize that coal mines and natural gas drilling sites kill wildlife, too.

There's no truly innocent party here. It's just that wind turbines and solar panels are held to a higher standard for this one simple fact: They're new. We're more afraid of what we *don't* know than the enemy we *do*.

And there are plenty of ways to mitigate these risks. Ecologists have found that much of the impact on wildlife related to wind turbines has to do with where, exactly, these turbines are built. If they can be kept out of (or at least mostly out of) major flyways, the number of birds lost during key migration periods can be drastically reduced. Ridgetop farms can also be problematic, since the red marker lights meant to alert planes to their presence often attract insects, which then attract bats and birds and lead to unwanted deaths. Avoid these, and we can mitigate a large quantity of deaths, even if not all of them.

Wind farms have found further ways to reduce bird deaths by altering when the turbines turn during migration season, turning only when fewer animals are flying, and by making power lines less attractive as perches. Turbines are built taller so that animals can fly beneath the blades, unharmed. Some even have bat sensors that halt the machinery if an animal gets too close, while others incorporate intelligent cameras that recognize large and rare birds of prey (like eagles) as they approach and shut down the turbines to avoid collisions.

On the ground, the impact may be a wash. One study in Finland found that 67 percent of terrestrial mammals are displaced from areas where turbines are installed.[44] However, the study had its own (self-admitted) limitations, including incomplete methodology that made it hard for researchers to gather how, why, and for how long animals were staying away from turbines. Other studies have also been inconclusive. Unfortunately, a large portion of the research, including one that took place in 2022 in India, on wind and wildlife doesn't have data on earlier biodiversity. We don't know the biodiversity of a site prior to wind, so it's difficult to measure how wind is impacting biodiversity.[45]

Well-managed solar and wind can create a pasture that not only provides food and shelter for grazing animals, but also habitat for birds, pollinators, and a greater diversity of plant species.

Some solar graziers build their entire business model around this concept. Arlo Hark of Cannon Valley Graziers launched his career doing targeted grazing and forest management. When he first started out, many people in his area used goats to manage buckthorn. "I wanted to figure out how I could have as specific an ecological benefit as possible," he said of his grazing operation in Minnesota.

Here, solar companies have strict regulations to abide by. As part of the "habitat-friendly" designation, they need to follow a checklist and

meet certain certification steps. For example, they must list what percentage of their seed mix is pollinator friendly.

When it comes to solar grazing, Arlo said, "You need to be able to
provide a full spectrum of services," and his operation does just that.
"We are seeing awesome biodiversity in terms of grass and flowering species.... It's a critical part of how we do business in the upper Midwest."

It's not just in the Midwest, either. Britain has studied the ecological
impact of agrivoltaics on biodiversity for years. A 2016 study looked
at eleven different solar sites that incorporated a variety of practices,
like grazing and pollinator friendly plants, comparing them with arable
control plots just outside the perimeter.[46] The study found consistently
greater biodiversity on the solar farms. The impact was highest in places
where wildflower mixes were sown, but even when agricultural grass
mixes were chosen, the impacts were profound.

Then there's the poop problem. One of the biggest head-scratchers
for conventional farmers these days is figuring out what to do with
manure. When animals are raised in barns—or even in outdoor feedlots—manure is typically disposed of in slurries, lagoons, or piles, leading to significant emissions of the greenhouse gas methane as well as a
number of other environmental and human health and safety issues.

When livestock are grazed rotationally—and moved often—the
manure problem is eliminated. There's no manure that needs to be shov-
eled or disposed of. It's deposited directly onto the ground, but in a bal-
anced and evenly distributed way. It's estimated that manure accounts
for 14 percent of greenhouse gas emissions from agriculture, which in
itself contributes to a lion's share of overall global emissions.[47]

But rotational grazing, since it doesn't rely on concentrating manure
in one single area, produces carbon dioxide with little or no methane
and recycles nutrients back into the soil before they are lost.[48] Rotational
grazing, when done correctly, allows the soil and the plants to recover
between grazings, keeping the carbon in the soil—where it belongs.

As we spoke, Arlo was en route to a solar site with a trailer load of lambs. Friendly and laid back (and, I might add, sporting quite an impressive mustache), Arlo is one of the country's best spokespeople for the myriad benefits of solar grazing. He practices regenerative grazing with his herd of sheep and goats through the work he does with his company, Cannon Valley Graziers, owned with partner Josie Trople. "It makes sense to stack benefits on these sites," he explained. "We are providing a top-notch service to our customers, improving soil and water quality, and providing meat and fiber to our community. It just makes sense."

It does make sense. But it's not perfect. Far from it. In fact, one of the current challenges with agri-energy is figuring out how sites can be made safe and secure for grazing animals like sheep, while also providing fencing that keeps out predators.

Another issue has to do with the potential endangerment of rare plants. One study found that solar panels can change the immediate microhabitat and have a detrimental impact on rarer plants. However, the study also notes that picking an area that's already disturbed (like farms) or introducing native plants after construction can help.[49]

Some states have regulations in place to address these issues already, ones that require developers to avoid areas of high native biodiversity and to allow for wildlife connectivity both now and in the face of climate change. But given the National Electric Code, which requires fencing that's at least seven feet high on utility-scale solar sites, these requirements can often still be an issue.[50]

Some facilities have experimented with wildlife-permeable fences, which have larger holes than chain link to allow medium-size animals (think raccoons, rabbits, and squirrels) to fit through. This fencing works well on some sites, but the problem arises on sites where larger wildlife passageways are allowed. When bears and coyotes are allowed to roam through a site where sheep are grazing, there are undoubtedly going to be some major headaches for the shepherd.

This is where more research is definitely needed. We need to figure out which design elements can maximize the benefit for livestock while mitigating the harm to wildlife. Considering avian and mammalian behavior, including migratory and flight patterns, can help reduce the overall impact these sites have on wildlife.

The issue is that performing wildlife research takes many years and can be quite expensive. Since the solar industry is still a nascent one, it's difficult to understand and evaluate long-term impacts. Development is moving faster than mitigation strategies can be created and implemented.

For some animals, there may not be a good or obvious solution. Fencing creates obstacles that are tough to work around. Nevertheless, some species of wildlife, like small burrowing reptiles and mammals, may find some relief from agri-energy regardless of what type of fencing is used.

Two of the biggest threats to tortoises, for instance, are damage to burrows and actual physical injury from heavy machinery like mowers. Pollinators are another area of concern. I'll talk more about pollinator health later on, in chapter 5, but rest assured that the net benefit here can be quite high.

According to the UK Energy Research Centre, five characteristics engender "solar parks" as exceptionally good places for nature and biodiversity: "Longevity—they will be in the landscape for 25–40 years; Secure & undisturbed—with the exception of maintenance vehicles solar parks are secure places with limited disturbance; Paid for—the land is paid for and thus there is no pressure to generate further income; Landscape—they are often in agricultural landscapes, where nature enhancements are needed most; Climate—the physical presence of the arrays provides climatic niches."[51]

It's going to be a long road ahead while we figure out what works well and what doesn't. But in an industry this new, experimentation is the name of the game.

Later, Arlo told me that he doesn't dislike the long drives to solar installations. He gets to listen to his satellite radio. His favorite artist, I was pleased to hear, is Willie Nelson. I'm a big fan of Willie Nelson myself, both for his music and his astute, often tongue-in-cheek sound bites. Perhaps one of my favorite quotes of his is "I think most art comes out of poverty and hard times."

Looking at a solar site, with sheep grazing and native plants blooming and pollinators buzzing and ground-nesting birds getting cozy in the grasses, it's easy to see the art. And for graziers like me and Arlo, who have found a thing of beauty amid harder times making a living as farmers, we appreciate that artwork even more.

"There's not another scalable way forward," Arlo told me. "We have enormous opportunities ahead of us. It's a big responsibility. We're the shoulders people are going to be standing on."

And not just people, either—but also wrens, robins, swallows, grouse, blackbirds, hawks, mice, voles, chipmunks, woodchucks, and so much more.

Agri-Energy for Fire Suppression

Not too long ago, I was scrolling mindlessly on my phone and stumbled upon a headline that I felt was probably clickbait. Naturally, I was baited. I clicked. The headline of the article: "Plant That's Everywhere Is Fueling a Growing Risk of Wildfire Disaster."

"Grass," I thought. "It's got to be some species of grass."

I was hoping the article would be a bit more specific in its indictment, perhaps calling out a specific species of grass to surprise me, but there wasn't a shock-and-awe factor here after all. It was just grass.

Nevertheless, the article cited a troubling statistic: Since 1990, the number of homes in the United States that have been destroyed by wildfires has more than doubled. Fires are burning bigger and hotter than ever, many of them fueled not by forests, but by grasses and shrubs.

Since the 1990s, wildfires can be blamed for 80 percent of the fires that burned homes in the US West.[52]

Grass is perhaps more deadly than forests when it comes to wildfires because it doesn't take long for it to turn into kindling. It's also more sensitive to weather—just look at how your lawn responds to a couple of weeks of no rain versus the trees' response. Your lawn gets crispy in a hurry.

Although grass and other vegetation are important when it comes to soil stability, particularly on solar sites, they can also serve as a hot spot—quite literally.

Solar farms aren't immune to fire. The most common causes of solar farm fires are related to error in design, faulty products, and poor installation practices. Direct-current isolators have the highest fire risk, leading to 30 percent of fires caused by solar equipment, but connectors and inverters aren't exempt either. It's typically not the panels themselves catching on fire, but instead, the other components.[53]

Those seven-foot-tall fences I mentioned earlier might protect the panels from intruders, but they don't do anything when it comes to fire.

Exactly how many fires there have actually been on solar farms is difficult to measure, particularly because solar installations on rooftops have increased just as ground-mounted units have—and that can, in itself, become sort of a chicken-and-egg debacle. Did the fire start in the panels and spread to the house, or the other way around? Similarly, photovoltaic (PV) fires tend to be lumped into an "other" category for reporting purposes, too, so they are a tough statistic to quantify.

One 2021 study in Germany found that of two million PV plants, 0.006 percent caused a fire resulting in major damage. Instead, most were related to faulty cabling and connections, which can occur in any electrical system (and aren't at all related to the panels).[54]

Similarly, it's estimated that about one in two thousand wind turbines catch on fire each year.[55] For context, improperly maintained or downed power lines (from all sources of electricity) account for about 3 percent of wildfires.[56]

The problem isn't the solar or wind farm itself; whenever there is electricity, there is a risk of a fire. The actual panels and components are no riskier than any other electrical component.

When a solar farm catches on fire, however, it's bad news for another reason—it burns incredibly hot, particularly when lithium batteries are involved.

This is an area where solar farms tend to attract the most criticism, with many concerned citizens taking to Facebook and the like to express their worry that fires like these are going to become increasingly common as we ramp up solar construction across the United States. Those concerns aren't unfounded, but they may be somewhat misdirected.

First, lithium batteries are found in just about everything—from the car you drive to the cell phone in your back pocket. Lithium-ion battery fires, many caused by e-bikes and e-scooters, in New York City alone accounted for a whopping 268 fires in just 2023.[57] Lithium-ion battery fires are difficult to put out because they can reignite easily and they burn hotter and faster than other types of fires. They need more water to put out, and batteries can explode, sending metal shrapnel flying in all directions.

Second, proper maintenance of solar sites plays a huge role in preventing these fires, just as properly maintaining and storing your devices is key to preventing lithium-ion battery fires elsewhere. No matter how well-maintained a solar site is, it's not impervious to the risk of wildfire—no more than any other structure is.

Fire isn't a new phenomenon. Natural fires happen from time to time and are actually beneficial for the ecosystem in many ways. But nobody wants a wildfire burning on a one-hundred-acre solar site.

Enter solar grazing.

Grazing for wildfire fuel breaks isn't something talked about often in the humid Northeast, but in the West, cattle and sheep have been used for centuries as a valuable rangeland fire protection tool.

Fuel breaks are simply blocks where vegetation has been fully removed or minimized to slow the spread of the flames, making it easier for firefighters to combat wildfires. Prescribed burns, chemical treatments, and mowing can all serve as forms of fuel breaks, but they can be costly and difficult to maintain.

Targeted grazing is the more sustainable alternative, particularly in areas like the Great Basin, where invasive annual grasses serve as major contributors to fire size and frequency. It's estimated that invasive annual grasses burn two to four times more frequently than their counterparts.[58]

This is where we can put sheep, the solar industry's newest volunteer firefighter, to work.

Ryan Indart, owner of Indart Solar Sheep Grazing in Clovis, California, reached what he thought was the end of the line in 2018. Low wool prices, high production costs, and increasing regulations (plus a drought year that made growing barley and wheat too expensive) were pushing Indart out of business. He'd maxed out his savings and his line of credit. "I was hemorrhaging assets," he told me.

But then he was contacted about grazing sheep on a large solar project in Fresno County, and the lifeline couldn't have come at a better time. His sheep were tasked with keeping the vegetation down when it needed to be kept down the most. Vegetation management on these solar sites was necessary for all the other reasons that have been discussed, but also for fire fuel load reduction. Grazed areas have been shown to burn less aggressively than uncleared ones.[59]

"We have a Mediterranean climate," he told me. "It's very rainy in the winter and dry in the summer." The vegetation growth comes on fast and strong at first but then doesn't come back. That's great for crops, he added, but not for fire risk.

Sheep don't start fires like mowers do. I've seen firsthand just by mowing my lawn with my old-as-dirt push mower that when you hit a rock, the contact creates a spark. In damp upstate New York, where the summer months often make it feel like we're living in a rainforest, that spark isn't a big deal. I seldom notice it. But if you're mowing a solar site that hasn't seen rain in weeks, that spark could turn deadly in a hurry.

Sheep grazing a California solar farm.
Credit: Indart Solar Sheep Grazing, California

Sheep don't create sparks—besides the spark of innovation, that is.

Ryan is now debt-free and grazing more than a thousand sheep around California, grazing sheep to help reduce the risk of fires. He and his "four-legged firefighters," as he calls them, graze four thousand acres in Kings County alone.[60] The solar sheep business isn't his only business; Ryan, a fourth-generation rancher, also grows oranges, cherries, almonds, and dry land wheat and barley. He shears thirty thousand pounds of wool that's sold through Roswell Wool and also raises lambs for meat.

"I just wish more people would have the 'innovation' attitude," he said.

Innovation, indeed, is the name of the game when it comes to agri-energy. As we think of creative ways to make the most of the land we have available (and to keep that land as safe and healthy as possible), it's important to remember that we're doing so not just for ourselves, but for all the other creatures that live there, too.

CHAPTER 5

Protecting Plants and Pollinators

The flower doesn't dream of the bee. It blossoms and the bee comes.
—Mark Nepo

N<small>OT JUST SHEEP, COWS, AND CHICKENS</small> benefit from the unique micro-climate created beneath solar panels. Plants happen to love it, too. It's another area where the "innovation attitude" is being displayed front and center.

"It's a playground for plant physiologists," Dr. Serkan Ates, an associate professor at Oregon State University's College of Agricultural Sciences, explained to me. Much of Ates's research has covered sheep behavior under solar, which makes sense given his PhD in animal nutrition. He's discovered that although forage production decreases, solar provides a protected environment for both animals and plants to thrive.

In the early spring, production under the panels is often reduced because of increased shading. But there are workarounds here, namely by adjusting the spacing between panels or using tilted or tracker panels that get more sun. And the shade, which proves to be a detriment in the spring, flips roles and provides a *benefit* in the summer, with increased forage production and the ability to increase grazing in dry climates.

Solar panels offer shelter to other animals that prefer the shade, like mice and moles, as well as predator protection. It also means plants bloom later—a boon for the bees—and creates an incredibly unique solar microclimate.[1]

Previously, it was thought that only cool-season crops in warmer climates (think brassicas in Virginia and farther south) could thrive in the shaded environment of solar farms. We now know that's just not the case.

Anna Clare explained to me that there are four distinct microclimate zones created here: beneath the panels, along the eastern and western drip edges, and in the rows (which tend to receive direct sun). According to a 2011 study, these systems have the potential to increase global land productivity by an impressive 35 to 73 percent.[2] There's also a 30 percent increase in economic value for those combining shade-tolerant crop production and solar-generated electricity, another study found.[3]

For a long time, the agrivoltaics conversation was dominated by an emphasis on shade crops like lettuce. Indeed, according to one study, "Some varieties of lettuce produce greater yields in shade than under full sunlight; other varieties produce essentially the same yield under an open sky and under PV [photovoltaic] panels."[4]

But it's not just about lettuce anymore. Just like it's not just about sheep.

Juli Burden works as a researcher for the Hawaii Agriculture Research Center. Since roughly 2021, she's grown crops in a small, shaded corner of a 230-acre solar farm in Mililani, on the island of Oahu. The project started with four commercial hydroponic troughs on a research demonstration site that was just half an acre or so in size, with five panels. She wanted to see how system designs could be optimized while she worked simultaneously to develop best practices.

Exploring everything from water-use efficiency to production to biodiversity, Juli wanted to figure out how we could get the best of both worlds. What are the ideal crops? What is the ideal spacing?

When I interviewed her, she told me that her team grows fourteen different crops: daikon, radish, kabocha squash, melons, cauliflower, broccoli, eggplant, bush beans, poha berries, bunching onion, sweet potato, strawberries, lavender, and dryland taro. She's even sown cover crops of buckwheat and cowpeas. And lettuce? They're growing five different varieties here.

They've also experimented with kalo, mushrooms, vanilla, basil, tomatoes, and even māmaki, which is a native rainforest understory crop that's used to make a ready-to-drink canned beverage.

All these crops, according to Juli, "love it under the solar panels."

Broccoli, she said, produced bountiful heads in the heat of full summer, something that doesn't typically happen in Hawaii's tropical climate. The vanilla plants, normally grown in greenhouses with misters to provide constant humidity, might even flower this year.

The United States is hardly the first country to experiment with agrivoltaics. In Japan, nearly two thousand agrivoltaic installations generate more than two hundred megawatts of electricity (enough to power 32,000-plus homes) and provide land to grow more than 120 types of crops.[5]

Even aquaponics (an aquaculture system in which waste produced by farmed fish "fertilizes" crops grown hydroponically up above) works well here. Juli works with producers who find that fish thrive in this setup. If there's too much direct sunlight, algae production in fishponds can increase. Algae deprives fish of the oxygen they need, so even a small amount of shade can offer a huge benefit.

Juli recognizes that not all sites lend themselves nicely to crops, just like not all sites are suited for grazing. Agrivoltaic systems can also involve more substantial up-front investments, but arguably more extensive benefits, as dual use makes it possible to grow plants and produce power on the same plot of land.

There's an unspoken sense of synergy on these sites. "The shade provided by solar panels can reduce water evaporation and create a more humid environment for crops, while the crops can also cool panels through evapotranspiration, increasing the panels efficiency," reads a statement on the Hawaii Agricultural Research Center's website.[6]

Juli believes that the costs associated with water, leases, and processing facilities could potentially be subsidized with the right partnerships. "The inherent problems in agriculture will still exist," she told me, referring to the issues related to getting projects up and running. "Making this work [at scale] is hard." There's also the risk of farmers getting bottlenecked into just a handful of crops, which explains much of the brassica-greens obsession on the mainland. But that's something Juli's hoping to fix with her research. She isn't just focused on one crop. She's studying more than a dozen.

When done correctly, the yields can be impressive. Farmers in places where land access is a challenge—like Hawaii—can farm with little to no money tied up in rent. "Agrivoltaics makes it easier for farmers to get long-term leases," she said, something that's virtually unheard of in Hawaii.

Juli is currently studying variables ranging from weed mat color—to get an idea of the benefits of different colors related to the albedo effect—to soil moisture. Most studies note significantly reduced temperatures under the panels, but Juli's curious about just how much of an impact this will have.

In most cases, according to a 2019 study, the crops that do best in agrivoltaics are those that benefit from "the added protection from sunlight or excessive evaporation."[7]

However, figuring out the best crops will be largely location (and site) dependent. Tomatoes will likely do well in sunny, hot climates like Hawaii, but may struggle in the Northeast, where sunlight's more limited and the shading serves as a detriment rather than a helping hand.

In Arizona, "partial shade from the panels has been incredibly beneficial, especially for tomatoes and peppers. We saw doubling of yield of tomatoes using 30 percent less water, and we saw tripling of yield for beans and peppers using half as much water. In these hot, arid environments, that partial shade from the solar panels can really have a beneficial effect on crop yields as well as reducing water demands," reported Jordan Macknick of the National Renewable Energy Laboratory in one interview.[8]

Large solar arrays can, unfortunately, contribute to an urban heat island effect, but this can be offset by vegetation. Plants release water through the process of transpiration as they take in carbon dioxide for photosynthesis. Research has indicated that the microclimate created under solar panels helps the panels produce about 2 percent more electricity and stay cooler by about 16 degrees Fahrenheit.[9] It's not just about what the panels can do for the crops; it's also about what the crops can do for the panels.

A 2019 study by Greg Barron-Gafford and colleagues found that agrivoltaic panels produced more energy in May and June compared to the noncropped versions while also helping the crops. Barron-Gafford and his team found that some types of peppers could produce three times as much fruit in an agrivoltaic system, likely due to the plants being less stressed by excessive sunlight.[10]

The relationship is more complicated for places that are colder and wetter, but that doesn't mean that the Northeast can't successfully pair crop production with solar. It's all about choosing the right crops. As Macknick noted in an interview for *The Counter*, "One of the challenges is many things in agrivoltaics are very site specific. You have to try very hard to be able to extrapolate results from one region to another region."[11]

Sometimes it might not be the best idea to plant a crop in the deepest shade. It might need to be placed on the outskirts of a panel or even in the alleys. That doesn't mean that agrivoltaics doesn't work—just that we need to be thoughtful about how we plan and implement our ideas.

It's not always going to be a win. In Italy, spinach yields decreased on one agrivoltaics site.[12] And in Maine, researchers explored how diversified crops like blueberries could perform in a photovoltaic setup. They didn't have the most favorable results.[13]

In the blueberry study, it wasn't a matter of retrofitting agriculture to an existing solar site, but instead, the other way around. The eleven-acre solar array was built on top of an existing blueberry patch managed by farmer Paul Sweetland. The first goal of the project was to form an understanding of how construction, in particular, would affect the blueberry plants, which are perennial shrubs. The panels were installed in three different sectors: one with a standard construction process (with no considerations given to the crops), one labeled "mindful" (with machinery required to stay on certain paths), and the third labeled "careful" (with mats placed over the plants and as few driving trips as possible).

Although the "careful" group obviously fared the best, all three sectors recovered just fine. The group continued the study over three years to compare the yield among the different microclimates—some plants fully shaded, some partially shaded, and some in full sun.

The results weren't what they had hoped: The plants directly underneath the panels produced just 9 percent of the blueberries compared to bushes planted in rows beneath the panels. The shaded areas also suffered from more disease and weeds.[14]

That's not to say the study didn't hold value. It demonstrated that construction around cropped sites *can* be done, particularly with a bit of forethought. It also showed the importance of modifying the specific approach to the specific setting. Blueberries ended up not being the best-case scenario for agri-energy in Maine, but that's not to say they wouldn't thrive in a different setup. Without trying, it's tough to say what will and won't work.

Some plants, like potatoes, surprise us. Typically, potatoes need at least six hours of direct sunlight per day, suggesting that the shading from solar panels might not be ideal. But one study out of Belgium found that solar panels can cool potato plants and help them grow in a dry climate, even with the lower light. The researchers were astonished to find that the potatoes had "the ability to adapt to shaded conditions and … compensate the reduction of PAR [photosynthetically active radiation] by a higher light harvesting capability."[15]

A similar study in Massachusetts researched cranberry production, this time with elevated panels spaced farther apart over working cranberry bogs. The project created nine megawatts of solar capacity while still allowing cranberries to be grown and harvested underneath the arrays.[16] The study found significant yield reduction (again, a place where we need to look at the overall picture instead of individual variables) in the cranberries, but there weren't necessarily any other red flags.

Cranberries, unlike blueberries, don't need as much sunlight to be productive, but they are typically grown on bogs or wetlands that can't be developed like hayfields can. In general, hand-picked crops are better suited for agrivoltaics because mechanically harvesting around photovoltaics can be tricky. There's also a trend toward putting solar over high-value crops like vineyards, orchards, berries, and even cannabis. Despite the yield reductions, cranberries might nevertheless be a good fit when it comes to maximizing our land use.

It's important to note that this approach has global potential, not just potential here in the United States, and as such, it's equally important to think about global food production systems holistically and internationally, rather than just about how things are done stateside. In South Korea, for example, researchers growing broccoli under solar panels found that the quality of the broccoli was just as high as that grown in traditional setups. Interestingly, it was also a deeper shade of green, which made it more appealing to consumers.[17]

In Kenya, agrivoltaics has helped rural farmers grow a greater range of high-value crops, where the coverage from the panels reduces water loss and mitigates ultraviolet stress while also providing energy independence along with food and water security to Kenya's people. This makes a huge difference for households in remote locations, such as Kajiado, where it's often not possible to grow horticultural crops because of the climate.[18]

Even fruit trees have potential. Colorado peach farm Talbott Farms received a grant through the US Department of Agriculture's Rural Energy for America Program, or REAP, to see how solar might integrate with a peach orchard. The tracking panels help protect the trees from frost and hail damage while the facility also powers the farm's entire packing and processing operations.[19]

And let's not forget the people tending the crops. Another reason agri-energy works so well for hand-harvested crops is that it can improve farmworker health. Farmworkers can now plan their harvesting around the time of the day when the panels provide shade, reducing heat stress and improving health outcomes.

Though best suited to hand-harvested crops, even mechanically harvested crops have some potential. Hay and silage weren't traditionally considered for agrivoltaics due to the shading impact beneath the panels as well as the difficulty of mechanically harvesting between the arrays. But that might be changing.

The Ohio State University recently completed a two-year research study demonstrating forage (hay) production between the rows of a photovoltaic facility. Funded by the US Department of Energy's Foundational Agrivoltaic Research for Megawatt Scale, or FARMS, program, the research was carried out on a 120-acre parcel of a 1,000-acre utility-scale solar site. The study found that hay production is entirely possible, particularly when developers put thought into designing a "hay-ready solar site" that considers spacing requirements, alley widths, and other design components. Furthermore, the yields of the alfalfa and cool-season hay crops grown in test plots on solar were "comparable to yields of newly seeded forage stands in an open field setting."[20]

You've witnessed me lament the overtaking of the American agricultural economy by corn and soy multiple times in this book, but I recognize that these crops are still important (albeit oversubsidized) elements. And believe it or not, even corn and soybeans can be grown in agrisolar systems. Per the Agrisolar Clearinghouse, "Shade and increased soil moisture can be particularly helpful in dry, hot years and areas that continue to face long-term droughts."[21]

Obviously, we have options. The key now is to avoid setting sites up in a way we can't retrofit later, Stacie Peterson from the National Center for Appropriate Technology told me. Her priority is figuring out how projects can be equally beneficial for farmers and solar developers alike, whatever the crop might be.

"Don't assume that all solar designs are the same," she said. From clear panels to tilting panels to solar greenhouses, the opportunities are endless—if we're open to the benefits and willing to work around the challenges.

She highlights, in particular, the immense benefit of agrivoltaics for water usage and crop health even as far north as Alaska. Although solar panels are often touted for their ability to shade and cool the crops beneath them, in colder climates, as the temperatures start to drop, they have the *opposite* effect. "Agrivoltaics can increase soil temperatures by two to three degrees Fahrenheit and add a few weeks of the growing season," she said, highlighting frost protection as yet another benefit.

When we move into the hot desert, that same element of shading presents another benefit in the form of water conservation. Some studies, according to Stacie, have shown up to 75 percent reduced water needs for crops grown on solar.

This fact highlights another key variable of agri-energy that we just aren't paying enough attention to: water usage. One Oregon State

University study found that adding solar to the land quadrupled the water efficiency while doubling the land's production.[22] In some dryland settings where agrivoltaics are implemented (and where water has traditionally been in short supply and a thorn in the side of farmers), some solar farmers are finding they now don't have to irrigate at all. Agriculture accounts for more than 69 percent of global water use, so that fact is more than significant.[23] As our population grows, we're running out of water. Why not make the most of what we have?

Too *much* water is seldom a concern on agrivoltaics sites, though there have been some concerns about how rain, diverted and directed into certain areas by the panels, might create additional puddling or erosion around crops. It's relatively easy to mitigate, however, by tweaking irrigation design.

At the end of the day, agrivoltaics—specifically, growing crops under solar panels—might only benefit a small percentage of sites. But it doesn't *need* to benefit every site. If we at least seriously consider dual use on each and every site, it might not matter if they don't all pan out; we'll still be making massive strides.

Protecting Pollinators

I'd be remiss if I didn't mention one of the smallest but perhaps most influential players in agrivoltaics: pollinators. Pollinators have been in the news a lot lately (they've gotten a lot of "buzz," if you will), but they've always been crucial to how our planet functions.

Around the world, roughly a thousand different plants that are grown for food, fiber, beverages, spices, and medicines need to be pollinated by animals (75 to 95 percent of all flowering plants require pollinators).[24] Everything from the coffee you drink in the morning to the blueberries you put in your pancakes requires pollinators. That amounts to about one of every three bites of food you eat.[25]

When we think about pollinators, our minds instantly go to honeybees, but there are many other creatures that serve as pollinators, too, including hummingbirds, bats, butterflies, moths, wasps, ants, beetles, and more.

Certain crops, like blueberries, are 90 percent dependent on honeybee pollination. Almonds depend entirely on honeybees for pollination at bloom time.[26] Even food products that don't require pollination to reproduce can still be affected by pollinators. Cattle, for instance, eat pollinator-dependent alfalfa and clover. Without a solid pollinator habitat, everything else will slowly but surely collapse.

As temperatures increase, adequate habitat for nectar foraging, along with nesting sites, becomes limited. Pollinators have begun shifting their ranges. Higher temperatures mean that both food and water resources are limited.[27]

Not only must pollinators shift their habitat to find adequate food sources, but they also face a famine of sorts as we plant nonnative species that aren't compatible with their diets. Flowering times are changing, too, so even when food sources happen to be present, seasonal pollinator cycles and feeding patterns haven't adapted quickly enough. Thus, pollinators are starving to death in areas where they could once easily find food.[28]

That's without even addressing extreme weather events or the misuse of pesticides. In 2023, for example, severe storms in California killed 60 percent of the western monarch butterflies there.[29]

Pesticides include insecticides, but they also include herbicides meant to kill weeds. Pesticides and herbicides most often kill pollinators when they're applied to crops or unwanted vegetation during the blooming period, but kills can also happen when they drift to nearby fields or when pollinators drink from contaminated water sources, including dew, on recently treated plants. Herbicides also affect pollinators when plants deemed as "weeds" or "unwanted" by us are sprayed and pollinators can no longer rely on them as a food source.

But pesticides aren't the only threat. All said and done, it's estimated that, even in undisturbed forests (where pesticides aren't being sprayed), pollinators are in steep decline. One study of forests in northeastern Georgia found that over a period of fifteen years, the number of pollinator species present had fallen by more than 40 percent. Pollinator populations naturally fluctuate, and "there's always a risk of misinterpreting natural fluctuations as evidence for alarming decline," one of the study's authors, Michael Ulyshen, reported of the findings, highlighting that the results and following analysis strongly indicate that populations of bees and butterflies alike have been in steep decline within the study area.[30]

The data is dismal, and in many cases, the threats facing pollinators are either beyond our control or simply beyond our current level of research and understanding.

But what *can* we do?

There are a few key tenets of pollinator protection, and they can easily be addressed with the right agri-energy set-up.

Different Types of Habitat and a Diversity of Plants

Kevin Campbell has long been a proponent of bees on solar. His background in agrivoltaics began with Shady Creek Lamb Farm in Ontario, Canada, where Chris Moore and Lyndsey Smith began grazing sheep in 2017 (as introduced in chapter 3). Their grazing season starts in late April or early May and continues through October.

As Smith noted in an episode of *Profitable Practices* on RealAgriculture, "There's a lot of corn and beans and this provides two hundred acres right in the middle of all that ground cover and flowering plants that's really important to the habitat here."[31]

One of the biggest problems associated with modern agriculture is sameness. Monocrop agriculture has been said to have the potential to feed billions of people (as I mentioned earlier, the quality of that claim as well as the quality of that mass-produced diet is up for debate), but we can't say the same about its ability to feed other species. According to researchers at Montana State University, "Monoculture provides bees with one nutrient source which results in poor bee health, increased transportation of hives, increased use of pesticides on crops and stress to search for diversity in food. It is imperative to increase crop diversity in order to decrease bee colony deaths."[32]

Monocropping—growing just one type of crop, like corn or soy—in one area isn't problematic just because of increased use of pesticides. It also results in a lack of nutritional diversity that leads to poor immune health in pollinators and makes them more susceptible to disease.

You could technically survive on just chicken nuggets (my four-year-old makes this case quite often), but you'd be missing out on a lot of important nutrients. Your immune system would suffer, and you'd be more susceptible to disease. You'd find yourself catching every single cold your child brought home from school.

Bees, bats, and butterflies are no different. While they might not need quite the diversity of food humans do, they still need a variety of nutrients. When we bulldoze a forest or a meadow to plant a field of corn, we are steamrolling their ability to access those diverse nutrients.

The good news is that when solar and wind farms are appropriately managed, energy can be produced while pollinators (and ideally, livestock) are still fed.

The sites grazed by Moore and Smith's sheep are also outstanding habitats for bees. The on-site apiarist produces two hundred to three hundred jars of honey each year. The bees are just slightly offset, raised in the areas leased to the solar farm that don't have panels on them, but many solar farms operate with bees directly under or around the panels, too.

"Bees forage up to two or three miles away," Kevin told me, "so there's potentially hundreds of acres of agriculture indirectly benefiting from solar, especially compared to fields that were previously farmed for corn or soy."

Corn and soy, two of the biggest cash crops produced in North America, take up more than 178 million acres in the United States alone.[33] Though they are important crops, corn and soy do not require pollinators. Corn is wind-pollinated, whereas soy is self-pollinating (though it can be argued that soybean fields are still important resources for pollinators).[34] With pollinator numbers in steep decline, a switch to agri-energy is a great add to boost their populations, especially if the land was previously cultivated for corn and soy.

Nevertheless, when a field that was previously being used to grow corn and soy is converted into solar, there are two options for revegetation: Plant it into whatever mix is cheapest and just mow it before it blooms, or plant it into a pollinator and grazing-friendly mix and manage it with rotational grazing (which allows pollinator species like clover to thrive). By combining the sheep with bees with solar, you have a winning blend.

It's not just agriculture or renewables that are problematic to pollinator populations. Consider human development. As our cities grow larger and our suburbs sprawl out of control, bees and butterflies and bats just don't have anywhere to go. It doesn't take an entomology degree to understand that when fields are paved over into parking lots, plants go away and so do pollinators' food sources.

There's no good in keeping farmland around if it can't be farmed, but this is one area where that argument of mine doesn't hold water. Even unused farmland is still beneficial to pollinators (perhaps more so if the fields are converted back into brushy meadows with a variety of species rather than monocropped corn). Yet, my counter to that is that allowing fields to lie fallow and unused for the sake of pollinators alone doesn't make much sense. That's especially true when it's more likely that that land will be converted into some sort of development and won't just remain unused. Instead, it will be turned into a parking lot, a housing project, a Dollar General—you get the idea.

"Solar farms can make exquisite, high-quality habitat," Michael Noble of Fresh Energy told me. He's a big proponent of prioritizing pollinator habitat perhaps over anything else, arguing, "We don't need more broccoli—we need more pollinators."

The beauty of agri-energy is that you don't have to choose. Nobody does. We can have our broccoli and our bees.

Rob Davis, who was named Eco-Solar Steward of the Year at the 2024 Solar Farm Summit, works tirelessly to promote pollinator-friendly solar. He contributed to the creation of a scorecard system for pollinators on solar. He's also the former director of the Center for Pollinators in Energy, the nation's leading clearinghouse of pollinator-friendly solar information and best practices.

The scorecard system was created in 2016 when Fresh Energy came together with the Minnesota Corn Growers and Audubon Minnesota to create a statewide standard for vegetation on solar sites.[35] The scorecard resulted from a bill with the goal of setting voluntary standards for solar sites that are friendly to pollinators and birds, specifying that sites should be planted with native plants. Audubon Minnesota is optimistic that this bill can be used as a template in other states. In Minnesota, 90 percent of planned solar sites are currently in row crops, not forests.[36]

Transitioning this acreage to pollinator-friendly sites with native plants would have a huge impact—the equivalent of more than two million homes with native plant gardens instead of mowed lawn.[37]

Other states have quickly followed suit. Today, fourteen more states (California, Illinois, Indiana, Maryland, Massachusetts, Michigan, Missouri, New York, North Carolina, Ohio, Oregon, South Carolina, Vermont, and Virginia) have some sort of publication regarding pollinators on solar, and most are drafted into state law. In addition, many states without their own standards have adopted scorecards from neighboring states.[38]

The language in each state's scorecard varies, but each is essentially a habitat assessment form that helps developers plan projects with pollinators in mind. Minnesota's landmark scorecard includes information about what percentage of the proposed site will be dominated by wildflowers (anywhere between 31 to more than 61 percent) and how much will be dominated by native species cover. There's also a section highlighting the planned cover diversity (from ten species to twenty-six or more species), as well as planned seasons with at least three blooming species present. The scorecard requires developers to cite available habitat components within a quarter of a mile (such as water sources, native trees and shrubs for nesting, and created nesting features) as well as stipulations for how the site will be planned and managed. There are additional criteria based on insecticide risk (with provisions made both for insecticide use on-site as well as the potential for drift from nearby areas). The scorecard even includes a section on seed mixes.[39]

Attracting pollinators isn't complicated. They need food and water, and they need to not be sprayed with chemicals. But it gets a little more complicated (not always just in a negative way) when you factor in the needs of the panels. On a typical solar farm, the different zones allow for different plant mixes. While you can't necessarily grow tall grasses and non-shade-tolerant species directly beneath the panels, many plants would thrive here—or at least could be grown around the perimeter of the arrays.

The beauty of this kind of plant diversity is that it also lends itself nicely to the establishment of healthy (and stable) soil on the site. Native, pollinator-friendly plants can improve water quality and reduce erosion.

According to Michael Noble, abiding by the terms of these scorecards can certainly "help the solar companies make more friends." For some, like MCE Clean Energy, pollinator-friendly ground cover isn't just a nice publicity stunt, it's a must. Under the company's feed-in tariff program and power purchase agreements, "new solar project partners [must] plant pollinator-friendly ground cover throughout the project site and submit a pollinator scorecard every three years."[40]

Rob Davis, when interviewed about this project, said that "requiring disclosure of what will be growing under and around PV solar panels is a critical and meaningful first step toward encouraging greater innovation in ground cover design and management."[41]

There's always been concern about greenwashing as it relates to pollinator-friendly habitat. Some people view it as yet another attempt by a money-hungry industry to garner public support by preying on hearts and minds. Don't we all want to save the bees and the butterflies?

Incorporating pollinator practices on solar is a phenomenal way to generate public support. Whether it's done solely as a great marketing tactic or not, it may not matter—the bees don't care who's on the cover of *Time*. We just need to make sure, for the sake of the consumer, that what's being advertised is, indeed, what's being sold.

Growing a diversity of plants and holding stakeholders accountable for what's being done to manage those plants is a great way to do it. Planting just a little patch of clover and calling it pollinator-friendly solar isn't enough, Michael Noble told me. The scorecards require us to take things one step further.

So, what exactly do these sites look like? At the forefront are native plants—lots of them and lots of different *types* of them.

Planting Native Plants

As developers go about planning their sites with pollinators in mind, the biggest question is, What should we grow? The answer almost always is native plants.

A native species is one that has been present in an area for a very long time. Generally, it has coevolved with the landscape over thousands of years. Pollinators, accordingly, have evolved right along with such species.

Some pollinators are generalists and have the ability to forage on different plant groups. Others rely on specific plant species; for example, the monarch butterfly is heavily dependent on milkweed.

Nonnative or invasive species are frequently introduced into an area either by accident or by design. They can severely disrupt biodiversity, outcompeting native plants and eliminating them entirely, and affect the sources of food that are then available to pollinators.

Our lawns are some of the biggest offenders here. We have more than forty million acres of lawn in the United States. Lawns are largely considered the biggest "irrigated crop" in the country. But a typical lawn gives nothing back to pollinators, which is why the Audubon Society strongly encourages homeowners to plant native plants.[42] The same is recommended for developers.

The most beautiful part about this recommendation is that it doesn't restrict developers in the slightest. Rather than saying that every site must be planted to a particular species, it gives freedom of choice based on the site location, layout, environment, climate, soil quality and type, and so much more—even whether animals are going to be grazed there.

Ernst Conservation Seeds began selling its Fuzz & Buzz seed mixture in 2020.[43] This mixture is formulated to meet the unique nutritional needs of sheep while providing a low-growing, easily maintained, and "sustainable vegetation" solution for solar farms. It includes species like perennial ryegrass, orchard grass, meadow brome, alsike clover, red clover, bird's-foot trefoil, and Kentucky bluegrass. While it's not the ideal mix for every site, it's a great starting point—a plug-and-play seed formulation for solar graziers on pollinator-friendly sites.

But it's not enough to just broadcast a few seeds and call it a day. That vegetation has to be appropriately managed. So what happens next?

Providing a Continuous Food Supply

One of the worst things you can do to pollinator habitat is to mow it down. Yet mowing is a requirement on solar sites to prevent vegetation from shading the panels. Or is it?

It's a tricky balance. I've already discussed how and why vegetation is such a critical necessity around solar. But when the vegetation grows too tall, it becomes a hindrance. Shading just a single cell in a solar panel can reduce output by up to 80 percent.[44] The solution is not avoiding vegetation, but making sure that the vegetation never becomes so tall that it blocks out light.

As part of the social media trend "No Mow May," homeowners are now encouraged to wait to mow their lawns for the first time in the spring until June or later, allowing these early spring "weeds" to flower and feed pollinators. We can follow a similar train of thought on solar farms. We can still knock down vegetation, we can still support pollinators, but we can do it in a less catastrophic way that we currently do. Rather than mowing three or four times a season with traditional equipment, we can send in sheep to handle the mowing for us.

Cornell University researcher Niko Kochendoerfer found that light grazing produces "abundant bees and wildflowers" while keeping the plants from shading the panels. She's even noticed some rare bee species turning up. Grazing, she added, is also typically less expensive than traditional site management. Lewis Fox of Agrivoltaic Solutions added, "Certain times of the year … the sites will be like a butterfly house in a zoo—there's just butterflies everywhere." In addition, researcher Maggie Graham has noted that pollinators not only frequent plants in the solar array, but also pollinate crops in nearby fields.[45]

Lewis, Maggie, and Niko aren't the only ones who've noticed the impact of sheep with pollinators. Arlo Hark has managed solar sites with sheep in what he calls his "new genre of grazing" for years, but with pollinators and biodiversity in mind. "Some people say grazing and pollinators aren't compatible, but that's not our experience," he told me, comparing the symbiosis between sheep and pollinators on solar to what you might see with cattle and birds in the American West.

When it comes to the relationship between agriculture and energy, it takes some hard work to figure out what will work well together and what won't. There's no perfect solution, which is why some developers, like Chad Farrell at Encore Renewable Energy, don't love the idea of legislation that's too prescriptive in regard to solar grazing and pollinator habitat even though that might be all that's preventing immense green-washing in an industry the public already generally distrusts.

"Solar can be a good neighbor," Chad said, referencing the pollution-free, noise-free mowing benefits that sheep can offer all while still supporting pollinators. He added that this model is likely the "least impactful and most aesthetically pleasing."

Pollinator solar sites don't just work better, they *look* better. Solar-centric arrays aren't attractive; for many, they're eyesores, distracting from the broad green landscapes for which agricultural towns are so famous. But flowering plants on solar sites offer a break and give passersby the opportunity to truly enjoy the beauty of nature, from hummingbirds to bees and everything in between. And the beauty of this model is that it doesn't rely on the typical fear-mongering techniques that the clean energy industry has been so fond of.

Rather than inspiring fear over a need to take immediate action to prevent climate change from killing us all, this model inspires hope. Hope that we can become more energy-independent. Hope that we can become more food-independent. Hope that we can support the pollinators we rely on to help us do both.

Most important is that it's hope that we no longer need to rely on an either-or solution to achieve our goals. Marcus Gray, who runs Grays LAMBscaping with his wife, Jess, in Virginia, knows a thing or two about pollinators; he served as the executive director of Sustainable Monarch, an organization that offers market-based solutions to landscape-level conservation and encourages environmental stewardship in communities. He joked with me that getting everyone to work together is akin to chaperoning a middle school dance. "I'd love to see more diversity for farming," he said. "It shouldn't have to be and/or—you can do sheep *and* pumpkins *and* hay *and* pollinators. You can combine things."

As we scale up energy production—and look for ways to build back up our pollinator populations and maintain our food supplies—we can't look at things as either-or. We need to be focused on the "and." We need to focus on how we can make that middle school dance a little less awkward, a little more natural and fluid for everyone on the dance floor.

But as we scale, there's somewhat of a hesitation in the solar community about how well grazing and pollinator habitat will work, both together and individually, on large, utility-scale sites. Sure, it works fine for community-scale sites that are only thirty acres, but what about the ones that are one hundred, five hundred, one thousand, two thousand acres?

These solutions *can* work, but they need to be done thoughtfully and with the site's individual characteristics in mind. For a long time, pollinator solar and grazed solar were viewed as two largely disparate entities: You could have pollinator habitat, or you could graze sheep, but not both.

As Marcus indicated, it's certainly possible to incorporate both. Farming can be integrated into pollinator-friendly solar sites, with benefits to everybody—and everything—involved.

Solar Apiaries: A Sweet Deal for Sheep

Remember, too, that as temperatures increase globally, suitable habitat and nesting sites for wildlife become limited. Our world is simply getting too hot—and too dry—for pollinators and other creatures to handle.

Solar panels, again, create a unique microclimate that offers increased humidity, reduced temperatures, and even shelter from severe weather events. Compared to conventional farmland, solar sites planted with pollinator-friendly native vegetation increased habitat quality threefold, with two-thirds more carbon-storage potential, 20 percent less water runoff, and 95 percent less soil erosion.[46]

When we think about what pollinators need and tailor our plantings accordingly, we can have a monumental impact both on their populations as well as whatever else is eating those plants.

Anna and Ben Freund, who own Open View Farm in New Haven, Vermont, have a 2.49-megawatt direct-current solar array. In addition to growing organic sheep and vegetables and producing maple syrup, they also prioritize pollinators on their solar farm. They seeded the ground with a sheep grazing mix that includes clover and bird's-foot trefoil—the soil was a heavy clay that dried out quickly in the arid weather of late summer, and the clover alleviates that. The clover, as you can imagine, has also done amazing things for the bees.[47]

The best part about grazing sheep on pollinator sites is that they don't knock everything down all at once. When the right rotational (and prescriptive) grazing techniques are applied, sheep can be let loose on a site only when the plants have already flowered, chew down the vegetation before it goes to seed, and then come back later in the season if there's more growth. They don't hit everything at once; instead, they nibble a bit of clover here, a bit of bird's-foot trefoil there, and a dandelion over yonder.

That's not to say that, done indiscriminately, sheep or other grazing animals couldn't have a negative effect on pollinator habitat. Left in one spot or allowed to graze without consideration of bloom times and unique site dynamics, it would be quite easy for a site to turn into a mud lot. It's all about understanding the layout of the land and the best rotational grazing practices.

Countless companies have now made themselves famous for the work they're doing with bees on solar. Bare Honey, for one, manages apiaries located just outside the fence on pollinator-friendly solar projects. The company has hives on dozens of sites around Minnesota and distributes honey throughout the upper Midwest. Not all these sites are solely designated to pollinator habitat; many are used to grow vegetables and other crops, too. It's no longer a choice between broccoli or bees—we can have them both.

Dustin Vanasse, owner of Bare Honey, said in an interview with *MPR News* that solar farms that include vegetables and other crops "provide direct health benefits for the bees by providing a variety of types of pollen.... You can think of it like eating just Trix cereal for your entire life as you're growing up, compared to having a variety of vegetables available and a varied diet."[48]

It's not just honey, either. In Hinesburg, Vermont, Bee the Change has beehives on its 1.67-megawatt Magee Hill solar farm—it sells honey and beeswax harvested from the apiary there and from others across the state—and even harvests milkweed fluff to use as insulation for neck warmers.

This venture opened up additional revenue streams while also benefiting the environment. Bee the Change noticed a significant increase in pollinator abundance at the solar sites. "By the end of year three, you can create a pollinator habitat equivalent to the most beautiful meadow you've ever walked through in the peak of summer. And it has impacts beyond the fence-lines," said Mike Kiernan, founder, when he was interviewed by Rob Davis for a Fresh Energy publication. Where, during initial site surveys, he would originally see a few dozen unique pollinators at a site, he will now see well more than two hundred.[49]

As another example, Clif Bar and Company (the same Clif Bar that makes the delicious energy bars as well as other products), recently opened a two-megawatt solar farm (about five acres) with designated pollinator habitat at its Twin Falls, Idaho bakery.

Overall, there's a growing interest in boosting pollinator habitat, and consumers are more than happy to support companies that are doing their part to protect butterflies and bees. They say that any press is good press, but when it comes to pollinator-friendly solar, it's really, really good press.

For an industry so hyperfocused on winning hearts and minds, attracting pollinators hosts another benefit. Michael Noble told me about projects where solar farms are now used as wildlife-viewing areas. Some have constructed boardwalks with benches and binoculars so community members and tourists can relax, watch birds and butterflies flitting around, and simply enjoy the beauty of this fabricated "nature"—in their own backyards.

Pairing sheep with pollinators on solar makes good sense, too. So why isn't that happening everywhere—as a default?

Again, it all comes down to a lack of knowledge and understanding—and to cost, or rather, fear of an increased cost, at least at the outset. After the first few years, native vegetation results in reduced maintenance costs, reduced soil erosion, and improved stormwater infiltration. But it can be more expensive to plant and maintain initially.[50]

Because of these fears, it's tough for lawmakers to come together. That's true for wind as well as solar, and pollinators can be just as affected by wind turbines. Take bats, for example, which are important pollinators that also eat pest insects and disperse seeds. They also reproduce slowly, birthing just a single pup per year, and are therefore sensitive to population declines.

Wind facilities can reduce mortalities in a number of ways, including through the use of ultrasonic and audible deterrents and visual deterrents.[51] Shutting down turbines at night, when the bats are most active, or setting them to spin only when wind speeds are high, can reduce bat deaths by up to 93 percent.[52] Since wind power tends to only be generated at high speeds, the impact on energy production (and there-fore company profits) tends to be quite low.

Unfortunately, because there's no clear standard for what should or should not be done to protect bats, the wind industry isn't terribly moti-vated yet to practice any mitigation strategies. It will cost money to implement these strategies, so although some companies have volun-tarily adopted these sorts of measures, others likely won't until they're required to do so.

Only a handful of states currently mandate pollinator consider-ations for renewables—and there's a great deal of division among those that don't. Interestingly, it's not an us versus them discussion, either. I expected to hear "No regulations" coming largely from the renew-able developer side and "More regulations" coming from the environ-mentalists and policymakers, but that's not always the case. Developers are often quite interested in additional regulations simply because they crave a clear benchmark to guide their decisions. If they know exactly what the state or locality is expecting in terms of pollinator provisions, it's much easier to meet the standard than if everything is left up to interpretation. Regulations also provide a level playing field. If every company is expected to design and build sites with pollinators in mind (or any other agricultural component in mind), every company must do it. If not, building sites so altruistically becomes challenging, because costs are increased for the developer and their projects then become less competitive.

When it comes to developing a project, the lowest price wins. Con-sumers don't want to pay any more than they already are for electricity, and so the company that can build a project for the lowest possible price is almost always going to win the bid, at least until states or towns (or even individual companies) start incentivizing agri-energy.

At the outset, agri-energy likely will cost a little more than "traditional" projects. There are additional (or more secure) fences to be built and, in some cases, irrigation systems to install. There are more hoops to jump through, meaning there's more labor, which will incur an additional cost, too.

Without regulation or incentivization, agri-energy may result in a slight increase in energy costs because the party producing that energy will have to pay more to get things established. So electricity may be marginally more expensive. At first.

Over time, those costs will be amortized. By investing in agri-energy, we're investing in our farmers. We're investing in our air quality. We're investing in our communities.

And yes, we're investing in the pollinators. That payout may not be evident immediately, however. It may take a few weeks, months, years—many years, perhaps—to really see a difference.

We also can't forget all those costs that are outside the scope of the balance sheets: the invisible toll that conventional agriculture and conventional energy are having on our planet and our children and our wallets. This invisible toll is created solely because we are so adamant about keeping these two things at odds with each other. Instead, we need to think about how spending a little more now, whether it's in terms of time or money, can pay off in the future.

It *will* pay off—for the pollinators, and for the sheep, and for everybody else—but only if we're aware of the challenges and are willing to face them head-on. If only we are willing to work together.

It's not "either-or," as Lauren Glickman, vice president of policy and communications are Encore Renewable Energy told me. "It's 'yes, *and* ...'"

CHAPTER 6

Not All Is Bright and Sunny

The art of life is a constant readjustment to our surroundings.
—Kakuzō Okakura

THE CONVERSATIONS I HAVE WITH FOLKS about agri-energy are becoming increasingly predictable. When the topic of grazing sheep on solar comes up, the other person will nod their head, sometimes listen a little bit to what I have to say, and then say, "Well, I'm glad that it works really well for you and is making a difference for your farm, but I don't think it will work on a larger scale."

Often, they reference how things work in the American West.

I'm told, "Solar grazing works here in New York"—where you aren't real farmers, is the subtext, because we don't have hundreds of miles of feedlots—"but it won't work in Kansas." Or Texas. Or Oklahoma. Or anywhere in the breadbasket.

I always bring up examples of the big guns—the people who are not only solar grazing or growing crops under solar in the West, but are doing it at volume. JR Howard, for instance, currently runs about thirty-five hundred ewes on utility-scale sites in Texas.

Or Amanda Stoffels, who grazes utility sites in Texas.

Or Ryan Indart in California.

Or any of the other hardworking shepherds and farmers I've talked to (and about) in this book.

The truth is that agri-energy can work everywhere, but it won't look the same everywhere. We love our monocrops, but agri-energy just isn't one of them. Every setup is going to look a bit different (or perhaps, very different). That's the beauty of it: It's diversified, and because it's diversified, it's more resilient.

And there are inherent challenges that need to be overcome, but these challenges already exist in energy and in agriculture when the two are operating independently of each other.

I think the misconception that some of my friends and family have about me is that I envision sheep on every solar site in North America, come hell or high water.

That's not my vision at all. I fully recognize the challenges that exist in agriculture and in energy and specifically in the marriage of the two. The difference is that I also recognize that for 90 percent of those challenges, there are solutions.

And for the other 10 percent? We might not have solutions right now, but simply being aware of the challenges and trying to find those solutions is far better than ignoring the problem and hoping it will all figure itself out eventually.

It's time to act, and the key to doing so is to put our problem-solving hats on.

Money Talks and … You Know the Rest

Problem one: the money.

I've come back to this theme countless times, and while I'd love to see solar companies implement agrivoltaics projects for all the other benefits we've talked about, it will always come down to the finances. What we tend to overlook is that it must make financial sense not only for the developer, but for the farmer and for everyone else involved.

Juli Burden of the Hawaii Agriculture Research Center told me that there are significant costs associated with setting up agrivoltaic systems, many of which the farmer must shoulder themselves. Even for farms that are already well-established, the expenses never seem to end, and there's a lot of risk involved.

In early 2024, Josh and I signed contracts to graze two new solar sites. Recognizing that we'd need extra sheep to fulfill the contract (numbers that wouldn't be met even after lambing), we purchased an additional seventy-five Katahdin ewes from a farm in Lowville, New York.

Looking back, it wasn't our smartest decision. We were referred to the seller by another solar grazier, and we paid relatively low prices for the ewes. We saw that good price and knew we needed to get a lot of sheep (fast and cheap) to fulfill those grazing contracts. But there were crucial pieces missing that we blindly ignored.

We were assured that the animals, though bred, probably weren't due for several more weeks. The seller didn't have the foggiest of what those due dates might actually be, but he was confident that time was on our side.

With that in mind, we scheduled a delivery to our farm. Although we weren't comfortable with not knowing exact due dates, we wholeheartedly believed that the fresh lambs wouldn't be expected for a month or so. We'd still have plenty of time to trim the ewes' hooves, vaccinate them, and do everything else we needed to do before they began to lamb. We even figured that this timeline would work with our somewhat unusual schedule that winter—normally, we don't travel much, especially not in the weeks preceding lambing. However, we had plans to travel to the Dominican Republic for our friends' wedding right after Valentine's Day and would be gone for a week. But, we reasoned, since our ewes (including these new ewes) weren't due to lamb for a while, we were comfortable leaving them with our farm sitter. We had plenty of time to get everything done once we returned. Nobody was due until March at the very earliest.

That was mistake number one—a mistake we realized upon their arrival, from the moment the sheep walked off the trailer. Looking at the ewes as they filed into the loading pen, their udders already heavy with milk, Josh shook his head, looked at me with wide eyes, and said, with an understandable slurry of expletives, "They're due any day now."

Sure enough, two days before we left for our trip, the first lamb was born.

A week or so later, we sat in the Montreal airport sipping beers, waiting for our flight to Punta Cana. On his phone, Josh pulled up the Lamb Cam app (a live feed from a wireless camera we have mounted in the barn to help us keep an eye on lambing). "Oh man," he said. We watched as the second lamb was born and ordered another round of beers to calm our nerves. The shepherd's relationship with the lambing barn is a tenuous one; things either go exceptionally well, or they require a great deal of intervention. Being fifty miles away from that lambing barn (and soon, nearly two thousand miles away) is not a great feeling.

Fortunately, all the births that occurred while we were gone were uncomplicated and didn't require any intervention. Doubly fortunate was that the friend we'd hired to farm-sit for us while we were gone has a background in midwifery—for human babies, of course, but this woman handled things beautifully while we were gone. All in all, we got lucky.

Yet because the timeline was thrown off and because the previous owner hadn't kept good records about which sheep had been bred, vaccinated, and dewormed (and when), we spent the rest of lambing season playing catch-up.

A couple months later, the really bad news hit. We learned that the two additional solar sites that we were supposed to graze—the whole reason for us spending more than $16,000 on our new ewes—were not yet up and running and probably wouldn't be ready for grazing until the next season. We had already spent enormous sums of money and needed a way to feed all these new sheep, which meant finding new pasture or buying more hay (which would cost us even more money). It was a tough pill to swallow but is one of the financial realities of getting started with agri-energy. There are already so many variables in farming that you can't control: commodity prices, the weather, and in many cases, your animals. Adding renewable energy, with its convoluted timelines and murky chain of command, only makes things more complicated.

The list of expenses doesn't end with the animals themselves. If you're moving animals on and off sites, you also need to consider handling systems, loading chutes, and trailers to truck them to and fro. Many graziers offer mowing as a supplement to grazing since it's not always possible to knock down the vegetation perfectly (and because most solar developers ask that graziers also maintain the area outside the fenced-in arrays, around the edges). So there's the cost of mowers, too, along with insurance (which typically is higher for solar grazing than many other farm enterprises, due to the high value of the panels you're maneuvering around) and other business expenses.

For this reason, it's important to manage different revenue streams in case sites fall through. We supplement our grazing with the sale of meat, not only from our lambs but also from beef cattle, pigs, chickens, and turkeys. As of this writing, Josh has, fortunately, now been able to quit his second job and farm full-time. And although I view my writing career as just that—a career, as well as something I'm deeply passionate about—I'd be foolish to think we could sustain ourselves on the income from the farm alone. Like most American households, we are a two-income one, and we recognize the importance of keeping multiple lines of income from multiple sources in case one falters.

Many people will read this story about our ill-advised sheep purchase and think, "That's really on the solar company—they shouldn't have strung you along like that." But they aren't truly to blame. Many variables influence whether and when a site goes online—something as seemingly simple as a shipping delay on one of the modules can push back a site's timeline by several weeks. US trade policy, permitting complications, and even delays in equipment testing can all affect a timeline, with fluctuations in the availability of building materials being the most common roadblock.[1] A Lawrence Berkeley National Laboratory survey discovered that between 2019 and 2024, about one-third of all solar and wind projects were canceled and half experienced delays of more than six months or more. Most of these interruptions occur in the permitting stage, but they can also happen when a project is already under construction.[2]

We were the only ones to blame in this situation, but as we ruminated on the problem, asking ourselves again as bills piled up in late April why we'd spent all that money, I gently reminded Josh that we'd made the best decision we could with the information we had available. Truly, that's all you can ever do.

Not just us, but solar developers are also tasked with making the best decisions they can with the limited information they have available surrounding agri-energy. "One of the biggest pushbacks [on agrisolar] is the money," Stacie Peterson of the National Center for Appropriate Technology told me. Although older solar sites can be retrofitted later, agrisolar "can be trickier, because some were built with arrays closer together, leaving less space for crops or equipment," she said. The National Renewable Energy Laboratory (NREL) had a cost estimator to help developers work out the dollars and cents of solar—and whether it would be worth it, but it's since been pulled from the lab's website. Several groups, including the American Solar Grazing Association, the AgriSolar Clearinghouse, and the Sierra Club, are either working on or have already published best practices guides for agrivoltaics. These resources can be helpful to all parties involved, but again, they are less of a direct blueprint and more of a list of suggestions. It's hard to provide prescriptions for managing agri-energy systems, and especially for designing them, because every site is so unique and mingles so many different variables and participants.

As an example, Stacie explained that "steel costs change with design." She added, "People always want a hard number. Ambiguity is difficult to live with." Some companies are hesitant to incorporate agri-energy projects from the outset because they don't want to raise the costs on the racking. In some cases, there's also the question of how deep components need to be buried so that equipment like plows and tractors can get through.

"The question," Robert Margolis of NREL said, "is, 'Is energy output going to be sufficient to pay for the costs?'" For right now, the answer isn't always yes—as much as we'd like it to be. There are still many situations in which grazing is more expensive than mowing or growing crops is more costly than spraying herbicides. But again, it's about finding a long-term solution, one that recognizes the necessary trade-offs for each industry. And as brand-new technologies come online and existing technologies become more refined, these solutions will, it is hoped, start to become more apparent. "Solar panels have gotten extremely cheap," Robert continued. "There are [also] vertical panels in Europe which don't offer as good of a production [rate], but it's a trade-off."

The cost of implementing agri-energy will always be a sticking point, at least until we get the hang of things. Yet it's clear, over the long term, that it is not only the best solution for the environment and the economy, but also for the bottom lines of both the developer and the producer.

The good news is that we, as farmers, already have grit. We're already used to working on shoestring budgets and having to fix everything with (sometimes literally) our own bootlaces. But we hope we don't have to do it for too much longer, because the longer it takes to implement agri-energy at the national level, the more small farms we'll see go out of business.

Incentivizing Companies to Do the Right Thing

The key to successfully implementing agri-energy at a large scale is exploring solutions that will make doing so more advantageous for everyone involved. Right now, though, there's just not enough money on the table for developers to do so on their own cognizance.

As of this writing, only a handful of companies manufacture solar panel racking. Many of the rack designs are the same, and most are more expensive when systems are designed with sheep or other livestock (increasingly, cattle) in mind. If there were more—and more afford-able—solutions, it likely wouldn't be as much of an expense to design a site with livestock considerations. But there's no real incentive for that to happen; sticking with the status quo is the most cost-effective option. If it ain't broke, don't fix it.

We need to offer a more tangible reward for the perceived risk of agri-energy. There's already a lot of risk involved in renewable energy. Projects are running behind schedule because materials are so hard to come by (we can thank our increasingly problematic supply chains for that). And in most places, additional regulations are being added to solar farm construction faster than we can keep up with them.

When it comes to lasting change, Stacie Peterson says that "local policy is the best," but adds that you need "financial mechanisms to make [the solar developer] do it." Best practices for a solar site should be tied to the site and to the permit to help reduce the likelihood of sites pitched at the planning meeting to be built with agri-energy components to be approved and then having the site approved, built, and sold before any agriculture actually takes place.

Stacie noted that there is a sevenfold increase in the acceptance of utility-scale solar when agri-energy is incorporated in some way. People like to think that local farmers—and so-called prime farmland—are being considered during the solar planning process.

However, many people express concerns about agri-energy being a form of greenwashing—in other words, solar companies saying that they'll develop projects with agrivoltaics in mind simply to gain public support and then not actually going through with it once the site is built, claiming that they couldn't find a farmer to fulfill the contract or that the site just wasn't well-suited for agri-energy after all. Alexis Pascaris of NREL told me that one of the best ways to reduce feelings of greenwashing is to get everyone involved. "People are more amenable if they're directly involved in the planning and design," she said.

That's easier said than done, unfortunately, since most community members don't know anything about a new site until they see posts being driven into the ground. Unless you're the landowner or you happen to be on the town planning board, these projects don't tend to be well advertised (even though they're typically open for public comment).

It makes people uneasy to know that solar and wind farms are popping up all around them, but when they discover that agriculture is being incorporated into the designs, they're much more relaxed about it. Conversations need to start happening early on—between the developer and the community as well as the developer and the farmer. We've been approached multiple times by developers who are planning projects near us that won't be finished for several years. We're often asked our thoughts on how a site should be designed in terms of water access, trailer access, panel spacing, and so on. We're more than happy to have these conversations, even though we aren't necessarily getting paid for hours.

One of the best pieces of advice I give to farmers who want to start grazing solar sites is to make sure the value is clear for both parties in the arrangement. Can you offer additional value to the solar company in some way? Many people believe, whether wrong or right, that we shouldn't have to incentivize solar companies just to do the right thing. They should just do it. These companies, the idealistic line of thinking goes, should be building in agri-energy considerations because it's the best for the environment, the land, the farmer, and the community. But we already have a massive bottleneck of projects that currently exist because there's so much regulation and red tape in place. More regulation might not always be the answer. If you tell a developer that they can't put in a site unless they're going to grow broccoli under the panels and then they can't find a farmer who actually wants to grow the damn broccoli, what happens then? At that point, much money has already been spent designing and building the site.

"What if I don't like broccoli?" Lexie Hain of Lightsource bp joked to me. "But 'We have to put broccoli between the rows.'" We need to make sure our agri-energy plans are flexible, ideally, with developers resourcing up and having people in house to help them understand nuances and forge partnerships.

Lexie is a big advocate for solar companies doing just that: having their own agri-energy experts on the team. She believes that there should be someone who can connect graziers with key people at a firm, integrating them with operations and maintenance managers, developers, and so on. And when that can't happen, it's hugely important for farmers and developers alike to do their own due diligence when it comes to thoughtfully incorporating agri-energy from the outset.

I don't know if more regulations will be the answer (or help encourage this early collaboration at any capacity), but I do think more incentives will. In a perfect world, everybody would do the right thing from the start. But we don't live in a perfect world. We live in a world where we need to work together and balance our own needs and preferences with the needs and preferences of everyone else, and we need to make sure conversations are happening early and often.

Avoiding Overregulation

How can we inspire larger, broadscale change, ideally at a nationwide level, without it becoming yet another victim to top-down micromanaging?

Many speculate whether we need incentives to make sure agri-energy actually happens. Developers need a reason to build projects out at this scale, especially when it's sometimes cost-prohibitive to do so. Solar and cattle is a great example. The benefits are there and the payout is clear—but it's still a risk to invest more money into pounding steel deeper into the ground. There has to be more of an up-front incentive.

There needs to be a quid pro quo here for legislators, too. They want to make sure that the payout is worth it and, as such, impose strict regulations that developers must follow to qualify for these kinds of funding.

As Chad Farrell of Encore Renewable Energy summed it up in a conversation with me, "We need to not be overly prescriptive." Regulations that mandate row spacing and racking heights might *seem* like they make sense, encouraging developers to do what's best for agri-energy to receive the incentives tied to the measures, but the problem with this approach is that it fails to recognize individual variables that might differ across sites.

One site might not be a good fit for growing broccoli, as Lexie highlighted, but it could be great for sheep and Runner ducks. Another site might not be well-suited for wide-spaced panels, meaning it might not be a good candidate for haying, but those tighter-spaced panels might make it the perfect choice for lettuce.

Juli Burden told me, "No two sites are alike, and not all sites will lend themselves nicely to crops or livestock." We need to figure out what makes a good site and figure out ways to make this work at scale. And, as mentioned earlier, we need to make sure farmers don't get bottlenecked into a few crops. "We need training for farmers on diversification," she said.

How productive can a site blending energy and food be? "It depends,"

Alexis Pascaris told me with a laugh. There are too many variables to quantify. "Where are you, what are you growing—all of this impacts the success of agrivoltaics," she said.

One study suggested that "a variety of farming activities are possible on solar installation land. Almost all the land—on the order of 95 percent—of a solar photovoltaic installation remains available for some type of cultivation or farming." Though that particular study ruled out commodity crops like corn and tobacco for solar sites, it said that "rotational sheep grazing, cultivating pollinator-friendly plants with or without apiaries, vegetable cultivation, berries, cattle grazing, mushroom production, and even saffron production (from crocus flowers) have all been done, although ... crop production is regionally specific and influenced by climate and conditions."[3]

At this point, it's really only grazing sheep and pollinator-friendly seed mixes that have been done at scale. We're still just dabbling because there's so much hesitation over what will work well. Fortune favors the bold, they say, and in this instance, I think those of us who are a little too cautious are going to find ourselves left behind.

And although incentives are certainly needed, we need to be mindful of not being too specific here. Goodhart's law—"when a measure becomes a target, it ceases to be a good measure"—is an adage that's a great example of this approach. This law, which has to do specifically with financial risk modeling, argues that "any observed statistical regularity will tend to collapse once pressure is placed upon it for control purposes."[4] I believe these are smart words to live by in the conversation about agri-energy policy, too.

We should use data to guide our actions and goals as they relate to renewables and agriculture. But we shouldn't live and die on that data. We need to use it to inform decisions, not to make those decisions for us. We also don't have any more time to waste. Ultimately, it's all about navigating the give-and-take.

The Give-and-Take

One of the biggest tug-of-wars that happens is the question of who gets paid and how much. Solar graziers are paid anywhere between $300 and $500 an acre (sometimes as much as $1,000 an acre) for their services, with variation in prices caused by site design, on-site resources (like water and interior paddocks), location, the local market, and so forth.

But most people agree that solar farmers, whether they're growing sheep or sweet potatoes, should be compensated somehow. In some cases, this payment is only in the form of free land to farm. These situations are becoming fewer and far between, however, said Juli. "There's more of a conversation about paying the farmers, since the solar farm doesn't need to do any weed management [if it's cropped]." This bit of payment can offset some of the initial costs of setting up an agri-energy system while providing the other aforementioned, ancillary benefits of farming under solar.

But there is a trade-off. "You lose a little production," Stacie Peterson admitted, "but you can use less water and energy."

The payment question isn't the only one that comes up as farmers and developers learn to play nice together. Regardless of which role you occupy, there are questions you need to ask yourself before you go into any conversation. What are your nonnegotiables? What can you budge on? (If you're a parent, you know the value of learning to pick your battles. This is no different. Your battles in this case, however, are more about what material the exterior fence should be made from and not about why we can't wear our shoes on the wrong feet).

Lexie's biggest piece of advice to aspiring graziers is to "just keep asking questions until you figure out what they [the solar company] are afraid of." Once you have an idea of what their fears are, you can then offer solutions to address them.

Most of the time, disagreement or conflict arises not because the other party is specifically and deliberately "out to get us." Instead, it's because something wasn't communicated clearly enough.

Johnny Rogers of North Carolina State University saw this situation all too clearly when he first put his sheep on a solar site. "One morning, I was drinking coffee and looked out [at the solar array] and just about had a heart attack," he told me. He had been stockpiling forage for his sheep, waiting to graze it until it was just the perfect height, and saw the solar company had sent out their own team to mow it down. The workers didn't realize what he was planning to do and thought they were helping by "cleaning up" the rest of the vegetation. They also applied herbicide, not realizing that Johnny had left the grass there on purpose. "You spray with glyphosate, something pretty tall will likely grow back as a result," he said.

It was a hard pill for Johnny to swallow, but fortunately, a bit of communication was all it took to rectify the situation. One conversation later, the problem was solved.

So much of agri-energy is about relationship building, Arlo Hark of Cannon Valley Graziers added, which can be a barrier to some folks. Some people just want to keep on farming, going about business as usual. But when it comes to a field as new and as unexplored as agri-energy, there's no such thing as business as usual.

"A lot of this is about how to get taken seriously," Arlo said. "Everybody has to figure out their own marketing." For him, having a focus on biodiversity and soil health is crucial. In other parts of the United States, focusing on pollinators might be the ticket. Some communities just want to know that their views are safe. In the West, fire mitigation might be the sticking point.

Whatever your sticking point might be, fight for it. Sell it. And if you're a farmer, remember that this involves not just communicating expectations and benefits to the solar company, but also to the public and to elected representatives.

Should We Hold for More Intel?

When I met with Michelle Hinchey, a New York state senator for the Forty-First Senate District, *her* biggest sticking point was that we need to wait to do anything until we have more information. I disagree.

Maybe it's because I'm a farmer. Farmers are, by our very nature, reactive creatures. You can plan and plan and plan—you can plan when you'll plant your seed, when you'll send your pigs to the slaughterhouse, how many lambs you're expecting to have. But you can't plan for what you can't plan. You never know when you're going to get a summer storm that dumps four inches of rain on your fields and washes away your seeds. You can't plan on a pandemic shutting down the slaughter-house for two months. You can't plan for a ewe that didn't take when she was bred.

Granted, we *do* need more research. We need more money, at both the state and federal levels, invested into studies on the feasibility of agri-energy across multiple contexts. On what sites do cattle work well? When are sheep better suited to a site? What's the best spacing between solar panels? "The field is relatively new," the Hawaii Agriculture Research Center's page on agrivoltaics reads. "More research is needed to optimize system designs and understand the best practices for different contexts."[5]

But we don't have time to wait.

A helpful bit of research that's encouraging solar developers to take the plunge into agri-energy is "The 5 Cs of Agrivoltaic Success Factors in the United States," a document of lessons compiled from the InSPIRE Research Study and put together by the National Renewable Energy Laboratory. The five Cs are climate, soil, and environmental conditions (C1); configurations, solar technologies, and designs (C2); crop selection and cultivation methods, seed and vegetation designs, and management approaches (C3); compatibility and flexibility (C4); and collaboration and partnerships (C5).[6]

These categories cover everything you would want to consider—both as a developer and as a farmer—when thinking about agri-energy. The lessons also come with ten specific recommendations from NREL to encourage "more successful agrivoltaics projects" and "more productive research" going forward.[7] This checklist gives us a framework to shoot for, an idea of things we should think about during the planning stages.

Although you could technically convert just about any solar site into an agri-energy site, it will function much better (and likely, much less expensively) if considerations are made from the outset. What does the water infrastructure look like? The spacing between panels? The gaps in the fence? Is there a tailored seed mix that can be used?

It's not perfect, but having conversations about agri-energy with this kind of framework in hand and these guiding principles in mind gives us a place to start. Anybody with more specific (particularly more commodity-specific) questions about agri-energy should visit the InSPIRE data portal. Here, you can search by development strategy (animal grazing, crop production, habitat—also known as ecovoltaics—greenhouse, crosscutting photovoltaics); by continent and geographic scope; and by topic (entomology, livestock, soil, hydrology, policy, siting, impact assessments, and so forth).

You might not find the exact information you're looking for, but it's a start. We can only use the information we have so far, but knowing where to look for this information helps.

Addressing Markets and Competition

My biggest question—and reservation—about agri-energy will always be one of the markets. We already have a limited market for the sheep that are being produced here, and selling lamb to a population that prefers beef has always been an uphill battle. Thank goodness I have a little training in marketing (though certainly not what I'd call actual skill), or our freezers would still likely be overflowing with unsold products.

It's a question for state departments of agriculture and markets; it shouldn't be one that's left to the producer. The most obvious solution to this supply chain issue would be to remove the barriers that exist when it comes to processing and distributing products. Our closest US Department of Agriculture–inspected slaughterhouse is a ninety-minute drive away. This inspection is required for us to sell lamb to a local restaurant, our biggest customer. We can sell custom-exempt lamb only to individual buyers; there simply isn't as much of a demand to sell an entire lamb as there is individual cuts.

If you aren't familiar, any beef, pork, lamb, or goat meat (poultry rules get even more convoluted, so I won't discuss them here) that is sold in a restaurant or a store must be processed and inspected in a federal USDA facility. Twenty-nine states (New York, where I live and do business, is not one of them) also operate their own state inspection facilities.[8]

If meat is inspected in one of these state facilities, it can generally be sold in the same way as if it were processed and inspected in a USDA facility, but cannot cross state lines (there are some exceptions to this as well, which I won't get into for the sake of brevity). Because New York does not operate state-level facilities, our only other option, then, is custom exemption. Under custom-exempt processing (and these rules vary within individual states), slaughter can be performed at a slaughter-house that does not have a USDA inspector on-site, but it cannot be sold as individual cuts. The meat must be marked "not for sale," and so, when an animal is sold and processed under custom exemption, it can only be sold by share (whole cow, half pig, for example). Quite techni-cally, the buyer is purchasing the live animal rather than the meat and therefore is responsible for processing costs and instructions.

If that description confused you, you aren't the only one. Processing laws, though all falling under the larger umbrella that is overseen by the USDA, still vary state to state and are, in my opinion, designed to accommodate only the largest of meat producers and not those wishing to supply meat locally. To make matters worse, the number of abattoirs in general is small. Even fewer is the number of USDA-inspected facilities; one report found that there's been a 36 percent decrease in USDA-inspected plants since 1990, and post-COVID, those numbers have likely gotten even worse.[9]

As you can see, a great deal of red tape is involved for small- to mid-sized producers like us. It is next to impossible to get slaughter appointments for our animals (we tend to book these at least one year out, if not more), and there's not enough financial incentive for custom-exempt slaughterhouses to pursue US Department of Agriculture certification. It's expensive and, as more than one slaughterhouse owner has told me, "a massive pain in the ass."

Until we have better markets for the animals raised in the United States, we may find that we reach our carrying capacity, but who knows? We continue to import millions of pounds of lamb each year, so clearly it's not an issue of customer demand but instead one of slaughtering capacity.

And then there's the other elephant in the room: Do we have enough sheep in the country to graze all these agri-energy projects? Right now, we do not. But the great thing about sheep is that they make more every day (just toss a few rams into your herd and you'll see). And again, we also shouldn't be putting all our eggs in the sheep basket. Just because many existing solar sites work well for sheep already, no modifications needed, that doesn't mean we can't think outside the box.

Seeing is believing, and a lot of people want to see these things in action before they believe that they'll work. Marcus Gray told me that it really takes the right person to want to get into agri-energy. He emphasized that there are so many logistical hurdles to overcome, from managing predators on-site (he said domestic dogs were his number one predator in Virginia) to the safety policies of the solar companies (Virginia has strict policies that require hard hats to be worn on every site, and Marcus also told me that he feels beholden to mark his electric fence every twenty-five feet because he's frequently witnessed technicians walk right into it.)

"People think anybody can do it," he said of agrisolar, but that's not the case. It's farming, but spicy farming. You get all the regular issues of raising livestock, and those problems don't go away on solar sites, just like predators don't.

There's just so much that goes into agri-energy—and so much of it is yet unexplored. As farmers, we need to know a lot about agriculture—something it's tough to be an expert in—while also knowing about photovoltaic systems.

And we're doing it all with a lot of unknowns. We don't know if we'll be able to sell the sheep we're raising at market. We don't know if we'll be able to get processing appointments. Perhaps most terrifying, we don't know how long we'll even be able to graze the sites, a topic that needs to come up between the farmer and the developer early on in the planning stages—specifically, how long is the contract for?

Most grazing contracts exist on a year-to-year basis. Some producers can net longer contracts, in some cases as long as six or seven years, but most of us are just hoping we make it until the next season.

The final issue is the concern that this market will become overcrowded, with everybody buying up a flock of sheep in hopes of getting a little cash from grazing a solar site. Others are worried about large cooperatives or companies buying up or hoarding grazing contracts and then doling out grazing allotments to whoever can do it at the lowest price, even if they don't have any experience grazing (or raising) sheep or other livestock. Despite agri-energy being a fledgling industry, the amount of infighting I've noticed within it already is shocking.

We can't let healthy competition turn into dissonance, however. We're all on the same team here: team agri-energy.

That is, after all, the beauty of this relationship. "There's so much bipartisan support for this," Alexis told me. "That's a real hallmark of its success. People on both sides coming together is a testament to the potential."

There's already enough disapproval and conflict over renewable energy to begin with. We're all told to love thy neighbor, but when it comes right down to it, it's hard not to feel bitter or jealous when your neighbor is offered a $20,000 per year solar or wind lease and you aren't.

Elizabeth Weise, in an article for *USA Today*, wrote, "The problem with wind, like the problem with oil" (and with solar, for that matter) "is that not everyone ends up with a turbine or a pump jack on their property because not every bit of land is right for wind or oil extraction." Such situations create bitterness, as farmer and legislator Jack Thimesch said for the Weise article, because "the ones that didn't get one don't see value. The ones that got 'em, see value."[10]

There will always be conflict when we perceive that someone else is getting some kind of benefit that we aren't. "Agrivoltaics is just one piece of the puzzle," Alexis reminded me. When it makes sense, it makes sense. And if it doesn't make sense for you yet? Give it time. We need to all work together to make sure renewable energy and agriculture can come together in the best way possible. Infighting and jealousy just don't have a place here.

Finding the Right Person for the Job

The final challenge in agri-energy is in forming the right partnerships—and in finding the right people for the job. Farming and energy have always been close siblings, so to speak, with energy being just another crop that farmers can now add to their portfolio of offerings. Yet we are too often looking at renewable energy, namely wind and solar, as methods to help "save" the American farmer, the knight on the white horse riding in to save the day.

Many of us disparage the solar industry for this exact viewpoint, and it's not just farmers. I've even spoken to some developers who disdain that the conversation is often seen as "developing land into solar as a way to help the struggling farmer."

This energy-giant-as-venerable-savior concept isn't anything new. Oil production has typically been the hero, swooping in to save farmers from whatever misfortune befell them. In the Weise *USA Today* article, Pete Ferrell, a farmer in Butler County, Kansas, said, "Dad allowed oil production here. There was a big drought in the 1950s. He said, 'In all honesty, it was the money from the oil that got us through.'" Today, Ferrell views wind energy not as the new savior, but as a new way to make money out of the land. He views it as "reminiscent of the side jobs and town jobs many farmers and ranchers have always needed to get by."[11]

Do farmers *have* to lease their land to solar or wind developers? No. Does a partnership make things a lot easier for both of them? Absolutely.

Many of the early adopters of agri-energy are producers who have been in the business for a while—farmers who are well established and perhaps don't have quite as much risk as the newbie with a hefty bank loan who's just getting started out, according to Alexis.

The key is not getting stuck in our old ways. "Farmers see the technological perspectives," she told me. "The livestock shading, the [ability for] trellising, the economics. They can satisfy their on-farm energy needs and get paid to lease the farmland."

It will take some creativity to get all these pieces to mesh, but if anyone has the mindset for ingenuity—and creative thinking—it's farmers.

"People don't know where to start," Stacie Peterson explained. It's overwhelming. This is a big, brand-new landscape, and nobody quite knows how to navigate it.

Perhaps the best place is to just go back to the beginning, to return to our roots.

Maybe we just need to do what we do best as farmers and think outside the box. Maybe we should explore solutions that sound just crazy enough to sound terrifying—but also just terrifying enough to work.

There will be challenges as we make this shift. But it's nothing a bit of baling twine and duct tape can't fix.

Managing Risk Without Succumbing to Fear

Fear is a powerful thing. It can paralyze us, making sure we don't do things we shouldn't. It can be caused by very real stimuli that create very real threats—the lion lurking in the shadows—or by the irrational triggering of the amygdala telling us there's a threat when it's really just our brains being a little too cautious. It's hard to shake fear when it's what we've always known, particularly when our fear is based on risks that we perceive as being real.

Josh Bennett, mentioned briefly in chapter 3, worked at EDF Renewables for sixteen years. Before that, he worked as a wind technician. He knows his way around renewables, and he knows his way around risk.

As soon as we started talking, I knew there was something different about him. His attitude about agri-energy was decidedly less risk-averse than pretty much anybody from his world that I'd talked to so far.

I'd been given his name by Kevin Campbell, also at EDF, and reached out via LinkedIn to see if we could chat. The only way he would agree to be interviewed, he told me, was if my book was going to give farmers fair representation.

"Don't worry," I told him. "That's the whole point."

"I don't want to build two-thousand-acre solar sites," he told me when I finally got him on the phone. "But I know we need to."

This reluctance was incredibly refreshing. We talk a lot about concerns over losing farmland, but strangely absent from these conversations is concern for the person actually doing the farming.

One of the biggest issues with solar development, said Josh, is that companies are "going into communities, thinking they're doing the Lord's work, bringing in renewables. It's a terrible way to do things, to develop an industry off the pain of another." It's tough to argue that farmers don't appreciate the several-thousand-dollar-a-year paycheck they get from leasing to solar. But it's often the only way out, an exit strategy. Farmers are hanging on by a thread, and solar developers come in, offering much more than what a farmer could get leasing or renting their land to anyone else, and it seems like the most viable option—because it is.

That's not to say that it's always the most desirable option. Some farmers want to lease the land and retire. Done. But others want to be able to continue to farm.

Agri-energy provides farmers who own land with a way to lease their land so that they can retire or move away or stop farming. It also presents farmers who don't own land with an opportunity to get on land and continue farming. Ultimately, it presents an opportunity to increase yields across the board. It's not just good for humans and our wallets. It's great for the crops and critters we're raising, too. And, as Josh said, "We don't have ten more years to figure this out."

His words resonated with me, particularly after the conversation I'd had with Senator Hinchey in which I urged her to let go of some of her hesitation over solar.

Indeed, since that conversation, a lot of great headway has been made. In addition to the Environmental Research Program the New York State Energy Research and Development Authority launched in June 2024, New York also made progress—under Hinchey's leadership—via the Agrivoltaics Research Program at Cornell University's College of Agricultural and Life Sciences. The goal of this program is to pioneer "strategies and technology to facilitate vital collaboration between the renewable energy and agriculture industries."[12]

Progress is certainly being made, and it seems as though developers, legislators, researchers, and farmers alike are finally warming up to the idea of colocating renewables with agriculture.

My fear, one that I share with Josh, is that it's not going to happen at the pace we need it to happen. And much of that has to do with a fear of the unknown.

CHAPTER 7

Counting Your Sheep— Are You Ready to Join the Agri-Energy Movement?

Seeing the bigger picture is not as important as knowing that there is one.
—Milos Tomusilovic

MY SON WAS BORN SMACK DAB in the middle of the COVID-19 pandemic. My older sister, Christan, took immediately to the role of auntie, coming up to visit at least every other weekend. She was my life raft during those times, taking the baby when I needed to shower or eat or just have a moment to breathe by myself.

Often, we would do jigsaw puzzles while the baby rocked in his swing. Like two old grannies, we sat at the kitchen table for hours, sipping coffee and laughing as we haphazardly tried to arrange the pieces together. The world was going to absolute shit outside the door, but we were just so solely focused on keeping that baby alive—and putting together those little cardboard pieces on the table—that none of it seemed to matter.

I like puzzles. I like looking at the bigger picture and trying to figure out how the pieces come together to create something beautiful. And

I like that there really isn't a winner. It's just about creating something beautiful.

As hard as I would try to finish those puzzles after my sister had left, I always struggled to find the motivation to do so. A puzzle would sit on the table for days before I finally got sick of the dog chewing on the pieces, and then I'd put the whole thing back in the box.

It's just easier to put the pieces together when more than one person is looking at the big picture.

As I look at the big picture of agri-energy, the image of the jigsaw puzzles is what keeps coming back to me. Whether speaking to a developer, a farmer, a community member, or an environmentalist, I've found that they all tend to have one thing in common: They get laser-focused on the finer details without stopping to consider the big picture.

Sure, planning a solar site to accommodate cattle might cost some money. The panels may need to be elevated, and the steel costs will be higher. We may need to fence off the panels to avoid damage. It's all going to take time and money to figure out.

From the farmer's perspective, it would be a lot easier to just graze a vacant field. There'd be no fencing off panels, no worrying about how to manage the cattle to prevent damage.

Looking individually at both of those things, it seems keeping them separate is the easiest way. It's the simplest. It requires the least brain juice.

But nothing in life is independent of anything else. We need renewable energy to power our homes and farms. Renewable energy needs farmers to continue growing food for us all to eat. It's all connected—we can't just take one puzzle piece out of the box and expect to get the complete picture. We need to dump the entire box of puzzle pieces out on the table and start seeing how we can fit them together, no matter how long it takes.

But we need to do it together.

In chapter 2, I wrote about my conversation with Phal Mantha, where he told me about raw sewage flowing from the top of the Hawaiian mountains into the open sea. What we do on one piece of land has a ripple effect many miles away and in ways we never might have pictured. So, as he said, "we need to manage our crap correctly," thinking "cradle to cradle versus cradle to grave."

Much of the agri-energy transition in the United States has been marked by fear, division, and politics. The Girouxs told me that the best advice they could give anybody who was thinking of leasing their land to solar (or wind, for that matter) is to work with a lawyer who has experience with leases for solar.

There's nothing wrong with consulting with someone who's got more legal expertise and understanding of the jargon. We want the grazing terms to be clearly defined and carefully defined; we need to know exactly what needs to be grazed and what doesn't, and we need to know what our obligations are in fulfilling the contract. Working with a lawyer is smart.

The problem is that some people will use the legal system strategically, to sow more division. We shouldn't be "lawyering up" as a way to protect our best interests, necessarily, but to make sure everybody understands what's on the table and how we can best serve the bigger picture (while still keeping our own interests and needs in mind). It's wise to look out for your own best interests. But also, make sure you are thinking about what the other party needs, too.

That's one of my deepest concerns about the future of agri-energy. The agri-energy industry is rife with bad actors, as is every industry. I've met with several farmers and graziers who are solely and exclusively focused on making sure they get the best possible price to graze or farm a piece of land but don't consider with equal weight the concessions the solar company is already making.

"Well, they're making enough money off these projects" is the scornful remark I always hear in return. "They can afford to put in a well for my sheep"—or fence off separate grazing paddocks, or pay $1,000 an acre, or ... you name it.

Sure, they might be able to. But until you've walked in another person's shoes, you have no idea of what their perspective actually is. I've spoken to so many developers who, independently, want badly for their sites to be grazed. But when they bring the numbers to the other stakeholders—many of whom may not even work for the same company—it just doesn't pencil out.

There might be other logistical hurdles in the way, too, some far outside the developer's control. We recently spoke with a developer who wanted us to graze a nearby site but said that the town was adamant on using chain link fence instead of woven wire for the perimeter. Why? "We have no idea," the developer told us. "But they will not budge on that."

Fortunately, chain link can still work for sheep as long as it's tight to the ground and at least six feet tall. We prefer woven wire for livestock, but chain link isn't the end of the world. We can work with that. *We* can budge.

My advice to anyone who's thinking about implementing agri-energy solutions, whether it's from the renewable energy side or the agriculture side, is to come up with a clear list of must-haves and nice-to-haves. What do you absolutely need? What can you live without?

For example, when George and Marcel Giroux's first solar farm was being built, they realized that they hadn't asked where the power would come out of the field. They didn't pay attention to the terms of the lease, they said, and before they knew it, it was being routed directly by Marcel's house. "At that point," George said. "It was too late. There was no way we could change it."

Was it a deal breaker? No. Was it something that probably could have been changed early on, without too much stress from either side? Most likely.

It all comes down to a conversation.

Getting Started as a Solutions Provider

If you're thinking about getting involved as what I call a "solutions provider"—if you're someone who wants to graze or farm on land that's being used for solar or wind but you aren't the primary landowner—the most important thing is to start the communication process early on.

"You need to learn to be a service business," Lewis Fox of Agrivoltaic Solutions told me, emphasizing that if you're going to graze, you need to have plans for how that's done. "If you don't have a good idea of what solar grazing looks like, it can be intimidating," he said.

Aspiring graziers should connect with the American Solar Grazing Association (ASGA), the premier source of information on how, why, and where to solar graze. In addition to hosting webinars and publishing studies on the benefits and challenges of agri-energy, ASGA is run by perhaps the nicest and most accessible group of people I've ever met in my entire life, many of whom I've interviewed while writing this book.

Forming a network is incredibly important, especially for new graziers who aren't familiar with the nuances of farming, let alone the nuances of farming solar. A network of professionals (ideally, a network comprising individuals from both the renewable and agriculture world, rather than just one sector) who have done this before and are entrenched in the industry provides you with the opportunity to learn and ask questions, and perhaps most importantly, a shoulder to cry on when things don't go as expected. And that, as you may have gathered, is more often than not.

Farming under solar is just like farming in general but with big, bulky panels in the way that are incredibly expensive and rife with liability. You need to make sure you have the proper insurance coverage, and you need to make sure you have a rock-solid contract.

I am not going to give any information on what kind of insurance or what kind of contract you need. Again, ASGA is a great resource for that, but it's individually focused. What I'm charging on a solar site and paying for insurance in upstate New York will likely look different for a site in northern California. But as you're working through a contract (which you absolutely must have, with no exceptions) with a developer, consider these talking points:

- Will there be water on-site (via a well or any other source) for my animals, or will I need to truck water in? (*We often graze sites without on-site water and that's fine, but we lower our bid prices if we can access water on-site since it reduces labor, trucking, and the burden on the well at our home farm.*)
- Will there be room to back a trailer into the site for loading and unloading? (*I have never encountered a situation where this was not the case, but it's always good to check.*)
- Can corrals, loading chutes, and other handling systems be installed on-site? If not, will there be ample space for me to set these systems up with portable units? (*As a grazier, bear in mind that handling systems can add significant cost to grazing and will need to be factored into your pricing.*)
- How much of the site will I be responsible for grazing? Will I need to maintain the vegetation around the outside of the exterior fence? (*In most cases, the answer here is yes, but it can be negotiated.*)
- What height must the vegetation be maintained to, or how many "mows" are you expecting me to make with my sheep per year? (*We try to shoot for about three "mows" per season, but it varies depending*

on the site and the seasonality. We try to keep the grass at about eighteen inches or shorter, below the leading edge of the panel.)

- What time span will the contract cover? *(Unfortunately, I've never had a contract for longer than one year at a time, but I know of many graziers who are landing three- to seven-year contracts. For your own farm planning and viability, the longer, the better, but bear in mind that longer contracts are riskier for the developer, particularly if you're new to solar grazing.)*

- Am I expected to graze the entire site, or can some areas be mowed in a hybrid fashion? *(We do have sites that employ a hybrid approach of mowing some of the stemmier vegetation that the sheep can't get to in time. Most developers allow and encourage this practice, but be transparent about it up front. You may need to invest in additional equipment—the mower—and if there are other considerations on a site, like maintaining pollinator habitat, as described below, mowing may not be ideal.)*

- Is this site also going to be designated a pollinator-friendly site? *(If yes, mowing decisions will need to be made. You, as the grazier, should come up with a plan for how often you will move the sheep to allow for optimal bloom times and improved pollinator health.)*

- Who is my point of contact for the duration of this project? *(Projects often change hands multiple times throughout the terms of a contract. Turnover is just as high in the renewables industry as it is elsewhere. Always strive to have multiple contacts for a project.)*

- What are the safety requirements? *(Utility-scale sites tend to have stricter regulations than many other sites in terms of safety. Even some community-scale sites are strict and require more comprehensive insurance policies. Many require safety gear, like hard hats and reflective vests, on-site. Others have reporting systems where you must tag in and out when entering and exiting the site. Develop a clear idea of these requirements and make sure you'll be able to comply.)*

- What is the timeline? *(A site will probably not be ready for grazing as soon as it is constructed. There will likely be a window when it needs to be revegetated and the vegetation needs a chance to catch up. Don't expect to be grazing as soon as a site goes online. Make sure your contract clearly outlines when you are expected to start grazing and when you should be done for the season.)*
- Who are the neighbors/landowner? *(Get to know the landowner and neighbors. Introduce yourself and explain what you're doing. You need allies, and the more people you have on your team, the better.)*
- Are there limitations to what I can do on-site? *(If you're rotationally grazing, you might not think twice about popping in fiberglass posts—but the asset owner might not be comfortable with that. Make sure you detail your plans in advance to avoid miscommunication.)*
- What's the price? *(This is where the claws really start to come out during conversations. I recommend graziers develop different tiers of pricing. Your most expensive rates should be on sites where there's going to be more labor involved—whether in terms of management of the sheep or trucking water—whereas the cheapest should be on the more plug-and-play sites.)*
- What paperwork do I need? *(To start grazing, you'll generally need a W-9, proof of insurance, and a contract. There might be other onboarding requirements per the developer.)*

All these considerations need to be outlined clearly in your contract. Payment and insurance terms also need to be crystal clear. We are required to have a $1 million liability policy as a minimum for most of our sites, but every company and site will be different. Some companies require much more than that for insurance, which can be prohibitive for new graziers.

Some graziers have banded together to form cooperative-esque systems (like United Agrivoltaics) to tackle these costs. Insurance—along with equipment for solar grazing like panels, corrals, and even trailers—can be prohibitively expensive. Joining a cooperative won't necessarily be a good solution for every grazier and every site, but if you're new to grazing and have limited resources and a limited network, it's an option.

Getting connected with decision makers is another barrier to getting started with agri-energy. As Lewis said, "Prepare to be patient." You need to find out who owns the site and who's managing it (often very different people). Looking up town board meeting minutes and finding the contact information can be helpful. Sometimes it just comes down to sending emails and cold-calling. He added, "Once you get the first, then you have a track record. The site owner will use your experience as good public relations, and time is just the other ingredient. You have to be really bullish on it."

Familiarize yourself with the ebb and flow of solar. In some cases, you might spend years emailing back and forth with a company's staff about a project, and they might seem enthusiastic, but then it dies at the last minute. "We've seen grazing passed over in favor of robotic mowers," Lewis said with a sigh. "It's your job to tell the story of what can be possible."

We've had sites fall through—or get delayed—and have been stuck holding the bag for hundreds of sheep we have suddenly had to feed without the acreage to do so. Fortunately, we have other revenue streams that help us continue to keep our business running in these situations (remember that diversification is key), but if you're totally dependent on grazing contracts for your cash flow and something falls through—or gets delayed—you're going to sink. Always have a plan with a backup plan and a backup plan for that backup plan.

Make sure solar grazing or agri-energy in general is a good fit for your farming operations and current goals. If you're farming part-time and working another job, it might not make sense for you to take on a two-hundred-acre utility-scale site an hour's drive from home. You'll have a hard time dedicating the time and resources to that. Think carefully about where you want your farm to be five, ten, fifteen, and twenty years from now. If it's just a hobby, agri-energy isn't necessarily off the table, but you may need to be more realistic about the size and scope of the projects you take on.

You also need to be prepared to sell yourself as much as possible. Now is not the time to be humble. Fortunately, when we got our first solar site, this was something we were already used to doing, having spent multiple years trying to educate our customers on the benefits of grass-fed lamb, pastured poultry, and woodlot pork.

You don't need a degree in marketing or a fancy advertising agency to sell yourself, either. The key to effective marketing lies in vivid storytelling. Think about what advantages you can offer as a grazier (or a vegetable farmer, or whatever it is you want to do) and market yourself like crazy. Set yourself apart. Who are you? What are your values? What makes you different from the next farmer down the road?

Look at your business from the outside in. Think about your customer: the solar developer. What value are you adding? What problems can you solve for that venture?

Throughout my career as a freelance writer, I've done quite a bit of sales-driven copywriting. In addition to writing social media posts, ads, articles, and blogs, I also frequently write website copy to help companies sell their products and services.

If I'm writing copy for a landscaping company, I could easily just write, "We mow lawns." That's great, and sure, it gets the point across. But why does it *matter*?

Instead, I focus on the value we provide. It's not just about mowing the lawn, but figuring out the value of having someone else mow your lawn for you. "We mow your lawn so that you can finally sleep in on a Saturday rather than getting out there early to get the chore done.

You can spend more time with your family while enjoying a gorgeous-looking backyard. You can finally host that backyard barbecue you've been putting off." We're focusing on what the *customer* needs and wants rather than what *we're* trying to sell.

The technique should be the same when marketing your business. Don't just think about what *you* want to get out of the conversation—the contract—but what you can offer the *developer*. Be customer-centric.

Think about the value you're bringing to the table and see if you can add any more. Are you improving pollinator health? Mention that. Reducing risk by avoiding mowing? Highlight that. Creating good PR? Say so. Can you offer mowing around the exterior fence, even if it's not required as part of the contract? Are you willing to do reseeding work? What about plowing snow to clear the access roads in the winter? Can you serve as a consultant on other projects, even those you might not be grazing yourself?

You don't need to stretch yourself too thin here—don't offer what you don't want to offer or don't feel comfortable doing (or, as is often our situation, what you don't have *time* to do). But see what's in reach, and if you can extend to offer additional value, do so.

Be visible. Go to conferences. Cold-call. Set up social media accounts highlighting your services. Connect with developers on LinkedIn. Pitch. Pitch some more.

But don't be too hard on yourself when things fall through. Remember that a lot of what happens at this stage is beyond your control. Permitting processes can become onerous and expensive for developers. Sometimes the project changes hands so many times that your name gets lost in the shuffle. That's when being persistent (Josh says I'm more like "obnoxious," but I think they mean the same thing) really pays off.

When referring to a single person on the development side advocating hard for solar, Lewis told me that a project is "most successful with one person wanting to take it on." With a point person you can really trust, the wheels start turning faster and more effectively than when you're working with a mix of people. But if that point person leaves or changes jobs, the work you've done to build that relationship disappears.

That's one reason lots of people in the agri-energy world, including Lexie Hain of Lightsource bp, advocate hard for each solar company to have its own team specifically dedicated to solar grazing. "There are many steps in the process, and one individual really can't manage it all," she said. "Developers need to know what the 'ask' is or what graziers need."

Ideally, each company would have a connection point that integrates early on with the grazier. Graziers need to be clear about what they need, from fences to watering systems and contract terms, but it helps if developers have at least a general idea of what the "ask" might be across the board (even if each individual site and grazier is a little different).

According to ASGA's 2023 census, we're close to one hundred thousand acres being grazed by solar sheep in the United States.[1] Farmland in the US has the technical potential to provide twenty-seven terawatts of solar energy capacity.[2]

There is a tremendous opportunity for us to grow together. But we need to make sure we're building the right connections, both with developers, with other graziers, and with community members.

Many solar graziers formally offer consulting work as part of their business. Others are happy to help answer questions and assist with site planning as a gesture of goodwill (and as a way to network).

Don't turn any opportunity for conversation away, even if it doesn't seem like it will help you out in the slightest. We've been approached by developers for sites that aren't remotely close to being within our range, but we've always helped answer their questions about site layout and sheep logistics.

It's just the neighborly thing to do.

Getting Started as a Landowner

There are already a number of well-documented resources for land-owners who want to install renewables on their own farms. Many are location-specific, varying widely by state and especially by town, so I encourage you to do your own research if this is something that interests you and will save you money. But to make the decision, ask yourself a few questions.

First, is your land even suitable for wind or solar (either or both)?

Solar panels perform best in direct sunlight, though they can still produce on cloudy days and even in the winter. They'll need at least four to five hours of direct sunlight, ideally with a southern exposure. Trees may need to be removed.

If you're mounting panels on top of a building, whether it's your home or a barn, you'll need to do so close to or equal to the latitude of your home, generally at a thirty- to forty-five-degree angle.

The condition of the roof is also exceptionally important. I don't recommend that you consider solar for an older building—a roof that needs to be rebuilt can be a problem. You can replace the roof and *then* add solar, but if you have the space for it, ground-mounted panels might be the better bet.

Think about the tax, legal, and financial obligations. Don't skimp on a good lawyer. Make sure you understand everything, even if it gives you a headache. Again, it differs by state. In New York, land used for wind or solar energy is exempt from an increase in property taxes for fifteen years following installation. After that period, property taxes will likely increase. Plan ahead.[3]

If you're not leasing to a solar or wind company, how will you pay for your renewables, and what benefit will they provide to you? How will you use them to power your farm or home? Will the benefits outweigh the cost? Can you secure funding?

Look into the programs—grants and tax credits—offered by your state or municipality. In the past, the US Department of Agriculture has offered Rural Energy for America Program (REAP) loans and grants. REAP offers guaranteed loan financing and grant funding to agricultural producers who wish to install renewable energy systems or make energy-efficient improvements (agrivoltaics can often fall under this umbrella). REAP funds can be used for the purchase and installation of renewable energy systems, including small- and large-scale solar and wind, as well as hydropower, geothermal, biomass, hydrogen, and ocean generation.[4] Although it's not clear whether this program will be offered in future years following the Unleashing American Energy Executive Order issued by President Donald Trump in January 2025, there may nonetheless be similar initiatives to explore down the road.[5]

If you're thinking about installing systems for your home and not necessarily your business, remember that the federal government also offers the Residential Clean Energy Credit, a tax credit equaling 30 percent of the costs of "new, qualified clean energy property for your home installed anytime from 2022 through 2032."[6] As I'm reviewing the final changes to this book in July 2025, however, there is a chance of those credits disappearing (as soon as 2026) under the auspices of the Trump administration's One Big Beautiful Bill.[7]

If you're not sure where to start with your research or are unsure of which programs are still currently being offered (as you can see, this is a highly volatile, rapidly changing area), talk to your accountant or visit your state's department of energy website to find local contractors. New York State Energy Research and Development Authority, or NYSERDA, is the go-to for New York; it publishes a list of state-approved installers who can give you more information about residential or agricultural installations. In Illinois, it's the Illinois Solar for All initiative, managed by the Illinois Power Agency. If you live in Pennsylvania, you can find more information via the Pennsylvania

Public Utility Commission or the Pennsylvania Solar Center. There are resources available no matter where you live, and this information is easy to find with a quick internet search.

Trying to find someone to lease your land to for wind or solar can be a bit trickier. In the state of New York, developers typically look for parcels of land that are at least ten contiguous acres, but this requirement can vary. In South Carolina, on the other hand, developers more often look for around twenty acres of land, whereas in Texas, one of the most active states for solar leasing, developers tend to look for larger plots of forty to one hundred acres or more. Again, it varies based on the state, the solar or wind company, the local utility, and perhaps the town.

Even if you have the right number of acreage, there will be limitations related to property lines and zoning. You also need to consider the proximity of electric and transmission lines.

Terrain matters, too. Flat land with good southern exposure is important for ground-mounted arrays, just as it is for rooftop panels. Does the land have any limitations in terms of flood zones, waterways, wilderness or national/state park areas, hazardous sites, National Forest Service land units, or grassland? All these can impede solar.

Even if it's still *possible* to install solar despite these limitations, it might not always be prudent or cost-effective for a developer, who may have more hurdles to overcome. You'll need to ask questions about what's a deal breaker.

You also need to consider how close you are to the electrical infrastructure. The farther your land is from the electrical grid, the higher the cost of interconnection. If you're adjacent to a transmission line, that's great; you'll likely get a higher lease rate per acre. If your land is located within a few miles of a substation, that's good news, too.

Lease payments also tend to increase if the voltage of the line or substation is in the range that's required for the project's desired capacity. Just because there's electrical infrastructure in place doesn't mean it can currently hold a project of any size. This issue currently affects many parts of the country where new projects are going in faster than the existing infrastructure can handle it.

As far as installation goes, if you're leasing to a solar company, it will handle those logistics for you. You shouldn't need to worry about being in compliance (though it's again smart to chat with a lawyer to make sure everything is on the up-and-up in terms of your contract). But if you're building solar construction you intend to own outright, you'll want to make sure you're working with a licensed contractor who's obtaining building permits that are in compliance with state and local standards. Get that outside help.

If you're not sure who to reach out to if you're interested in leasing your land, the planning board is again a great place to start. Read meeting minutes and ask your community members if they know anybody who's been contacted by a developer. If so, it means a developer is already canvassing the area looking for properties. If they aren't able to help you, they may know of another solar company that can.

These examples are all very solar-specific, but in general they also apply to wind. The process essentially works the same way—the exception being what's required for siting. A single wind turbine can require up to eighty acres of land with access roads and other features considered. Wind turbines are exceptionally heavy, so the soil needs to be stabilized prior to construction. If you're planning to install just a small turbine to power your farm or home, your spatial needs may be small as well, but you'll want to make sure the land you have supports such an installation. Again, get an opinion from a contractor who deals in this kind of construction specifically.

The exclusion zones, such as grassland, national parks, waterways, and flood zones, are similar for wind as they are for solar. Again, for projects that will be tied into the grid, you also (obviously) need access to that power grid.

Where you live perhaps matters a bit more for wind, too, because the East Coast has incentivized wind generation more than other parts of the United States.

As you can see, there's a lot of "it depends" involved in this process. If you think you want to add solar or wind to your property, ask yourself the following questions:

- Do I have enough room for wind or solar or for just solar (since solar requires significantly less space)?
- Do I want to own the system outright, or do I want to lease my land to a developer?
- How will I pay for this system? Do I plan to pay out of pocket, or will I seek financing? Will I apply for grants or loans?
- What are my energy goals? Do I simply want to produce another "crop" on my land by leasing to a developer, or do I want to tap into that renewable energy myself to fulfill my residential or agricultural needs?
- If I'm installing my own system, what zoning laws and regulations do I need to follow?

Once you've decided on the answers to these questions, start having conversations with the people who can help you meet the goals of your project. Everything starts with a conversation, whether it's with an installer, a developer, or even just a friend who can get you connected with the right people.

Just Start Talking

Many people stress the need for more government involvement in the agri-energy arena. Indeed, regulation and policy development are well under way in many places. In late 2022, the US Department of Energy granted $8 million to projects integrating solar with farming. These include the Rutgers University project I discussed in chapter 1,[8] as well as projects in Alaska studying the benefits of agrivoltaics in high-latitude underserved communities and in Arizona studying climate-smart agrivoltaics.

Like I've said several times throughout this book, we know that sheep and pollinators work well. Now, it's time to see what else is possible.

We aren't going to meet our energy goals with solar alone. We aren't going to meet our agri-energy goals with *sheep* and solar alone. We need to diversify our energy diets just as we need to diversify our agricultural markets.

Can we raise cattle under wind installations? Chickens under solar panels? Where does cabbage fit in?

We need all kinds of food—and we need all kinds of energy. Let's stop thinking "This won't work" and start thinking, "Sheep won't work here, but maybe cattle will."

It's about finding individual solutions to individual problems rather than trying to paint everything in broad strokes. "Regulation can be supportive of agrivoltaics," Lexie Hain told me, "but it can also be a burden."

Additional funding unfortunately won't come without more regulation. The government won't experiment with agrivoltaics unless we can demonstrate the potential for a real return and the smallest amount of risk possible. I suppose that's just the cost of doing business.

So how do we make sure agri-energy doesn't become a trend that eventually just withers and dies on the vine?

For one, we need to make sure the conversations keep going. Don't fall victim to the "This will never work" narrative. If you find yourself feeling defeated or jaded, go splash some water on your face. When it comes to agri-energy, we all need to maintain a sort of childlike optimism.

Agri-energy might not always work in the way you envisioned it, but it can almost always work. We just need to keep talking, and to keep asking the right questions. Most important, we must connect. George Bernard Shaw famously wrote, "The single biggest problem with communication is the illusion it has taken place."[9]

We might not all agree about the topic at hand when we sit down to have the conversation, but what *can* we agree on? What do we have in common? Let's focus on those commonalities instead of the differences.

After all, we already have plenty of research that shows how well agri-energy works. I'm all in favor of more research and more exploration—I'm glad the government is committing more resources to doing so, even if those incentives do come tied to more regulation.

But there comes a time, as I tried explaining to New York State Senator Michelle Hinchey in our November 2023 meeting, that research just stops cutting it. There comes a time when you've collected all the knowledge you can and it's time to just take a leap of faith.

If you want to see the future of agri-energy take full form, the best things you can do, whether you're a farmer, a developer, or anybody else reading this book, are to keep those lines of communication open. And act. Don't stop talking and don't stop learning, but jump. Just do it.

I feel strongly that agri-energy is the best way to solve the energy and food crisis in this country. If you agree, don't keep your thoughts to yourself. Speak up. Get in touch with your legislators. Tell them about agri-energy and why it's so important. Explain what you read in this book. Read about your state's requirements for agri-energy projects. Go to planning meetings for your town and explain how agri-energy can help your small town thrive. Learn more about how you can support your local farmers.

Research. Read. Ask questions. Ask the right questions. Investigate. Don't just opine. Do.

On a bright May day when I was writing this book, Josh and I drove to one of the solar farms we graze to check the sheep. When we first pulled into the site, the glare of the sun reflecting off the panels was blinding. I put my sunglasses on and blinked a few times.

"Ugh," my first thought was as I looked around at all the metal and wires. "Those panels sure can be gaudy sometimes." But as my eyes adjusted to the light and I walked onto the solar farm, stepping deeper into the shadows of the arrays, those feelings slowly began to dissipate.

A cool breeze played with the hair around my ears. The sun didn't feel so harsh. A butterfly tickled my arm as I passed the water troughs, making my hair stand up on end as it idly passed me by.

I saw sheep lounging under the panels, stretching contentedly as they got up lazily to move to a new spot. Lambs grazed on grass near their mothers but didn't bolt away. Instead, they eyeballed us cautiously but kept enjoying the bright green grass, chewing loudly.

Looking down, I saw honeybees landing on a small patch of clover and heard the screams of hawks overhead. Back down by my feet, a small vole rushed for cover, not wanting to be made the hawk's next meal.

Looking back up into the sky, I saw the sun—the massive engine powering all this life down below. And gazing directly ahead, I saw hundreds of sheep protected from the elements and from coyotes and from any threat of harm, their only job for the day to eat and nap in the shade. I looked at my feet and saw pollinators, dozens of them, helping produce food for the next generation of livestock and plants on this solar farm.

And I saw my own shoes making dim imprints in the soil—soil that was growing stronger and more fertile by the day. Those shoes encased feet, very human feet, feet of a species who for so long has been viewed as nature's greatest enemy.

I don't think we are nature's greatest enemy, but we've certainly done some damage. And we need to undo that damage—or at least start to repair some of what we've broken. We need to begin to heal our injured and fragmented planet.

To start fixing things, we don't have to abandon who we naturally are as humans. We don't need to separate ourselves from nature. We just need to start seeing ourselves as pieces of the bigger puzzle, to start putting together some of those broken pieces. To come together.

When I look at the solar farm, it's easy to *just* see the panels, the imposing, anthropogenic structures we've created to meet our own goals and fulfill our own needs. Rows and rows of panels.

Lambs and ewes grazing a New York solar site. Credit: J&R Pierce Family Farm

But here's what else I see: I see how we can use those same structures to meet the needs of sheep. I see how we can meet the needs of honeybees and butterflies, of hawks and woodchucks and voles. Those rows and rows of panels are home, shelter, food.

The old saying is that we need to see the forest for the trees. Perhaps it's time to start thinking about how we can see the *solar farm* for the *panels*. Or for the wildlife, the pollinators, and the food.

We need to stay curious and creative. Our eyes need to stay open to what's possible if we want to find creative solutions to our twenty-first-century—and beyond—problems.

We can't let the wool get pulled over our eyes.

Close those eyes of yours. Now open them. There are so many possibilities, but only if we choose to see them. Our climate needs to be healed. Our food supply needs to be fixed. Agri-energy is the solution that can save them both.

Acknowledgments

In this book, I talk a lot about the importance of community. I have always believed that the whole is truly greater than the sum of its parts, and to that end, I have many people to thank. Without them, this book, my career as a writer, and our farm would not be possible.

This list is massive, but my gratitude is larger.

First and foremost, I thank the people who rolled the dice and trusted a starry-eyed freelancer with just a few years of writing experience to write an actual book. I thank Lisa Amstutz at Storm Literary Agency for her endless patience and tenacity in helping me find the perfect audience for this crazy idea of mine.

I also thank Emily Turner and Annie Byrnes at Island Press for all their hard work in ideating, editing, polishing, and perfecting this book. As a technologically challenged writer who struggles with properly formatted footnotes and cogent outlines, I fully recognize the magic in what these two talented women do every single day.

I am forever indebted to all those who lent me their wisdom, photos, and memories and, perhaps more importantly, offered me detailed explanations of the more technical and scientific aspects of agri-energy.

For an English major and former high school teacher who hadn't taken a single science class since high school, this help was key.

Most notably, I extend my heartfelt thanks to Nick Armentrout, Dr. Serkan Ates, Jonathan Barter, Josh Bennett, Juli Burden, Kevin Campbell, Juliet Caplinger, Rob Davis, Alex DePillis, Chad Farrell, Lewis Fox, Linda Garrett, Paul Gipe, Lauren Glickman, Marcus Gray, Lexie Hain, Arlo Hark, Will Harris, Ryan Indart, Byron Kominek, Amber Lessard, Dr. Arjun Makhijani, Phal Mantha, Robert Margolis, Dr. Anna Clare Monlezun, Michael Noble, Alexis Pascaris, Stacie Peterson, Johnny Rogers, Elie Schecter, Caleb Scott, David Specca, Amanda Stoffels, and Marguerite Wells. Words cannot describe how thankful I am to all these individuals for donating hours of their time to answer my questions and share their thoughts on the present and future state of agri-energy. Without their input, this book simply would not exist.

I'd also like to specifically acknowledge Ken Lehman of Kendall Sustainable Infrastructure and Tim Stout of GreenSpark Solar. Along with their teams, they gambled on our farm, trusting J&R Pierce Family Farm to graze our first site in Plattsburgh even though we had zero experience in solar grazing to call on. Had we not stepped foot on that site, we would still be blind to the countless benefits of agri-energy.

I must also call out the farmers in my community who have lent not only their wisdom to this book, but have been immeasurably generous with their time, resources, and advice as we've grown our farm. As young farmers with no experience or family background in agriculture, having mentors in our local community to guide us has been an incredible blessing.

I'll start by thanking Tony LaPierre, whose leadership within the Farm Bureau has been an inspiration. His advocacy for the local agricultural community is a godsend.

I also thank George and Marcel Giroux. From helping us get on our first solar site to assisting us with herding sheep, these brothers have become wonderful mentors and friends. I cannot thank them enough for their generosity (and for not laughing at our many mistakes, even though I'm sure they wanted to).

Two other mentors I thank are Gary and Connie Menard. There aren't many people you can call in the middle of the night with panicked questions about calf scours, and most people who answer the phone probably wouldn't sound happy when they do. But the Menards have never failed to be there for us, to teach us what we don't know, and to provide us with much-needed moral support.

Another massive thank-you goes to the Davis family (Norm, Chad, and Amelia). The saying is that there are friends, there is family, and then there are friends that become family, and I'd say these three fall into the last category. With open arms, they welcomed us into their home, their farm, and their story. Norm passed away in the summer of 2025, and we will miss him (and his dry, hilarious commentary) immensely. More than he could ever have realized, he's left a profound legacy on our farming community.

I also thank my parents, Paul and Theresa, who nurtured my love of writing at a very young age and who have always been supportive of my dreams, no matter what they happened to be at the time (even when those dreams involved me traveling abroad alone, moving to Manhattan, quitting teaching to pursue my writing career, or, yes, starting a farm. As a parent myself now, I'm not sure I would have the patience and grace you both did!). I also thank my sisters, Christan and Corinne, who have, at this point, donated several years' worth of ear time (and several bottles of wine) to listen to me stress and muse over the contents of this book.

Another thank-you goes to Molly Bowen, the only person I entrusted to read my cobbled-together manuscript before it was completed. She has been one of my greatest cheerleaders and is the best conversationalist I know. Her superpower is challenging each and every idea (but without losing any ounce of warmth or kindness), and I'm so lucky to have her in my corner.

A special thank-you goes to Leta Pierce. Not many women can say that they are friends with their mother-in-law, but I'm one of the few. I thank her for her endless support, for many hours of babysitting, for all the advice she's given our business, and for welcoming me without hesitation into her family.

Which leads me to my most important acknowledgment: to Josh and Lew. I love you both more than words can describe.

These two are my reason for everything, to say nothing of my reasons for writing this book. Josh is, without a doubt, the kindest, strongest, and smartest person I know. When I was seventeen years old, he gave me a tiny charm necklace. The charm was shaped like a book. He believed in my dream of becoming a writer far sooner (and far more) than I ever believed in myself. No matter what we've gone through, whatever challenge we have faced, I've never felt like we were up against something impossible. We were, and are, in this together.

And then there's Lew. From the moment he was born, I knew he was going to be my explorer, my feral child with skinned knees and a wild imagination. And he is. Every day, his awe motivates me to try to understand the world a bit better. He's too young to read these words now, but I hope that one day, he will know how much of an inspiration he is to me every single day.

Finally, I thank everyone who has contributed to this journey by either helping me write this book or simply taking the time to read it. I am so fortunate to know you all and to have you along with me on this wild adventure.

Notes

Introduction

1. "Farm Household Income Estimates." USDA ERS—Farm Household Income Estimates, January 27, 2025. https://www.ers.usda.gov/topics/farm-economy/farm-household-well-being/farm-household-income-estimates/

2. Semuels, Alana. "'They're Trying to Wipe Us Off the Map.' Small American Farmers Are Nearing Extinction." *Time*, November 27, 2019. https://time.com/5736789/small-american-farmers-debt-crisis-extinction/

3. Winikoff, J. B., and Maguire, K. *The Role of Commercial Energy Payments in Agricultural Producer Income* (Report No. EIB-271). US Department of Agriculture, Economic Research Service, 2024. https://doi.org/10.32747/2024.8374827.ers

4. Mintert, James, and Langemeier, Michael. "Farmer Sentiment Declines to Lowest Level Since June 2022 Amid Weakened Financial Outlook." Purdue University, May 7, 2024. https://ag.purdue.edu/commercialag/ageconomybarometer/farmer-sentiment-declines-to-lowest-level-since-june-2022-amid-weakened-financial-outlook/

5. "Cost of Renewable Energy." Inspire Clean Energy, 2020. https://www.inspirecleanenergy.com/blog/clean-energy-101/cost-of-renewable-energy

6. Laws, Forrest. "Can Agrivoltaics Help Solar Energy and Agriculture Co-Exist?" FarmProgress, October 22, 2024. https://www.farmprogress.com/conservation-and-sustainability/can-agrivoltaics-help-solar-energy-and-agriculture-co-exist-

7. Laws, "Can Agrivoltaics Help?"

Chapter 1: A Cash Crop

1. Zeballos, Eliana, and Wilson Sinclair. "Budget Share for Total Food Remained 11.2 Percent in 2023." US Department of Agriculture, Economic Research Service, June 27, 2024. https://www.ers.usda.gov/data-products/chart-gallery/chart-detail

243

?chartId=76967; Johnson, David S., et al. "A Century of Family Budgets in the United States." Bureau of Labor Statistics, May 2001. https://www.bls.gov/opub/mlr/2001/05/art3full.pdf

2. Weise, Elizabeth. "Like A 'Second Wife': Wind Energy Gives American Farmers a New Crop to Sell in Tough Times." *USA Today*, February 16, 2020. https://www.e-mc2.gr/el/news/second-wife-wind-energy-gives-american-farmers-new-crop-sell-tough-times

3. "Farm Household Well-Being—Farm Household Income Estimates." US Department of Agriculture, Economic Research Service, December 3, 2024. https://www.ers.usda.gov/topics/farm-economy/farm-household-well-being/farm-household-income-estimates

4. "Farm Household Well-Being."

5. "Farm Household Well-Being."

6. "Small Farms, Big Differences." US Department of Agriculture, May 18, 2010. https://www.usda.gov/about-usda/news/blog/small-farms-big-differences

7. Souza, Kim. "Tyson Foods' CEO Pay Up 33%; Company Makes Management Changes." Talk Business and Politics, January 3, 2023. https://talkbusiness.net/2022/12/tyson-foods-ceo-pay-up-33-company-makes-management-changes/

8. Bekkerman, Anton, et al. "Where the Money Goes: The Distribution of Crop Insurance and Other Farm Subsidy Payments." American Enterprise Institute, January 2018. https://www.aei.org/wp-content/uploads/2018/01/Where-the-Money-Goes.pdf?x91208

9. "Census of Agriculture." United States Department of Agriculture National Agricultural Statistics Service, 2017. https://www.nass.usda.gov/Publications/AgCensus/2017/Full_Report/Volume_1,_Chapter_1_US/

10. "New York State New Farmers Grant Fund: Guidelines." State of New York, October 2018. https://esd.ny.gov/sites/default/files/2018Guidelines-New-Farmers-GF.pdf; Pershing, Don, and J. H. Atkinson. "Figuring Rent for Existing Farm Buildings, Purdue University. https://www.extension.purdue.edu/extmedia/ec/ec-451-w.html

11. Biscontini, Tyler. "Small Scale Agriculture." EBSCO, 2024. https://www.ebsco.com/research-starters/agriculture-and-agribusiness/small-scale-agriculture

12. Wedell, Katie, et al.. "Midwest Farmers Face a Crisis. Hundreds Are Dying by Suicide." *USA Today*, March 9, 2020. https://www.usatoday.com/in-depth/news/investigations/2020/03/09/climate-tariffs-debt-and-isolation-drive-some-farmers-suicide/4955865002/

13. "Northeastern Region Land Values Report." Cornell Cooperative Extension, August 10, 2021. https://senecacountycce.org/agriculture/northeastern-region-land-values-report

14. Halvorson, Jodi. "Is the Allure of Farming Irresistible?" US Department of Agriculture, June 16, 2021. https://www.usda.gov/media/blog/2021/06/16/allure-farming-irresistible

15. "Employment in Agriculture (% of Total Employment) (Modeled ILO Estimate)."

World Bank, February 7, 2024. https://data.worldbank.org/indicator/SL.AGR
.EMPL.ZS

16. Halvorson, "Is the Allure of Farming Irresistible?"

17. Fahy, Jennifer. "How Heirs' Property Fueled the 90 Percent Decline in Black-Owned Farmland." Farm Aid, February 28, 2022. https://www.farmaid.org/blog/heirs
-property-90-percent-decline-black-owned-farmland/

18. Winikoff, J. B., and K. Maguire. *The Role of Commercial Energy Payments in Agricultural Producer Income* (Report No. EIB-271). US Department of Agriculture, Economic Research Service, 2024. https://doi.org/10.32747/2024.8374827.ers

19. Brannstrom, Christian, et al.. "Spatial Distribution of Estimated Wind-Power Royalties in West Texas." *Land* 4, no. 4 (December 2, 2015): 1182–99. https://doi.org
/10.3390/land4041182

20. Morrison, Liz. "Wind Wisdom: 5 Questions to Ask Before Signing a Wind-Energy Lease." FarmProgress, March 1, 2012. https://www.farmprogress.com/technology
/wind-wisdom-5-questions-to-ask-before-signing-a-wind-energy-lease

21. "Solar Leases." Cornell Cooperative Extension, Steuben County, November 21, 2022. https://putknowledgetowork.org/energy/solar-leases

22. Breen, Kayla. "Farms Everywhere Are Hurting: Farmers Seek Stronger Safety Net in Federal Farm Bill." *Press Republican* (Plattsburg, NY), March 1, 2018. https://www
.pressrepublican.com/news/local_news/farms-everywhere-are-hurting/article
_13323799-5f7d-510a-b4cb-7f3ea91621a4.html

23. "Year-on-Year Growth in Residential Electricity Prices in the United States from 2000 to 2023, with a Forecast Until 2025." Statista, October 15, 2024. https://www
.statista.com/statistics/201714/growth-in-us-residential-electricity-prices-since-2000/

24. "Net Metering." Solar Energy Industries Association. https://www.seia.org/initiatives
/net-metering

25. Gipe, Paul. *Wind Energy for the Rest of Us: A Comprehensive Guide to Wind Power and How to Use It.* Wind-works.org, 2016, 290.

26. "Solar Renewable Energy Credits." Solar United Neighbors, June 28, 2024. https://
solarunitedneighbors.org/resources/solar-renewable-energy-credits-srecs/

27. "Solar Energy Equipment Credit." New York State Department of Taxation and Finance, December 16, 2019. https://www.tax.ny.gov/pit/credits/solar_energy
_system_equipment_credit.htm

28. "Solar Tax Credits in South Carolina." South Carolina Renewable Energy Co., 2020. https://screc.org/understanding-tax-credits-1

29. "Small Wind Guidebook." Office of Energy Efficiency and Renewable Energy, 2019. https://windexchange.energy.gov/small-wind-guidebook

30. "Wind Energy in Denmark." International Energy Agency, 2022. https://iea-wind.org
/about-iea-wind-tcp/members/denmark/

31. Gipe, *Wind Energy for the Rest of Us*, 480–81.

32. Giblin, "Wind Generation Benefits Farmers, Rural Communities, and the Environment." American Farm Bureau Federation, September 13, 2017. https://www.fb

.org/focus-on-agriculture/wind-generation-benefits-farmers-rural-communities-and
-the-environment

33. Watson, Delbert. "Farming the Wind: Wind Power and Agriculture." Union of Concerned Scientists Fact Sheet, September 2019. https://www.ucsusa.org/sites/default
/files/2019-09/agfs_wind_2003.pdf

34. Gipe, *Wind Energy for the Rest of Us*, 4.

35. Gipe, *Wind Energy for the Rest of Us*, 9.

36. "Biochar." Climate Hubs, US Department of Agriculture, 2023. https://www.climate
hubs.usda.gov/hubs/international/topic/biochar

37. "NRCS Biochar Funding Quick Guide for US Producers." Colorado State Extension,
January 2024. https://extension.colostate.edu/wp-content/uploads/2024/01/biochar
_funding_for_US_producers_quick_guide_-2.pdf

38. "Recovering Value from Waste: Anaerobic Digester System Basics." US Environmental Protection Agency, 2011. https://www.epa.gov/sites/default/files/2014-12/docu
ments/recovering_value_from_waste.pdf

39. AgriSolar Clearinghouse. "Case Study: Winston Cone Optics and Dairy Processing,"
August 17, 2023. https://www.agrisolarclearinghouse.org/case-study-winston-cone
-optics-and-dairy-processing/

40. Chikaire, J., et al. "Solar Energy Applications for Agriculture." Department of
Agricultural Extension, Federal University of Technology, Owerri, September 2010.
https://www.matchinggrants.org/global/pdf/doc122-89.pdf

41. Gipe, *Wind Energy for the Rest of Us*, 266.

42. "Guide to Farming Friendly Solar." Vermont Agency of Agriculture, Food, and
Markets. https://solargrazing.org/wp-content/uploads/2019/06/On-Pasture-Co
-location-of-solar-agriculture.pdf

43. "Introduction to Solar PV on Farms Under the SMART Program." University of
Massachusetts Amherst, Center for Agriculture, Food, and the Environment, 2020.
https://ag.umass.edu/clean-energy/research-initiatives/solar-pv-agriculture

44. Makhijani, Arjun. "Exploring Farming and Solar Synergies." Institute for Energy and
Environmental Research, February 2021. https://ieer.org/wp/wp-content/uploads
/2021/02/Agrivoltaics-report-Arjun-Makhijani-final-2021-02-08.pdf

Chapter 2: Energizing Communities

1. "Governor Cuomo Signs Accelerated Renewable Energy Growth and Community
Benefit Act: Practical Law." Practitioner Insights News and Analysis, April 9, 2020.
https://content.next.westlaw.com/practical-law/document/I0c1abdc179b911ea
80afece799150095/Governor-Cuomo-Signs-Accelerated-Renewable-Energy-Growth
-and-Community-Benefit-Act?viewType=FullText&transitionType=Default&con
textData=(sc.Default)

2. Le Coz, Emily, et. al. "New York Community Divided Over Wind Farm." USA Today
Network, December 13, 2017. https://stories.usatodaynetwork.com/windfarms/the
-community-rift/

3. Le Coz et. al. "New York Community Divided."

4. "St. Lawrence County—Quick Facts." US Census Bureau, 2024. https://data.census .gov/profile/St._Lawrence_County,_New_York?g=050XX00US36089#income-and -poverty

5. Shrider, Emily. "Poverty in the United States: 2023." US Census Bureau, September 10, 2024. https://www.census.gov/library/publications/2024/demo/p60-283.html

6. "Franklin County—Quick Facts." US Census Bureau, 2024. https://data.census.gov /profile/Franklin_County,_New_York?g=050XX00US36033

7. Sommerstein, David. "Like Most Rural Places, the North Country Lost Population in 2020 Census." North Country Public Radio, August 26, 2021. https://www.north countrypublicradio.org/news/story/44368/20210826/like-most-rural-places-the -north-country-lost-population-in-2020-census

8. Le Coz et. al. "New York Community Divided."

9. Rosenthal, Lauren. "A Small Town in SLC Just Got Cut from a Multimillion-Dollar Wind Deal. Its Reaction? 'Relief.'" North Country Public Radio, January 25, 2018. https://www.northcountrypublicradio.org/news/story/35507/20180125/a-small -town-in-slc-just-got-cut-from-a-multimillion-dollar-wind-deal-its-reaction-relief

10. Iaconangelo, David. "Why Do People Dislike Wind Power? What a DOE Lab Found." Energy Wire, March 15, 2022. https://www.eenews.net/articles/why-do -people-dislike-wind-power-what-a-doe-l

11. Rueter, Gero. "Wind Power Critics: What's the Truth About Their Claims?" DW, December 15, 2021. https://www.dw.com/en/wind-power-critics-whats-the-truth -about-their-claims/a-60048961

12. "How Loud Is a Wind Turbine?" General Electric, August 2, 2014. https://www.ge .com/news/reports/how-loud-is-a-wind-turbine

13. Rueter, "Wind Power Critics."

14. "Wind Energy Projects and Safety." Office of Energy Efficiency and Renewable Energy, 2019. https://windexchange.energy.gov/projects/safety

15. "Transformative Power Systems." Office of Fossil Energy and Carbon Management. US Department of Energy, 2022. https://www.energy.gov/fecm/transformative -power-systems

16. "Gas and Coal Power Has Broken Down 114 Times So Far This Year, Fair Dinkum." Australia Institute, October 23, 2018. https://australiainstitute.medium.com/gas -coal-power-has-broken-down-114-times-so-far-this-year-fair-dinkum-1c87043 a9251

17. Clemente, Jude. "Do Wind Turbines Lower Property Values?" *Forbes*, October 3, 2015. https://www.forbes.com/sites/judeclemente/2015/09/23/do-wind-turbines -lower-property-values/

18. David, Leonardo, et al. "How Much Do Solar Panels Increase Home Value? (2024 Guide)." EcoWatch, July 26, 2024. https://www.ecowatch.com/solar/solar-panels -increase-home-value

19. Kiger, Brandon. "Life Cycle Assessment and Photovoltaic (PV) Recycling: Designing

a More Sustainable Energy System." National Renewable Energy Laboratory, April 19, 2016. https://www.nrel.gov/solar/market-research-analysis/blog/posts/life-cycle-assess ment-and-photovoltaic-pv-recycling-designing-a-more-sustainable-energy-system

20. Woody, Todd. "Most Coal-Fired Power Plants in the Us Are Nearing Retirement Age." QZ.com, July 21, 2022. https://qz.com/61423/coal-fired-power-plants-near -retirement

21. "New Reports From NREL Document Continuing PV and PV-Plus-Storage Cost Declines." National Renewable Energy Laboratory, November 12, 2021. https://www .nrel.gov/news/program/2021/new-reports-from-nrel-document-continuing-pv-and -pv-plus-storage-cost-declines.html

22. "IKEA U.S. Announces Commitment to Clean Energy with New Solar Installation and Large-Scale Renewable Heating and Cooling Projects." IKEA, September 12, 2023. https://www.ikea.com/us/en/newsroom/corporate-news/ikea-u-s-announces -commitment-to-clean-energy-pub780defe0

23. Gerdes, Justin. "Community Wind Projects Poised to Take Off in Denmark." *Forbes*, October 22, 2012. https://www.forbes.com/sites/justingerdes/2012/10/22/com munity-wind-projects-poised-to-take-off-in-denmark/

24. "Governor Cuomo Signs Accelerated Renewable Energy Growth and Community Benefit Act."

25. "Wind Power Facts and Statistics." American Clean Power, September 13, 2024. https://cleanpower.org/facts/wind-power/

26. "Kansas Property Tax Exemptions." Kansas Department of Revenue, 2019. https:// www.ksrevenue.gov/pvdptexemptions.html

27. Harris, Will. *A Bold Return to Giving a Damn: One Farm, Six Generations, and the Future of Food*. Viking, 2023.

28. Gipe, Paul. *Wind Energy for the Rest of Us: A Comprehensive Guide to Wind Power and How to Use It*. Wind-works.org, 2016, 527.

29. Otway, H. J. "Nuclear Power Plant Safety." International Atomic Energy Association, 1974. https://www.iaea.org/sites/default/files/publications/magazines/bulletin/bull 16-1/161_202007277.pdf

30. Gipe, *Wind Energy for the Rest of Us*, 59.

31. Lakhani, Nina. "A Just Transition Depends on Energy Systems That Work for Every-one." *The Guardian*, November 13, 2022. https://www.theguardian.com/environ ment/2022/nov/12/cop27-dash-for-gas-africa-energy-colonialism

32. Gipe, *Wind Energy for the Rest of Us*, 342.

33. Jordan, Erin. "Solar Developers Willing to Adapt Projects, Pay Neighbors." *The Gazette* (Cedar Rapids, IA), October 13, 2023. https://www.thegazette.com/iowa -ideas/solar-developers-willing-to-adapt-projects-pay-neighbors/

34. "How Renewable Energy Can Help Save America's Struggling Farms." Generation180, July 28, 2021. https://generation180.org/blog/how-renewable-energy-can-help-save -americas-struggling-farms/

35. "Reg 1-109, Community-Based Energy Development Projects." Nebraska Depart-

ment of Revenue, 2011. https://revenue.nebraska.gov/sites/revenue.nebraska.gov/files/doc/legal/regs/1-109.pdf

36. Jordan, "Solar Developers Willing to Adapt Projects."

37. "Clean Energy Is Building a New American Workforce." Environmental Defense Fund, March 15, 2017. https://www.edf.org/report/clean-energy-building-new-american-workforce

38. Olano, Maria Virginia. "Chart: Which States Have the Most Solar and Wind Power Jobs?" Canary Media, July 7, 2023. https://www.canarymedia.com/articles/clean-energy-jobs/chart-which-states-have-the-most-solar-and-wind-power-jobs

39. "What Is U.S. Electricity Generation by Energy Source?" US Energy Information Administration. https://www.eia.gov/tools/faqs/faq.php?id=427&t=3

40. Tierney, Susan, et al. "Setting the Record Straight About Renewable Energy." World Resources Institute, May 12, 2020. https://www.wri.org/insights/setting-record-straight-about-renewable-energy

41. Torpey, Elka. "Green Growth: Employment Projections in Environmentally Focused Occupations." US Bureau of Labor Statistics, April 2018. https://www.bls.gov/careeroutlook/2018/data-on-display/green-growth.htm

42. Tierney et al. "Setting the Record Straight About Renewable Energy."

43. "US Doubles Renewable Subsidies to $15.6 Billion in Last Seven Years, EIA Says." Reuters, August 2, 2023. https://www.reuters.com/business/energy/us-doubles-renewable-subsidies-156-billion-last-seven-years-eia-2023-08-02/

44. "Senator Whitehouse on Fossil Fuel Subsidies: 'We Are Subsidizing the Danger.'" US Senate Committee on the Budget, May 3, 2023. https://www.budget.senate.gov/chairman/newsroom/press/sen-whitehouse-on-fossil-fuel-subsidies-we-are-subsidizing-the-danger-

45. Gipe, *Wind Energy for the Rest of Us*, 520.

46. "Hawai'i Clean Energy Initiative." Hawai'i State Energy Office, 2025. https://energy.hawaii.gov/hawaii-clean-energy-initiative/

47. Jung, Yoohyun. "Hawaii Has a Lot of Agricultural Land. Very Little of It Is Used for Growing Food." Civil Beat, February 2021. https://www.civilbeat.org/2021/02/hawaii-grown-maps/

48. "Increased Food Security and Food Self-Sufficiency Strategy." Office of Planning, Department of Business Economic Development and Tourism in Cooperation with the Department of Agriculture, State of Hawaii, October 2012. https://files.hawaii.gov/dbedt/op/spb/INCREASED_FOOD_SECURITY_AND_FOOD_SELF_SUFFICIENCY_STRATEGY.pdf

49. "World Must Sustainably Produce 70 Percent More Food by Mid-Century—UN Report." UN News, United Nations, December 3, 2013. https://news.un.org/en/story/2013/12/456912

50. "U.S. Food System Factsheet." University of Michigan Center for Sustainable Systems, 2023. https://css.umich.edu/publications/factsheets/food/us-food-system-factsheet

51. Kassel, Kathleen, and Annika Martin. "Ag and Food Sectors and the Economy." US

Department of Agriculture, January 8, 2025. https://www.ers.usda.gov/data
-products/ag-and-food-statistics-charting-the-essentials/ag-and-food-sectors-and
-the-economy

52. Kaufman, James. "Agricultural Trade." US Department of Agriculture, April 1,
2025. https://www.ers.usda.gov/data-products/ag-and-food-statistics-charting-the
-essentials/agricultural-trade

53. Davis, W., et al. "Vegetable and Pulses Data." US Department of Agriculture, March
18, 2025. https://www.ers.usda.gov/data-products/vegetables-and-pulses-data

54. Shahbandeh, M. "U.S. Total Lamb and Mutton Production from 2000 to 2024."
Statista, March 7, 2024. https://www.statista.com/statistics/194699/us-total-lamb
-and-mutton-production-since-2000/

55. Shahbandeh, M. "U.S. Total Lamb and Mutton Imports and Exports from 2006 to
2024 (in million pounds)." Statista, March 7, 2024. https://www.statista.com
/statistics/194707/us-total-lamb-and-mutton-imports-and-exports-since-2001/

56. Carey, Anne, and Ajay Nair. "Spinach Production Under Midwest Growing Conditions." Iowa State University Extension and Outreach, September 2022. https://
store.extension.iastate.edu/product/Spinach-Production-Under-Midwest-Growing
-Conditions

57. Workman, Daniel. "Top Fresh Spinach Exports by Country." World's Top Exports,
2023. https://www.worldstopexports.com/top-fresh-spinach-exports-by-country

58. "Crops and Livestock Products." Food and Agriculture Organization of the United
Nations, February 27, 2025. https://www.fao.org/faostat/en/#data/QCL

59. Carter, Rachel. "The True Cost of Local Food." UVM Food Feed—Sustainable Systems and University of Vermont, January 24, 2017. https://learn.uvm.edu/food
systemsblog/2017/01/24/true-cost-of-local-food/

60. Kaufman, "Agricultural Trade."

61. Kaufman, "Agricultural Trade."

62. Lacko, Allison. "The Pandemic Disrupted a Decade-Long Decline in Food Insecurity
in 2020, but Government Policy Has Been a Critical Support." Food Research and
Action Center, September 2022. https://frac.org/blog/food-insecurity-and-2022
-poverty-reports

63. Lacko, Allison. "Pandemic Disrupted a Decade-Long Decline."

64. "Fast Facts About Agriculture and Food." American Farm Bureau Federation, 2024.
https://www.fb.org/newsroom/fast-facts

65. Zumkehr, A., and J. E. Campbell, "The Potential for Local Croplands to Meet US
Food Demand." *Frontiers in Ecology and the Environment* (June 1, 2015). https://doi
.org/10.1890/140246

66. "How Much Land Will a Renewable Energy System Use?" Frontier Group, November
21, 2022. https://frontiergroup.org/resources/land-use-renewable-energy-system

67. "PV FAQs." US Department of Energy, Energy Efficiency and Renewable Energy,
2004. https://www.nrel.gov/docs/fy04osti/35097.pdf

68. Weaver, John Fitzgerald. "Solar-Plus-Food in Ethanol Fields Could Fully Power the

United States." *PV Magazine*, March 11, 2022. https://www.pv-magazine.com
/2022/03/11/solar-plus-food-in-ethanol-fields-could-fully-power-the-united-states/

69. Weaver, "Solar-Plus-Food in Ethanol Fields."

70. Lark, Tyler J., et al. "Environmental Outcomes of the US Renewable Fuel Standard."
Proceedings of the National Academy of Sciences 119, no. 9 (February 14, 2022).
https://doi.org/10.1073/pnas.2101084119

71. Gipe, *Wind Energy for the Rest of Us*, 528.

72. McAvoy, Audrey. "83,000 Hawaii Homes Dispose of Sewage in Cesspools. Rising
Sea Levels Will Make Them More of a Mess." Associated Press, July 6, 2023. https://
apnews.com/article/hawaii-cesspools-rising-sea-levels-climate-change-61b72be5
dcae1aff25945d17117cc873

73. McAvoy, Audrey. "Rising Sea Levels a Concern for Hawaii's 83,000 Cesspools."
Maui News, July 7, 2023. https://www.mauinews.com/news/local-news/2023/07
/rising-sea-levels-a-concern-for-hawaiis-83000-cesspools/

74. Sherwood, Leah. "UH Hilo Scientists Document How Rainfall Brings Harmful
Bacteria into Hilo Bay." University of Hawai'i Hilo, October 23, 2019. https://hilo
.hawaii.edu/chancellor/stories/2019/10/23/harmful-bacteria-hilo-bay/

75. "Electricity (HS: 2716) Product Trade, Exporters and Importers." Observatory of
Economic Complexity, 2023. https://oec.world/en/profile/hs/electricity

76. "Electricity Imports to the United States from Canada in Selected Years from 2000
to 2024." Statista, January 6, 2025. https://www.statista.com/statistics/189029/us
-electricity-imports-from-canada-since-1999/

77. Yousif, Nadine, "Ontario Says It Will Slap a 25% Surcharge on US-Bound Electricity." BBC, March 10, 2025. https://www.bbc.com/news/articles/c5yrpnr6kr2o

78. "Mobile Agrivoltaics: Harvesting Crops and Energy on Farmland." H2arvester, 2024.
https://www.h2arvester.nl/?lang=en

79. "United States Imports of Wool, Animal Hair, Horsehair Yarn." Trading Economics,
July 2024. https://tradingeconomics.com/united-states/imports/wool-animal-hair
-horsehair-yarn

80. Shahbandeh, M. "Total Shorn Wool Production Value in the U.S. 1999–2019."
Statista, March 15, 2024. https://www.statista.com/statistics/194423/total-wool
-production-value-in-the-us-since-1999/

81. Shahbandeh, "Total Shorn Wool Production Value"; Savage, Barry. "Key Factors
Impacting Wool Consumption and Valuation." Sheep Industry News, May 2023.
https://www.sheepusa.org/wp-content/uploads/2023/05/Wool-Market-Update
-Spring-2023.pdf

82. "Textile Exchange's Annual Materials Market Report Shows Further Growth in the
Overall Production of New Materials, Including Fossil-Based Synthetic Fibers."
Textile Exchange, December 1, 2023. https://textileexchange.org/news/textile
-exchanges-annual-materials-market-report-shows-further-growth-in-the-overall
-production-of-new-materials-including-fossil-based-synthetic-fibers/

83. Salfino, Catherine. "Consumers: It Matters Where Fashion Is Made." *Sourcing*

Journal, June 30, 2022. https://sourcingjournal.com/topics/lifestyle-monitor/made-in-usa
-fashion-grown-and-sewn-rob-magness-gitman-bros-353188/

84. Smith, Peter. "Tom Chappell." *Maine,* March 2010. https://www.themainemag.com
/1199-tom-chappell/#close

85. "Case Study: Jack's Solar Garden." AgriSolar Clearinghouse, August 10, 2022. https://
www.agrisolarclearinghouse.org/case-study-jacks-solar-garden/

86. O'Brien, Kelly. "Adirondack School Goes Solar." WCAX, September 18, 2018.
https://www.wcax.com/content/news/Adirondack-Solar-Farm-ribbon-cutting
-ceremony-494602091.html

87. "Clean Energy Systems Exemption." New York City Department of Finance. https://
www.nyc.gov/site/finance/property/clean-energy-systems-exemption.page

88. Saunders, Arabella, and Julia Rock. "What's an IDA? Local Agencies Hand Out $1b
in Tax Breaks Across New York." North Country Public Radio, March 6, 2024.
https://www.northcountrypublicradio.org/news/story/49468/20240313/what-s-an
-ida-local-agencies-hand-out-1b-in-tax-breaks-across-new-york

89. "New York State Solar Guidebook for Local Governments." NYSERDA, May 2021.
https://www.nyserda.ny.gov/All-Programs/Clean-Energy-Siting-Resources/Solar
-Guidebook

90. "Real Property Tax Law (RPTL) § 487." NYSERDA. https://www.nyserda.ny.gov
/Contacts/Energy-System-Taxation-Exemption

Chapter 3: Developing a Renewable Future

1. "Assemblymember Barrett and Senator Hinchey: SITED Act Signed into Law." NY
Assemblymember Didi Barrett, Assembly District 106, January 8, 2024. https://
nyassembly.gov/mem/Didi-Barrett/story/108681

2. "Farmland Solar Policy State Law Database." Farm and Energy Initiative, 2023.
https://farmandenergyinitiative.org/projects/farmland-solar-policy/state-law-database/

3. "Farmland Solar Policy State Law Database." Farm and Energy Initiative.

4. "The Potential of Agrivoltaics for the U.S. Solar Industry, Farmers, and Communities." US Department of Energy, April 17, 2023. https://www.energy.gov/eere/solar
/articles/potential-agrivoltaics-us-solar-industry-farmers-and-communities

5. "Maryland House Bill 1039 (2022)." American Farmland Trust, 2022. https://farm
landinfo.org/law/maryland-house-bill-1039-2022/

6. "Solar Massachusetts Renewable Target (SMART)." Commonwealth of Massachusetts, 2017. https://www.mass.gov/solar-massachusetts-renewable-target-smart

7. "Senators Hinchey and Harckham Send Letter to ORES Outlining Threats to Farmland and Environment by Proposed Copake Solar Development." New York State
Senate, August 25, 2023. https://www.nysenate.gov/newsroom/press-releases/2023
/michelle-hinchey/senators-hinchey-and-harckham-send-letter-ores

8. Ritchie, Hannah. "What Are the Safest and Cleanest Sources of Energy?" Our World
in Data, July 2022. https://ourworldindata.org/safest-sources-of-energy

9. Helman, Christopher. "How Green Is Wind Power, Really? A New Report Tallies Up

the Carbon Cost of Renewables." *Forbes*, April 14, 2022. https://www.forbes.com /sites/christopherhelman/2021/04/28/how-green-is-wind-power-really-a-new -report-tallies-up-the-carbon-cost-of-renewables/

10. "What Is the Carbon Footprint of Offshore Wind?" Orsted, 2024. https://us.orsted .com/renewable-energy-solutions/offshore-wind/seven-facts-about-offshore-wind /carbon-footprint

11. "Theodore Roosevelt Quotes." Theodore Roosevelt Center, Dickinson State University. Accessed June 20, 2025. 79. https://www.theodorerooseveltcenter.org/Learn -About-TR/TR-Quotes?page=79

12. Newburger, Emma. "The U.S. Passed a Historic Climate Deal This Year—Here's a Recap of What's in the Bill." CNBC, December 30, 2022. https://www.cnbc.com /2022/12/30/2022-climate-recap-whats-in-the-historic-inflation-reduction-act.html

13. "A Decade of Growth in Solar and Wind Power: Trends Across the U.S." Climate Central, April 3, 2024. https://www.climatecentral.org/report/solar-and-wind -power-2024

14. Jensen, Derrick, et al. *Bright Green Lies: How the Environmental Movement Lost Its Way and What We Can Do About It.* Rhinebeck, NY: Monkfish Book Publishing, 2021.

15. "Renewable Energy—Powering a Safer Future." United Nations Climate Action. https://www.un.org/en/climatechange/raising-ambition/renewable-energy

16. Bertrand, Savannah. "Fact Sheet: Climate, Environmental, and Health Impacts of Fossil Fuels (2021)." Environmental and Energy Study Institute, December 17, 2021. https://www.eesi.org/papers/view/fact-sheet-climate-environmental-and-health -impacts-of-fossil-fuels-2021

17. Bertrand, "Fact Sheet."

18. "Renewable Energy—Powering a Safer Future."

19. Kennedy, Ryan. "Hail Damage and Toxicity Risks in Solar Power Plants." *PV Magazine*, April 16, 2024. https://www.pv-magazine.com/2024/04/17/hail-damage-and -toxicity-risks-in-solar-plants/

20. "Why You Don't Need to Worry About Broken Solar Panels." Solar Energy Industries Association, April 15, 2024. https://seia.org/blog/why-you-dont-need-worry-about -broken-solar-panels/

21. "Can Hail Damage Solar Panels? Everything You Need to Know." Velo Solar, June 13, 2024. https://www.velosolar.com/can-hail-damage-solar-panels/

22. "Power Generation Costs." IRENA, 2022.https://www.irena.org/Energy-Transition /Technology/Power-generation-costs

23. Enkhardt, Sandra. "Agro Solar Europe Unveils Agrivoltaic Mounting Kit with Organic Materials." *PV Magazine*, March 20, 2024. https://www.pv-magazine.com/2024/03 /20/agro-solar-europe-unveils-agrivoltaic-mounting-kit-with-organic-materials/

24. Jamil, Uzair, et al. "Solar Photovoltaic Wood Racking Mechanical Design for Trellis-Based Agrivoltaics." *PLOS ONE* 18, no. 12 (December 1, 2023). https://doi.org/10 .1371/journal.pone.0294682

25. "State Renewable Portfolio Standards and Goals." National Conference of State Legislatures, August 13, 2021. https://www.ncsl.org/energy/state-renewable-portfolio-standards-and-goals

26. Cotnam, Hallie. "Sheep Farmers, Solar Company Form Powerful Partnership." CBC News, July 1, 2019. https://www.cbc.ca/news/canada/ottawa/solar-energy-panels-weeds-sheep-lambs-farming-grazing-1.5190376

27. Gipe, Paul. *Wind Energy for the Rest of Us: A Comprehensive Guide to Wind Power and How to Use It.* Wind-works.org, 2016, 68.

28. "Siting of Large-Scale Renewable Energy Projects." US Department of Energy. https://www.energy.gov/eere/siting-large-scale-renewable-energy-projects

29. "$5 Million Is Now Available for Demonstration Projects That Co-Locate Solar and Agricultural Operations in New York State." NYSERDA, June 7, 2024. https://www.nyserda.ny.gov/About/Newsroom/2024-Announcements/2024_06_07-NYSERDA-Announces-5-Million-is-Now-Available-For-Demonstration

30. Conlon, Kevin. "Growing Competition: Best Farmland for Crops Also Popular for Solar Farms." *Adirondack Daily Enterprise*, August 8, 2022. https://www.adirondackdailyenterprise.com/news/2022/08/growing-competition/

31. Huffstutter, P. J., and Christopher Walljasper. "Insight: As Solar Capacity Grows, Some of America's Most Productive Farmland Is at Risk." Reuters, April 29, 2024. https://www.reuters.com/world/us/solar-capacity-grows-some-americas-most-productive-farmland-is-risk-2024-04-27/

32. Conlon, "Growing Competition."

33. Pascaris, Alexis S., et al. "Do Agrivoltaics Improve Public Support for Solar? A Survey on Perceptions, Preferences, and Priorities." *Green Technology, Resilience, and Sustainability* 2, no. 1 (October 23, 2022). https://doi.org/10.1007/s44173-022-00007-x

34. "Pollinator-Friendly Solar Scorecards." Fresh Energy, accessed June 20, 2025. https://fresh-energy.org/beeslovesolar/pollinator-friendly-solar-scorecards

35. "Solar Massachusetts Renewable Target (SMART)."

36. McCall, James, et al. "Vegetation Management Cost and Maintenance Implications of Different Ground Covers at Utility-Scale Solar Sites." *Sustainability* 15, no. 7 (March 28, 2023): 5895. https://doi.org/10.3390/su15075895

37. McCall et al., "Vegetation Management Cost."

38. Weaver, John Fitzgerald. "The Economics of Solar Grazing." *PV Magazine*, August 3, 2023. https://www.pv-magazine.com/2023/08/03/the-economics-of-solar-grazing/

39. McCall et al., "Vegetation Management Cost."

40. "Dr. Pavao-Zuckerman Discovers Solar Heat Island Effect Caused by Large-Scale Solar Power Plants." University of Maryland, November 4, 2016. https://enst.umd.edu/news/dr-pavao-zuckerman-discovers-solar-heat-island-effect-caused-large-scale-solar-power-plants/

41. "Solar Panels Can Heat the Local Urban Environment, Systematic Review Reveals." Physics World, January 30, 2022. https://physicsworld.com/a/solar-panels-can-heat-the-local-urban-environment-systematic-review-reveals/

42. "How Do Temperature and Shade Affect Solar Panel Efficiency?" Boston Solar, October 15, 2023. https://www.bostonsolar.us/solar-blog-resource-center/blog/how-do-temperature-and-shade-affect-solar-panel-efficiency/

43. Koundal, Aarushi. "Heat Waves Bring Down Solar Panel Efficiency by Up to 1.5 Per Cent Per 5°C Temp Rise: Experts." ET Energy World, June 24, 2024. https://energy.economictimes.indiatimes.com/news/renewable/heat-wave-brings-down-solar-panel-efficiency-by-up-to-1-5-per-cent-per-5c-temp-rise-experts/111210308

44. Bellini, Emiliano. "Well-Irrigated Roofs with Vegetation Have Cooling Effect on PV Systems." *PV Magazine*, August 8, 2023. https://www.pv-magazine.com/2023/08/08/well-irrigated-roofs-with-vegetation-have-cooling-effect-on-pv-systems/

45. Williams, Henry J., et al. "The Potential for Agrivoltaics to Enhance Solar Farm Cooling." *Applied Energy*, 332, February 2023, 120478, https://doi.org/10.1016/j.apenergy.2022.120478

46. Kochendoerfer, N. et al. "Effect of Stocking Rate on Forage Yield and Vegetation Management Success in Ground Mounted Solar Arrays Grazed by Sheep." Cornell Nutrition Conference, October 2022. https://ecommons.cornell.edu/items/f9432d3c-3bc1-492a-b890-cf4ddefad5db

47. Apadula, Emily. "The State of Solar Decommissioning Policy: Then and Now." DSIREinsight, October 29, 2023. https://www.dsireinsight.com/blog/2023/10/27/the-state-of-solar-decommissioning-policy-then-and-now

48. Apadula, "State of Solar Decommissioning Policy."

49. "Financial Calculator." InSPIRE, January 2023. https://openei.org/wiki/InSPIRE/Financial_Calculator

50. Sahoo, Sanjib. "Walking the Line Between Risk and Failure." Enterprisers Project, June 9, 2016. https://enterprisersproject.com/article/2016/5/walking-line-between-risk-and-failure

Chapter 4: Powering Healthy Landscapes

1. "Global Greenhouse Gas Overview." US Environmental Protection Agency, April 11, 2024. https://www.epa.gov/ghgemissions/global-greenhouse-gas-overview

2. Melillo, Jerry. "Soil-Based Carbon Sequestration." MIT Climate Portal, April 15, 2021. https://climate.mit.edu/explainers/soil-based-carbon-sequestration

3. Miller, Daegan. "Midwestern US Has Lost 57.6 Billion Metric Tons of Soil Due to Agricultural Practices." University of Massachusetts Amherst, March 16, 2022. https://www.umass.edu/news/article/midwestern-us-has-lost-576-billion-metric-tons-soil-due-agricultural-practices

4. "Soil in Midwestern U.S. Eroding 10 to 1,000 Times Faster Than It Forms." US National Science Foundation, January 10, 2023. https://new.nsf.gov/news/soil-midwestern-us-eroding-10-1000-times-faster-it

5. Lal, Rattan. "Erosion-Crop Productivity Relationships for Soils of Africa." *Soil Science Society of America Journal* 59, no. 3 (May 1995): 661–67. https://doi.org/10.2136/sssaj1995.03615995005900030004x

6. Scharping, Nathaniel. "Agricultural Lands Are Losing Topsoil—Here's How Bad It

Could Get." *Eos*, June 11, 2024. https://eos.org/articles/agricultural-lands-are-losing -topsoil-heres-how-bad-it-could-get

7. "One-Third of Farmland in the U.S. Corn Belt Has Lost Its Topsoil." Yale School of the Environment, February 18, 2021. https://e360.yale.edu/digest/one-third-of -farmland-in-the-u-s-corn-belt-has-lost-its-topsoil

8. Schoeck, Michael. "U.S. Court Orders Developer to Pay $135.5 Million in 100 MW Solar Property Damage Case." *PV Magazine*, May 10, 2023. https://www.pv-maga zine.com/2023/05/10/u-s-court-orders-developer-to-pay-135-5-million-in-100-mw -solar-property-damage-case/

9. Rose, Michael T., et al. "Impact of Herbicides on Soil Biology and Function." *Advances in Agronomy* 136 (2016): 133–220. https://doi.org/10.1016/bs.agron.2015.11 .005

10. Machmuller, Megan B., et al. "Emerging Land Use Practices Rapidly Increase Soil Organic Matter." *Nature Communications* 6, no. 1 (April 30, 2015). https://doi .org/10.1038/ncomms7995

11. Walston, Leroy J., et al. "Modeling the Ecosystem Services of Native Vegetation Management Practices at Solar Energy Facilities in the Midwestern United States." *Ecosystem Services* 47 (February 2021): 101227. https://doi.org/10.1016/j.ecoser .2020.101227

12. South, Amber. "Franklin County's Newest Solar Farm Sparks Controversy in Rural Community." *Chambersburg Public Opinion*, March 20, 2024. https://www.public opiniononline.com/story/news/2024/03/20/some-worry-path-valley-solar-farm-will -generate-too-much-development/72870719007/

13. "Lamb—Food Source Information." Colorado State University, 2023. https://www .chhs.colostate.edu/fsi/food-articles/animal-products/lamb-2/

14. "Agriculture and Aquaculture: Food for Thought." US Environmental Protection Agency, October 2020. https://www.epa.gov/snep/agriculture-and-aquaculture -food-thought

15. Quinton, Amy. "Cows and Climate Change: Making Cattle More Sustainable." University of California, Davis, June 27, 2019. https://www.ucdavis.edu/food/news /making-cattle-more-sustainable

16. Bosch, D. J. "Effects of Rotational Grazing on Carbon Dioxide Emissions and Greenhouse Gas Credits." *Journal of Soil and Water Conservation* 63, no. 2 (March 1, 2008). https://doi.org/10.2489/63.2.51a

17. McCabe, Conor. "Why Do Cattle Produce Methane, and What Can We Do About It?" Clarity and Leadership for Environmental Awareness and Research at University of California, Davis, April 22, 2024. https://clear.ucdavis.edu/explainers/why-do -cattle-produce-methane-and-what-can-we-do-about-it

18. Fountain, Henry. "Belching Cows and Endless Feedlots: Fixing Cattle's Climate Issues." *New York Times*, October 21, 2020. https://www.nytimes.com/2020/10/21 /climate/beef-cattle-methane.html

19. Rotz, Clarence. "Impact of Beef Cattle on the Environment, Abstract." American

Dairy Science Association Proceedings, April 12, 2023. https://www.ars.usda.gov
/research/publications/publication/?seqNo115=402563

20. Bogaerts, Meghan, et al. "Climate Change Mitigation Through Intensified Pasture
Management: Estimating Greenhouse Gas Emissions on Cattle Farms in the Brazilian
Amazon." *Journal of Cleaner Production* 162 (September 2017): 1539–50. https://doi
.org/10.1016/j.jclepro.2017.06.130

21. "Public Land Statistics 2022." US Department of the Interior, Bureau of Land Management, June 2023. https://www.blm.gov/sites/default/files/docs/2023-07/Public
_Lands_Statistics_2022.pdf

22. "About the BLM Oil and Gas Program." US Department of the Interior Bureau of
Land Management. https://www.blm.gov/programs/energy-and-minerals/oil-and
-gas/about

23. Penrod, Emma. "BLM Proposes to Open 22 Million Acres in Western States to Solar
Development." Utility Dive, January 18, 2024. https://www.utilitydive.com/news
/blm-solar-development-roadmap-west/704855/

24. "Senate Bill S7899A." New York State Senate, May 13, 2025. https://www.nysenate
.gov/legislation/bills/2025/S7899/amendment/A

25. Harris, Lissa. "New York State: Leading the Flock." American Solar Grazing Association, January 15, 2022. https://solargrazing.org/new-york-state-leading-the-flock/

26. Kampherbeek, Emma W., et al. "A Preliminary Investigation of the Effect of Solar
Panels and Rotation Frequency on the Grazing Behavior of Sheep (Ovis Aries)
Grazing Dormant Pasture." *Applied Animal Behaviour Science* 258 (January 2023):
105799. https://doi.org/10.1016/j.applanim.2022.105799

27. Andrew, Alyssa C., et al. "Herbage Yield, Lamb Growth and Foraging Behavior in
Agrivoltaic Production System." *Frontiers in Sustainable Food Systems* 5 (April 29,
2021). https://doi.org/10.3389/fsufs.2021.659175

28. Cloete, S. W. P., et al.. "The Effects of Shade and Shearing Date on the Production
of Merino Sheep in the Swartland Region of South Africa." *South African Journal
of Animal Science* 30, no. 3 (March 1, 2000). https://doi.org/10.4314/sajas.v30i3
.3848

29. Kendall, P. E., et al. "The Effects of Providing Shade to Lactating Dairy Cows in a
Temperate Climate." *Livestock Science* 103, no. 1–2 (August 2006): 148–57. https://
doi.org/10.1016/j.livsci.2006.02.004

30. Andrew, et al., "Herbage Yield, Lamb Growth and Foraging Behavior."

31. Brown, Aston. "Farmers Who Graze Sheep Under Solar Panels Say It Improves Productivity. So Why Don't We Do It More?" *The Guardian*, June 12, 2024. https://
www.theguardian.com/australia-news/article/2024/jun/13/farmers-who-graze-sheep
-under-solar-panels-say-it-improves-productivity-so-why-dont-we-do-it-more

32. Bridge, Ashley. "There Are Many Ways to Solar Graze." Cornell Small Farms Program,
October 20, 2020. https://smallfarms.cornell.edu/2020/10/there-are-many-ways-to
-solar-graze/

33. Florentino, Sabrina, et al. "Raising Livestock and Crops Under Solar Panels." Univer-

sity of Minnesota Extension, 2024. https://extension.umn.edu/livestock-operations/what-are-agrivoltaics#research-summary-3602860

34. Heins, Brad, and Kirsten Sharpe. "Agrivoltaics and Grazing Dairy Cattle Under Solar Panels." *Progressive Publishing*, February 14, 2023. https://www.agproud.com/articles/57002-agrivoltaics-and-grazing-dairy-cattle-under-solar-panels

35. Farr, Marigo. "How to Expand Solar Without Losing Farmland? Send in the Sheep." *Grist*, March 10, 2022. https://grist.org/looking-forward/solar-grazing-expand-solar-without-losing-farmland-send-in-the-sheep/

36. "Bird Mortality at Renewable Energy Facilities Have Population-Level Effects." US Geological Survey, May 19, 2022. https://www.usgs.gov/news/science-snippet/bird-mortality-renewable-energy-facilities-have-population-level-effects

37. Smallwood, K. Shawn, et al. "Dogs Detect Larger Wind Energy Effects on Bats and Birds." *Journal of Wildlife Management* 84, no. 5 (March 26, 2020): 852–64. https://doi.org/10.1002/jwmg.21863

38. Smallwood et al., "Dogs Detect Larger Wind Energy Effects."

39. Merriman, Joel. "How Many Birds Are Killed by Wind Turbines?" American Bird Conservancy, January 26, 2021. https://abcbirds.org/blog21/wind-turbine-mortality

40. Merriman, Joel. "How Many Birds Are Killed by Wind Turbines?"

41. Loss, Scott R., et al. "Refining Estimates of Bird Collision and Electrocution Mortality at Power Lines in the United States." *PLOS ONE* 9, no. 7 (July 3, 2014). https://doi.org/10.1371/journal.pone.0101565

42. "Wind Energy Fact Check." Queensland Government Department of Energy and Climate, May 22, 2025. https://www.energyandclimate.qld.gov.au/energy/types-of-renewables/wind-energy/fact-check

43. Loss, S., et al. "The Impact of Free-Ranging Domestic Cats on Wildlife of the United States." *Nature Communications* 4, 1396 (2013). https://doi.org/10.1038/ncomms2380

44. "Review: Several Groups of Birds and Mammals Avoid Wind Turbines." Luke Natural Resources Institute Finland, December 18, 2023. https://www.luke.fi/en/news/review-several-groups-of-birds-and-mammals-avoid-wind-turbines

45. Kumara, Honnavalli N., et al. "Responses of Birds and Mammals to Long-Established Wind Farms in India." *Scientific Reports* 12, no. 1 (January 25, 2022). https://doi.org/10.1038/s41598-022-05159-1

46. Montag, Hannah, et al. "The Effects of Solar Farms on Local Biodiversity: A Comparative Study." Clarkson and Woods and Wynchwood Biodiversity, April 2016. https://helapco.gr/wp-content/uploads/Solar_Farms_Biodiversity_Study.pdf

47. "Agriculture Sector Emissions." US Environmental Protection Agency, March 31, 2025. https://www.epa.gov/ghgemissions/agriculture-sector-emissions

48. "Sources of Greenhouse Gas Emissions." US Environmental Protection Agency, March 31, 2025. https://www.epa.gov/ghgemissions/sources-greenhouse-gas-emissions

49. Tanner, Karen E., et al. "Microhabitats Associated with Solar Energy Development

Alter Demography of Two Desert Annuals." *Ecological Applications* 31, no. 6 (May 20, 2021). https://doi.org/10.1002/eap.2349

50. Kalies, Liz. "Making Solar Wildlife-Friendly: Creating Solutions to Maximize Conservation Benefit from Solar Production." The Nature Conservancy, July 10, 2023. https://www.nature.org/en-us/about-us/where-we-work/united-states/north-carolina/stories-in-north-carolina/making-solar-wildlife-friendly/

51. Armstrong, Alona. "Managing Solar Parks for Nature: Delivering to the Climate and Ecological Emergencies." UK Energy Research Centre, July 15, 2020. https://ukerc.ac.uk/news/managing-solar-parks-for-nature-delivering-to-the-climate-and-ecological-emergencies/

52. "Plant That's Everywhere Is Fueling a Growing Risk of Wildfire Disaster." *CBS News*, March 21, 2024. https://www.cbsnews.com/amp/sacramento/news/plant-thats-everywhere-is-fueling-a-growing-risk-of-wildfire-disaster/

53. Olano, Gabriel. "Fire a Major Hidden Danger for Solar Farms." *Insurance Business*, September 8, 2022. https://www.insurancebusinessmag.com/us/risk-management/news/fire-a-major-hidden-danger-for-solar-farms-419868.aspx

54. Wirth, Harry. "Recent Facts About Photovoltaic in Germany." Fraunhofer Institute for Solar Energy Systems, March 4, 2024. https://www.ise.fraunhofer.de/en/publications/studies/recent-facts-about-pv-in-germany.html

55. Krcmar, Angela. "The True Cost of Wind Turbine Fires and Protection." Wind Power Engineering and Development, September 8, 2020. https://www.windpowerengineering.com/the-true-cost-of-wind-turbine-fires-and-protection/

56. Archibold, Randal C. "Damaged Power Lines Blamed for Wildfires." *New York Times*, September 4, 2008. https://www.nytimes.com/2008/09/04/us/04fires.html

57. "Lithium-Ion Battery Safety." New York City Fire Department, accessed June 20, 2025. https://www.nyc.gov/site/fdny/codes/reference/lithium-ion-battery-safety.page

58. "Targeted Grazing for Wildfire Fuel Breaks." US Department of Agriculture Climate Hubs, 2022. http://www.climatehubs.usda.gov/hubs/northwest/topic/targeted-grazing-wildfire-fuel-breaks

59. "Grazing." UC ANR Fire Network, 2025. https://ucanr.edu/statewide-program/ucanr-fire-network/grazing

60. Gutierrez, Kassandra. "Property Owners Urged to Clear Weeds Ahead of Peak Fire Season." ABC30, April 22, 2024. https://abc30.com/growing-weeds-tall-vegetation-fire-season-wet-weather/14717367/

Chapter 5: Protecting Plants and Pollinators

1. Graham, Maggie, et al. "Partial Shading by Solar Panels Delays Bloom, Increases Floral Abundance During the Late-Season for Pollinators in a Dryland, Agrivoltaic Ecosystem." *Scientific Reports* 11, no. 1 (April 2, 2021). https://doi.org/10.1038/s41598-021-86756-4

2. Dupraz, C., et al. "Combining Solar Photovoltaic Panels and Food Crops for Opti-

mising Land Use: Towards New AGRIVOLTAIC Schemes." *Renewable Energy* 36, no. 10 (October 2011): 2725–32. https://doi.org/10.1016/j.renene.2011.03.005

3. Dinesh, Harshavardhan, and Joshua M. Pearce. "The Potential of Agrivoltaic Systems." *Renewable and Sustainable Energy Reviews* 54 (February 2016): 299–308. https://doi.org/10.1016/j.rser.2015.10.024

4. Marrou, H., et al. "Microclimate Under Agrivoltaic Systems: Is Crop Growth Rate Affected in the Partial Shade of Solar Panels?" *Agricultural and Forest Meteorology* 177 (August 2013): 117–32. https://doi.org/10.1016/j.agrformet.2013.04.012

5. Turrentine, Jeff. "Made in the Shade: The Promise of Farming with Solar Panels." National Resources Defense Council, February 23, 2022. https://www.nrdc.org/stories/made-shade-promise-farming-solar-panels

6. "Agrivoltaic—Hawaii Agriculture Research Center." Hawaii Agriculture Research Center, 2024. https://www.harc-hspa.com/agrivoltaic.html

7. Apostoleris, Harry, and Matteo Chiesa. "High-Concentration Photovoltaics for Dual-Use with Agriculture." *AIP Conference Proceedings* 2149 (2019): 050002. https://doi.org/10.1063/1.5124187

8. Lydersen, Kari. "Maine Farmer Pairs Solar Panels with Wild Blueberries. Will It Bear Fruit?" Energy News Network, September 1, 2022. https://energynews.us/2022/09/01/maine-farmer-pairs-solar-panels-with-wild-blueberries-will-it-bear-fruit/

9. "Largest Agrivoltaic Research Project in U.S. Advances Renewable Energy While Empowering Local Farmers." *Solar Power World*, June 10, 2021. https://www.solarpowerworldonline.com/2021/06/largest-agrivoltaic-research-project-in-u-s-advances-renewable-energy-while-empowering-local-farmers/

10. Barron-Gafford, Greg A., et al. "Agrivoltaics Provide Mutual Benefits Across the Food–Energy–Water Nexus in Drylands." *Nature Sustainability* 2, no. 9 (September 2, 2019): 848–55. https://doi.org/10.1038/s41893-019-0364-5

11. Malloy, Chris. "Why Combining Farms and Solar Panels Could Transform How We Produce Both Food and Energy." *The Counter*, March 30, 2021. https://thecounter.org/agrivoltaics-farmland-solar-panels-clean-energy-crops/

12. Thompson, Elinor P., et al. "Tinted Semi-Transparent Solar Panels Allow Concurrent Production of Crops and Electricity on the Same Cropland." *Advanced Energy Materials* 10, no. 35 (August 2, 2020). https://doi.org/10.1002/aenm.202001189

13. Gartner, Emmett. "Can a Farm Generate Solar Power and Blueberries at Once?" *Maine Monitor*, March 17, 2024. https://themainemonitor.org/farm-solar-power-blueberries/

14. Gartner, "Can a Farm Generate Solar Power and Blueberries at Once?"

15. Willockx, Brecht, et al. "Combining Photovoltaic Modules and Food Crops: First Agrovoltaic Prototype in Belgium." International Conference on Renewable Energies and Power Quality, June 2020. https://www.agrisolarclearinghouse.org/combining-photovoltaic-modules-and-food-crops-first-agrisolar-prototype-in-belgium/

16. Shemkus, Sarah. "Cranberry Farmers Look to Sweeten Income by Pairing Crops with Solar Panels." Energy News Network, May 28, 2021. https://energynews.us/2021/05/28/cranberry-farmers-look-to-sweeten-income-by-pairing-crop-with-solar-panels/

17. Chae, Seung-Hun, et al. "AGRIVOLTAIC Systems Enhance Farmers' Profits Through Broccoli Visual Quality and Electricity Production Without Dramatic Changes in Yield, Antioxidant Capacity, and Glucosinolates." *Agronomy* 12, no. 6 (June 12, 2022): 1415. https://doi.org/10.3390/agronomy12061415

18. Kamadi, Geoffrey. "Kenya to Use Solar Panels to Boost Crops by 'Harvesting the Sun Twice.'" *The Guardian*, February 22, 2022. https://www.theguardian.com/global -development/2022/feb/22/kenya-to-use-solar-panels-to-boost-crops-by-harvesting -the-sun-twice

19. West, Dan. "Talbott Farms Gets $700k Grant for Agri-Voltaic System." *Daily Sentinel* (Grand Junction, CO), July 4, 2024. https://www.gjsentinel.com/news/western _colorado/talbott-farms-gets-700k-grant-for-agri-voltaic-system/article_9b517cc6 -3978-11ef-ad5d-13a13704fcae.html

20. "Intercropping Hay Systems in Utility-Scale Solar: Equipment and Design Consider- ations for Hay Production." Ohio State University, October 2023. https://energize ohio.osu.edu/sites/energizeohio/files/imce/BTR%20Equipment%20FINAL%20 %28V_10.0%29.pdf

21. Peterson, Stacie, and Heidi Kolbeck-Urlacher. "Fact Sheet: Making the Case for Crops + Solar." Center for Rural Affairs, March 2024. https://www.agrisolarclearinghouse .org/wp-content/uploads/2024/03/Factsheet_Making_the_Case_for_Crops_and _Solar_03052023.pdf

22. "Oregon State University Research Shows Bright Future for Agrivoltaics." Oregon Department of Energy, February 3, 2021. https://energyinfo.oregon.gov/blog/2021 /2/3/oregon-state-university-research-shows-bright-future-for-agrivoltaics

23. Heinke, Jens, et al. "Water Use in Global Livestock Production—Opportunities and Constraints for Increasing Water Productivity." *Water Resources Research* 56, no. 12 (December 2020). https://doi.org/10.1029/2019wr026995

24. "Pollination." Pollinator Partnership, 2016. https://www.pollinator.org/pollination

25. "About Pollinators." Pollinator Partnership, 2016. https://www.pollinator.org/pollin ators

26. "Pollination Facts." American Beekeeping Federation, 2023. https://abfnet.org/pollin ation-facts/

27. "Threats to Pollinators." Pollinator Partnership, 2024. https://www.pollinator.org /threats

28. "Threats to Pollinators."

29. "Threats to Pollinators."

30. Ulyshen, Michael, and Scott Horn. "Declines of Bees and Butterflies Over 15 Years in a Forested Landscape." *Current Biology* 33, no. 7 (April 10, 2023): 1346–50.e3. https://doi.org10.1016/j.cub.2023.02.030. Epub 2023 Mar 3. PMID: 36870330

31. Tobin, Bernard. "Profitable Practices: Solar Grazing With Shady Creek Lamb Co." RealAgriculture, *Profitable Practices* podcast, September 25, 2023. https://www .realagriculture.com/2023/09/profitable-practices-solar-grazing-with-shady-creek -lamb-co/

32. Bassier, Abby. "Monoculture's Effect on Bees." Montana State University, accessed June 20, 2025. https://www.montana.edu/hhd/graduate/dietetics/blog_posts/mono culture_and_bees.html

33. Hanrahan, Ryan. "USDA Projects Decreased 2024 Planted Acreage." Farm Policy News, University of Illinois, February 26, 2024. https://farmpolicynews.illinois .edu/2024/02/usda-projects-decreased-2024-planted-acreage/

34. Lindsey, Laura, et al. "Pollinator Ratings in Soybean Varieties." Agronomic Crops Network, Ohio State University Extension, 2022. https://agcrops.osu.edu/newsletter /corn-newsletter/2022-42/pollinator-ratings-soybean-varieties

35. "Best Practices and Training." Fresh Energy, 2020. https://fresh-energy.org/beeslove solar/best-practices-and-training

36. O'Donnell, Jenna. "10 Major Audubon Conservation Wins from 2016." National Audubon Society, December 27, 2016. https://www.audubon.org/news/10-major -audubon-conservation-wins-2016

37. "Pollinator-Friendly Solar: Everybody Loves It." Fresh Energy, May 15, 2017. https:// fresh-energy.org/pollinator-friendly-solar-everybody-loves-it

38. "Pollinator Friendly Solar Scorecards." Fresh Energy. https://fresh-energy.org/beeslove solar/pollinator-friendly-solar-scorecards

39. "Pollinator Friendly Solar Scorecards."

40. "Pollinator-Friendly Ground Cover Now Required for New Solar Projects." MCE Clean Energy, February 12, 2020. https://mcecleanenergy.org/pollinator-friendly -ground-cover-now-required-for-new-solar-projects/

41. "Pollinator-Friendly Ground Cover Now Required."

42. "Bringing Nature Home." Maine Audubon Society, 2025. https://maineaudubon.org /projects/plants/

43. "Fuzz & Buzz Mix—Standard." Ernst Seeds, 2020. https://www.ernstseed.com /product/fuzz-buzz-mix-standard/

44. Lee, Sharon. "Avoid Solar Panel Shading: How to Minimize Its Impact." Velo Solar, December 16, 2022. https://www.velosolar.com/solar-panel-shading/

45. Flesher, John, and Tammy Webber. "Bees, Sheep, Crops: Solar Developers Tout Multiple Benefits." *AP News*, November 4, 2021. https://apnews.com/article/climate -science-business-lifestyle-environment-and-nature-8f388056808946fbc1aa9a4d6 bbc812e

46. Walston, Leroy J., et al. "Modeling the Ecosystem Services of Native Vegetation Management Practices at Solar Energy Facilities in the Midwestern United States." *Ecosystem Services* 47 (February 2021): 101227. https://doi.org/10.1016/j.ecoser .2020.101227

47. "Guide to Farming Friendly Solar." Vermont Agency of Agriculture, Food, and Markets. https://solargrazing.org/wp-content/uploads/2019/06/On-Pasture-Co-location -of-solar-agriculture.pdf

48. Marohn, Kirsti. "Mixing Solar and Farming Could Be Key to Clean Energy Future."

MPR News, November 7, 2023. https://www.mprnews.org/story/2023/11/07/farming-and-solar-landsharing-could-be-key-to-clean-energy-future

49. Davis, Rob. "600 Acres and 100 MW of Pollinator-Friendly Solar." Fresh Energy, June 21, 2021. https://fresh-energy.org/600-acres-and-100-mw-of-pollinator-friendly-solar

50. McCall, James, et al. "Vegetation Management Cost and Maintenance Implications of Different Ground Covers at Utility-Scale Solar Sites." *Sustainability* 15, no. 7 (March 28, 2023): 5895. https://doi.org/10.3390/su15075895

51. "Minimization: Deterrence." Renewable Energy Wildlife Institute, December 27, 2022. https://rewi.org/guide/chapters/04-minimizing-collision-risk-to-wildlife-during-operations/

52. Arnett, Edward B., et al. "Altering Turbine Speed Reduces Bat Mortality at Wind-energy Facilities." *Frontiers in Ecology and the Environment* 9, no. 4 (November 2010): 209–14. https://doi.org/10.1890/100103

Chapter 6: Not All Is Bright and Sunny

1. "US Electric Power Sector Reported Fewer Delays for New Solar Capacity Projects in 2023." US Energy Information Administration, May 8, 2024. https://www.eia.gov/todayinenergy/detail.php?id=62003

2. Nilson, R., et al. "Survey of Utility-Scale Wind and Solar Developers Report." Lawrence Berkeley National Laboratory, January 2024. https://emp.lbl.gov/publications/survey-utility-scale-wind-and-solar

3. Makhijani, Arjun. "Exploring Farming and Solar Synergies." Institute for Energy and Environmental Research, February 2021. https://ieer.org/wp/wp-content/uploads/2021/02/Agrivoltaics-report-Arjun-Makhijani-final-2021-02-08.pdf

4. Mattson, Christopher, et al. "'When a Measure Becomes a Target, It Ceases to Be a Good Measure.'" *Journal of Graduate Medical Education* 13, no. 1 (February 1, 2021): 2–5. https://doi.org/10.4300/jgme-d-20-01492.1.

5. "Agrivoltaic Systems: Our Project." Hawaii Agriculture Research Center, April 2025. https://www.harc-hspa.com/agrivoltaic-info.html

6. Macknick, Jordan, et al. "The 5 Cs of Agrivoltaic Success Factors in the United States: Lessons from the InSPIRE Research Study." National Renewable Energy Laboratory, August 2022. https://solargrazing.org/wp-content/uploads/2023/09/5-cs-of-agrivoltaics-.pdf

7. Macknick et al., "The 5 Cs of Agrivoltaic Success Factors."

8. "States With and Without Inspection Programs." US Department of Agriculture, October 4, 2022. https://www.fsis.usda.gov/inspection/state-inspection-programs/states-and-without-inspection-programs

9. "Overview of the United States Slaughter Industry." US Department of Agriculture, October 27, 2016. https://downloads.usda.library.cornell.edu/usda-esmis/files/b5644r52v/jd473028z/7w62fc23r/SlauOverview-10-27-2016.pdf

10. Weise, Elizabeth. "Like a 'Second Wife': Wind Energy Gives American Farmers a New Crop to Sell in Tough Times." *USA Today*, February 16, 2020. https://

www.e-mc2.gr/el/news/second-wife-wind-energy-gives-american-farmers-new-crop-sell-tough-times

11. Weise, "Like a 'Second Wife.'"

12. Hinchey, Michelle. "Hinchey, Kelles Bill to Create Agrivoltaics Research Program at Cornell Signed Into Law." New York State Senate, January 2, 2024. https://www.nysenate.gov/newsroom/press-releases/2024/michelle-hinchey/hinchey-kelles-bill-create-agrivoltaics-research

Chapter 7: Counting Your Sheep—Are You Ready to Join the Agri-Energy Movement?

1. "ASGA Call 76 Replay: How Big Is Solar Grazing in the U.S.? (ASGA Census Results)." American Solar Grazing Association, April 4, 2024. https://solargrazing.org/asga-call-76-replay-how-big-is-solar-grazing-in-the-u-s-asga-census-results/

2. "Farmers Guide to Going Solar." US Department of Energy, Office of Energy Efficiency and Renewable Energy, accessed June 22, 2025.https://www.energy.gov/eere/solar/farmers-guide-going-solar

3. "Leasing Your Farmland for Wind and Solar Energy Development: A Beginner's Guide for Farmers." New York Farm Bureau, December 2016. https://www.nyfb.org/application/files/2014/9780/6349/file_y349d211hx.pdf

4. "Rural Energy for America Program Renewable Energy Systems and Energy Efficiency Improvement Guaranteed Loans and Grants." US Department of Agriculture, 2024. https://www.rd.usda.gov/programs-services/energy-programs/rural-energy-america-program-renewable-energy-systems-energy-efficiency-improvement-guaranteed-loans

5. "Unleashing American Energy." White House, January 20, 2025. https://www.whitehouse.gov/presidential-actions/2025/01/unleashing-american-energy/

6. "Residential Clean Energy Credit." Internal Revenue Service, May 29, 2025. https://www.irs.gov/credits-deductions/residential-clean-energy-credit

7. Iacurci, Greg. "House, Senate Tax Bills Both End Many Clean Energy Credits: 'It's Just a Question of Timeline,' Expert Says." *CNBC*, June 20, 2025. https://www.cnbc.com/2025/06/20/gop-big-beautiful-bill-would-end-many-clean-energy-tax-credits.html

8. "DOE Announces $8 Million to Integrate Solar Energy Production with Farming." US Department of Energy, December 8, 2022. https://www.energy.gov/articles/doe-announces-8-million-integrate-solar-energy-production-farming

9. As quoted in Lyman, R. K. "How to Increase the Odds of People Paying Attention to Your Communication." University of North Carolina Kenan-Flagler Business School, November 21, 2022. https://execdev.unc.edu/how-to-increase-the-odds-of-people-paying-attention-to-your-communication/

About the Author

Rebekah Pierce is a freelance writer in upstate New York. She and her husband own J&R Pierce Family Farm, which specializes in regenerative agriculture and solar grazing. They raise sheep, cattle, pigs, chickens, and turkeys.